The Great Literacy Debate

The nature of literacy is an issue of global debate. When the National Literacy Strategy (NLS) was introduced into UK schools it was arguably the most ambitious educational reform programme in the world, and the controversy necessarily intensified. How can the impact of such reforms be assessed?

In its ten-year history the NLS affected every primary and secondary teacher in the country and, therefore, every child. The initiative provoked a widespread recognition of the importance of literacy for all children and attracted the attention of many other governments. This book is the first definitive and objective review and evaluation of the impact of these literacy reforms. With contributions from the most respected experts on literacy and English from the UK and from across the world, this unprecedented critical examination explores:

- how teaching policy and practice were impacted by the reforms
- how the NLS came into being, how it was operated and what it did and did not achieve
- what we can learn from its successes and failures
- the most important aspects of the reforms, from policing grammar to the impact of 'The Literacy Game' and 'informed prescription' on teaching.

Whether you are a policy maker or classroom teacher, this book is an invaluable resource to anyone concerned about literacy. It provides readers from around the world with a genuine and evidence-based perspective on this immense initiative, lucidly evaluating the lessons learned from both its ambitions and its failures.

Andrew Goodwyn is Head of the Institute of Education, University of Reading.

Carol Fuller is at the Institute of Education, University of Reading.

The Great Literacy Debate

A critical response to the Literacy Strategy and the Framework for English

Edited by
Andrew Goodwyn
and
Carol Fuller

Routledge
Taylor & Francis Group

LONDON AND NEW YORK

First published 2011
by Routledge
2 Park Square, Milton Park, Abingdon, Oxon OX14 4RN

Simultaneously published in the USA and Canada
by Routledge
711 Third Avenue, New York, NY 10017

Routledge is an imprint of the Taylor & Francis Group, an informa business

British Library Cataloguing in Publication Data
A catalogue record for this book is available from the British Library

Library of Congress Cataloging in Publication Data
The great literacy debate: a critical response to the literacy
strategy and framework for English/edited by Andrew Goodwyn
and Carol Fuller.
p. cm.
Includes bibliographical references.
1. Literacy – Government policy – Great Britain. 2. Literacy
programs – Great Britain – Evaluation. I. Goodwyn, Andrew,
1954–. II. Fuller, Carol (Carol L.)
LC156.G7G74 2011
379.2'40941 – dc22
2010050591

ISBN: 978-0-415-59763-0 (hbk)
ISBN: 978-0-415-59764-7 (pbk)
ISBN: 978-0-203-81424-6 (ebk)

Typeset in Galliard
by Florence Production Ltd, Stoodleigh, Devon

UNIVERSITY OF CHICHESTER

MIX
Paper from
responsible sources
FSC® C004839
www.fsc.org

Printed and bound in Great Britain by
CPI Antony Rowe, Chippenham, Wiltshire

Contents

List of contributors   vii

Introduction: 'informed prescription' or 'deformed
restriction'?   1
Andrew Goodwyn

1 Beyond the heuristic of suspicion: the value of media literacy   8
   Andrew Burn

2 What happened to teachers' knowledge when they played
   'The Literacy Game'?   27
   Viv Ellis

3 Policing grammar: the place of grammar in literacy policy   45
   Debra Myhill and Susan Jones

4 The origins, evaluations and implications of the National
   Literacy Strategy in England   63
   Roger Beard

5 New Zealand's literacy strategy: a lengthening tail and
   wagging dogs   87
   Stephanie Dix, Gail Cawkwell and Terry Locke

6 NLS1 and NLS2: implications of a social literacies perspective
   for policies and practices of literacy education   106
   Brian Street

7 The impact of the Framework for English: teachers' struggle
   against 'informed prescription'   117
   Andrew Goodwyn

8 The great literacy debate as makeover television: notes on genre
proliferation   136
  Adam Lefstein

9 The public, the personal, and the teaching of English,
language and literacy   157
  Dominic Wyse

  Index   171

Contributors

Roger Beard taught in primary schools and at the Universities of Northampton and Leeds before becoming Professor of Primary Education and Head of the Department of Early Childhood and Primary Education at the Institute of Education, University of London. He has published widely on both reading and writing and has written research reviews for the National Literacy Strategy in England and for the Brazilian and European Parliaments. He has also given invitation lectures and undertaken consultancies in the USA, Greece, Spain, Portugal and Cyprus. His most recent research has been an ESRC-funded study of children's writing development in the 9–11 age-range, with publications in the *Journal of Research in Reading, Literacy,* and *Language and Education.*

His books include *Children's Writing in the Primary School, Developing Reading 3–13, Teaching Literacy: Balancing Perspectives, Rhyme, Reading and Writing, Developing Writing 3–13* (all published by Hodder & Stoughton), *Reading by Apprenticeship?* (with Jane Oakhill, published by NFER), *Reading Development and the Teaching of Reading* (with Jane Oakhill, published by Blackwell), and he was the lead editor of *The SAGE Handbook of Writing Development,* which was based on an ESRC-funded international seminar series.

Andrew Burn is Professor of Media Education at the Institute of Education, University of London, and Associate Director of the Centre for the Study of Children, Youth and Media. He has researched and published work on many aspects of the media, including the textuality of computer games, young people's production of computer games, digital video and animation in schools, and media literacy. He taught English, media and drama in secondary schools for over twenty years. His most recent book is *Making New Media: creative production and digital literacies* (New York: Peter Lang).

Stephanie Dix, Gail Cawkwell and Terry Locke are members of the Faculty of Education at the University of Waikato, New Zealand. Stephanie Dix is a senior lecturer teaching and researching in literacy, children's writing and their revision practices, and New Zealand children's literature. She is particularly interested in classroom-based research supporting teacher pedagogy. Gail Cawkwell is a senior lecturer teaching and coordinating courses in children's literature and literacy education. Her research interests and teaching at postgraduate level are the development and effects of English and literacy policy on teachers' expertise. Professor Terry Locke is Chairperson of the Arts and Language Education Department. His research interests include constructions of English as a subject, teacher professionalism, the teaching of literature and writing, and the nexus between technology and literacy.

Viv Ellis is University Lecturer in Educational Studies at Oxford University and a Fellow of St Cross College. In his research he maintains a focus on learning, subject English, and the education of teachers with a theoretical perspective derived from Vygotsky known as cultural-historical activity theory. Recently, with Edwards and Smagorinsky, he edited *Cultural-Historical Perspectives on Teacher Education and Development* (Routledge, 2010) and his work on professional creativity has appeared in the international journal *Mind, Culture and Activity* (2011).

Andrew Goodwyn is Professor of Education and head of the Institute of Education at the University of Reading. He is chairman and International Representative for the National Association for the Teaching of English (NATE) and member of the Subject Associations Working group. He has a keen interest in theory and practice in the teaching of English and has published extensively in this area. His most recent publications are *The Expert Teacher of English, The status of literature: a case study from England* and *English teachers in the digital age: a case study of policy and expert practice from England* (forthcoming).

Susan Jones is a lecturer in education at the University of Exeter. Her research interests include gender and achievement, classroom interaction and the developing writer. She is the co-author of *Talking, Listening, Learning: Effective Talk in the Primary Classroom* (Open University Press) and *Using Talk to Support Writing* (Sage).

Adam Lefstein is Senior Lecturer in Education at the Ben-Gurion University of the Negev (Israel). His current research focuses on continuity and change in classroom interactional patterns, dialogic pedagogy and teacher learning from video recordings of classroom practice. Recent publications include: Lefstein, A. & J. Snell (2011), 'Professional vision and the politics of teacher learning', *Teaching and Teacher Education*, 27(3), 505-514; Lefstein, A. & J. Snell (2011), 'Playing *X-factor* in a Writing Lesson: Promises and Problems of Teaching with Popular Culture', *Reading Research Quarterly, 46* (1), 40-69; and Lefstein, A. (2008), 'Changing Classroom Practice through the English National Literacy Strategy: A Micro-Interactional Perspective', *American Educational Research Journal*, 45(3), 701-737.

Debra Myhill is Professor of Education at the University of Exeter, and is Acting Dean for the College of Social Sciences and International Studies. She leads the PGCE Secondary English programme and her research interests focus principally on aspects of language and literacy teaching, particularly writing and grammar, and talk in the classroom. She is the author or co-author of several books, including *Talking, Listening, Learning: Effective Talk in the Primary Classroom*, *Using Talk to Support Writing*, *The SAGE Handbook of Writing Development* and *Writing Voices: Creating Communities of Writers* (forthcoming).

Brian Street is Emeritus Professor of Language in Education at King's College, London University, and Visiting Professor of Education in the Graduate School of Education, University of Pennsylvania. He has a commitment to linking ethnographic-style research on the cultural dimension of language and literacy with contemporary practice in education and in development. Over the past 25 years he has undertaken anthropological field research and been consultant to projects in these fields in countries of both the North and South (e.g. Nepal, S. Africa, India, USA, UK).

His publications include *Literacy in Theory and Practice* (CUP, 1984), *Cross-Cultural Approaches to Literacy* (editor; CUP, 1993; shortlisted for the BAAL Book Prize), *Social Literacies* (Longman, 1995; winner of the David S. Russell Award, NCTE), and *Literacy and Development: Ethnographic Perspectives* (editor; Routledge, 2001: shortlisted for the BAAL Book Prize). He is also involved in research projects on academic literacies (co-editor; *Student Writing in the University: Cultural and Epistemological Issues,* Benjamins, 2000) and on home/school literacy and numeracy practices (co-author; *Navigating Numeracies: Home/School Numeracy Practices,* Kluwer, 2005). Recent publications include: Street, B. and Lefstein, A. (2007), *Literacy: an advanced resource book,* Routledge: London; and Heath, S.B. and Street, B. (2008), *On Ethnography: Approaches to Language and Literacy Research,* National Conference on Research in Language and Literacy, Teachers College Press: Columbia.

He is currently involved in development projects in South Asia and Africa using ethnographic perspectives in training literacy and numeracy teachers, and in a Widening Participation Programme for EAL students in the London area as they make the transition from school to university. He has just been awarded the National Reading Conference's Distinguished Scholar Lifetime Achievement Award. In 2009 he was elected Vice-President of the Royal Anthropological Institute and he has been Chair of the Education Committee of the RAI since 2006. He has published a total of 18 books and 120 scholarly papers.

Dominic Wyse is a Senior Lecturer in primary and early years education and a member of the Centre for Commonwealth Education at the University of Cambridge. He is a Fellow and Director of Music-Making at Churchill College Cambridge. He was a primary teacher for eight years which included posts in London, Bradford and Huddersfield. Following his work as a teacher he lectured in primary education at Liverpool John Moores University for eight years, latterly as a Reader.

Dominic's research focuses on curriculum, pedagogy and policy. A major strand of this is his work on the teaching of English, language and literacy. He also works on creativity and educational innovation. His current research includes a project funded by the National Gallery in London. Dominic gave evidence in relation to England's National Curriculum to the House of Commons' Committee for Children, Schools and Families, and was consulted for the government review of the national curriculum in 2011. He has spoken about policy and pedagogy on BBC *Newsnight* and BBC Radio 4 *Today*.

Dominic is editor (with Richard Andrews and Jim Hoffman) of *The Routledge International Handbook of English, Language and Literacy Teaching* and editor of *Literacy Teaching and Learning: a SAGE major work*. The third edition of his influential book *Teaching English, Language and Literacy* (with Russell Jones) is due in 2012. He is also editor of the forthcoming series of books about primary education to be published by Routledge. He is Associate Editor of the *Cambridge Journal of Education* and a member of the editorial boards of *Teaching and Teacher Education: An International Journal of Research and Studies* and *Writing and Literacy*.

Introduction

'Informed prescription' or 'deformed restriction'?

Andrew Goodwyn

There is only one agreement about the nature of literacy and that is that there is no exact agreement about what it is. There are many definitions that have much in common and so some differences are subtle but others are deep and ideological, hence literacy engenders debate and so the *raison d'être* for the title of this volume. Debates can, sometimes, be concluded, but the debate about literacy shows no signs of abating. When something as vast and important as a National Literacy Strategy (NLS) comes along, affecting every child and every teacher in England, then the debate necessarily intensifies. This is a global debate. In some countries the debate is at a different stage as governments struggle to resource even the 'simpler' forms of literacy. But in countries more comparable to England such as the USA, Australia, New Zealand and many other European countries, the debate takes on a more complex and highly politicised dimension.

This book does not take on the task of producing a history of literacy; there are other sources that cover that territory, although they in themselves do not agree on what the history of literacy has been (see Street, 1984; Barton, 1994; Holme, 2004). The focus of this book is to review and evaluate the importance of the NLS between 1997 and 2010 and to offer some perspective, from a range of researchers, on what we may learn from how the NLS came into being, how it was operated and what it did and did not achieve. Certainly one specific reference point in the genesis of this book was the publication of Stannard and Huxford's *The Literacy Game* in 2007. Its title is a homage to Michael Barber's *The Learning Game* (1996), written when he was the most influential adviser on education to New Labour whilst still in opposition and then when the National Literacy Strategy was created. For some of the authors in this volume the connotation of the term 'game' as applied to something so serious and fundamental as literacy, conveys in itself a sense of gimmickry and populism. This is not po-faced academic solemnity; one of the deepest flaws in the NLS was its oversimplification of literacy and the teaching of literacy, and its attempt to make political capital from implying that teachers had been at fault for a number of years and that the NLS was coming to 'save' them.

The idea of some kind of national focus on literacy was in fact conceived by the Conservative government in its last two years and they had set up a Literacy

Task Force in 1995. Their concern was that there had been a fall in reading standards since they had introduced the National Curriculum in 1988. Research was to demonstrate, as much as it is possible, that this 'concern' was ill-founded and certainly not based on evidence (Brooks, 1998). It is worth noting how history and debates about literacy repeat themselves. In 1973, the then education secretary, one Margaret Thatcher, claiming that reading standards were falling, commissioned a review of the teaching of reading to be chaired by Sir Alan Bullock. His report, often known simply as the Bullock Report (1975), was in fact entitled *A Language for Life*. Its recommendations, although popular with schools, many of which developed their own 'Language Across the Curriculum' policies, were never backed by government and its momentum was gradually lost.

The NLS was very different: it did not recommend, it demanded. Equally there is no equivalent to a report, like Bullock's, outlining the thinking and research evidence that underpinned it; instead all we really have is *The Literacy Game* and its hindsight. However, one party having manufactured a crisis in standards of literacy gave the incoming party the perfect ammunition for their own literacy blunderbuss. As *The Literacy Game* so fulsomely describes, New Labour became profoundly evangelical about the need to raise standards generally and their essential mission was to begin by rapidly improving the literacy of every child in the country. In itself this is a laudable aim and, it might be argued, even if there was no crisis, surely at the end of the twentieth century we needed an increasingly literate population in a fast-changing world? No one does, or did, argue with that fundamental aim.

What the authors here in *The Great Literacy Debate* demonstrate is why the NLS did not succeed and how. This is not an 'I told you so' response but it is a thoroughly critical evaluation and in that spirit there is much discussion of some of the better points of the overall strategy.

In 1999, two years after the NLS was fully underway, Roger Beard, a contributor to this volume, published a review of research which offered a rationale for the NLS. This somewhat tardy review can be explained chiefly by the political process and this is borne out by *The Literacy Game*'s description of the hectic and frenzied nature of the first couple of years of the New Labour government. Essentially a political decision was taken to capitalise on what the Conservative government had done, that is the setting up of a Task Force on Literacy and to act on the pilot work long before it was completed. Ten local educational authorities were trying out a diverse range of approaches to focusing on literacy and these experiments were only part way through their first year; there were no 'findings'.

The next important factor was a much more grounded and genuine one. It seemed possible that the introduction of a subject-based National Curriculum into primary schools in the late 1980s had not only disrupted the topic-based approach adopted by most schools in England, but had reduced attention to literacy itself. The argument was that primary teachers were busy getting their students to engage with subject matter in so many competing subjects that they were not having time for 'the basics'. Intriguingly this somewhat later led to the introduction of the National Numeracy Strategy (NNS) following the logic of the argument about literacy having been squeezed out of a subject-dominated curriculum. This 'initiative' was on a much smaller scale and was much lower profile and barely contentious. However it is worth noting that the NNS also missed the point. What else could explain why, in 2008, the government launched a proper review of Mathematics teaching, the Williams Review (Williams, 2008). This report identified a genuine crisis in mathematical knowledge in England, especially the quality of teaching of Maths in all schools. One recommendation which was acted on was that every primary school in England should have a Maths Champion by 2019; the additional training programme for this began in 2009. There is absolutely no evidence to suggest that this 'model' of change, that is identifying and training a change agent, was created as a deliberate contrast to the 'one size fits all model' of the NLS.

To return to the concern, shared by primary teachers, that the primary curriculum was overly determined by subjects, it was clear that initially these teachers were enthusiastic about a literacy strategy of some kind, as was demonstrated through the evaluations of the NLS and NNS (see comments below). The both symbolic and practical outcome of this loose consensus was the requirement for a Literacy Hour, to be taught every day of the school year without exception (see Stannard and Huxford, 2007, Chapter 4). In this volume there is some discussion of the Literacy Hour, its 'meaning' and its impact. Here we will simply note that producing an image of a clock with prescribed times on it for a sequence of activities to be followed slavishly positions teachers, regardless of experience and seniority, as if they were primary children themselves in some nineteenth-century classroom.

And this leads inexorably to the underpinning ideology, not evidence, of the NLS. Michael Barber's book outlines the need for 'informed prescription' and this idea of telling teachers what to do and how to do it without having to convince them of any rationale is that ideology. Whitty (2006: 2) analyses how Barber argued that 'informed prescription' was needed because of the two previous phases of the last 20 years:

- *Uninformed professionalism* – the period prior to the 1980s, often regarded as the golden age of teacher autonomy but when, according to Barber, teachers lacked appropriate knowledge, skills and attitudes for a modern society.
- *Uninformed prescription* – the period following the election of Margaret Thatcher's Conservative government in 1979 and, in particular, its imposition of a National Curriculum in 1988 for political rather than educational reasons.
- *Informed prescription* – the period following the election of Tony Blair's New Labour government in 1997, bringing with it (in Barber's view) 'evidence-based' policies such as the Literacy and Numeracy Strategies and Standards-based teacher training.

However, the much-mentioned evidence was never seriously forthcoming. In fact, teachers were conceptualised as the problem; the whole point of the NLS was to force teachers to change to fit the content and pedagogical model, the whole class approach, of the Literacy Hour.

The three evaluations of the NLS (Earl *et al.*, 2000, 2001, 2003), and to a much lesser extent of the NNS, carried out by an internationally independent team from the Ontario Institute of Education, 2001–3, were very clear in their findings. In years 1 and 2 the combined effect of teacher effort, focused training and additional classroom material and external 'support' from Strategy consultants led to a rapid rise in test scores, that is informed prescription can be highly effective in the short term. By year 3 the evaluators were arguing that the whole NLS needed not just a renewed effort but a different approach otherwise the temporary change to test scores would first plateau and then slip back, as indeed happened and as chapters in this volume attest. Instead of any genuine rethinking, the Strategy approach was simply to layer on top a number of additional demands such as Guided Reading, Guided Writing and so on. These additional demands certainly kept primary teachers busy but with only tiny gains in test scores.

And therein lies another of the critical failures of the NLS, its obsession with test scores. The NLS was never 'statutory', that is to say that whereas the National Curriculum is a legal framework which schools are accountable for providing, the NLS is technically only advisory. This might be seen as a cynical ploy, in that Ofsted inspectors were judging schools on their delivery of literacy and the public were judging schools on their place in performance league tables, with the implication that if you were not using the approach evangelised by the NLS then what were you doing that could possibly be better? The very great majority of schools treated the NLS as if it were 'the law', not least because of pressure, not only from inspection but from the local consultants. These consultants, employed within local educational authorities, were charged with ensuring that schools were constantly improving the levels achieved by children. These achievements were reified into the outcome of the Key Stage 1 and 2 tests in primary and the Key Stage 3 English test in secondary schools. At the micro level, head teachers set targets for individual teachers, at the meso level consultants set targets for individual schools and at the macro level, local authorities set targets for their schools collectively. At the policy level, various politicians set targets for the nation's schools, promising to resign if they were not met. Such a system of narrowly conceptualised, high stakes testing had a truly deadening effect, first on the primary and then, from 2001, on the secondary curriculum. Teaching to the test became imperative given that nothing else counted in measuring the success of a school and of the entire system. Meanwhile the Programme for International Student Assessment (PISA) tests suggested that England was performing at best modestly against countries where literacy was treated in an entirely different way, Finland being a much-quoted example.

One of the striking findings of the PISA tests was how little children in England enjoyed reading in primary schools, and this miserable finding was echoed by a survey of secondary teachers and student teachers in 2007 (Goodwyn, 2010) where teachers felt there was so little opportunity for students to enjoy literature, especially whole texts. This effect can be explained by the 'imperative to secure progression' so much promoted by the Strategy. This, it can be argued, is a blind obsession with measuring all children's progress by a series of tests linked to level descriptors all of which are performative; such an approach might work especially well in the training of dogs to perform tricks, at least if you do not care too much about how the dogs themselves are feeling. If your need is simply to produce dogs who can do impressive tricks, then informed prescription is what you need for the trainers. Primary schools and parents became increasingly disenchanted by the NLS and its performative obsessions, and the monumental Alexander Review has collected a huge amount of evidence to show how narrow and unengaging the primary school has become in the early twenty-first century.

The NLS was followed in 2000 by the Framework for English (FWE). In the period 1997–2000, there is clear evidence that secondary schools were busy preparing for the first cohorts of children coming up from the Literacy Hour environment (Goodwyn and Findlay, 2002). English teachers visited primary schools to observe the Literacy Hour and were much impressed by the energy of the teaching and the competence of the children in using linguistic vocabulary (ibid.). The FWE did not specify a Literacy Hour at secondary level but it was as dogmatically prescriptive about a pedagogical model of starter, whole class teaching, development and plenary, that exactly mirrored the Literacy Hour's formulation. Between 2000 and 2003 English teachers were angered and disenchanted by the patronising training model and the total disregard for flexibility and teacher autonomy displayed by the Strategy's secondary consultants (Goodwyn, 2003). After that initial reaction they settled into a superficially compliant mode ensuring that what the consultants wanted could be seen in classrooms for some of the time. However, during this period there was increasing teacher, teacher union and public pressure building up against the stultifying effects of the Key Stage 3 test; it was finally abolished in 2008, like a dam bursting with flood water. But during that period whilst complying with Strategy pressure, English teachers were becoming deeply dissatisfied with the 'imperative towards progression' that meant endless superficial coverage and the constant use of extracts to teach very limited teaching objectives as spelt out in the FWE document. They, and also student and beginning teachers, were especially unhappy with the reduction of time for real personal engagement with literature and for the difficulties of giving students an enjoyable experience of longer texts. One of the striking findings of research from this period (Goodwyn, 2010) is that English teachers did not want the term 'literacy' added to their job titles or to the name of their school subject. This contrasts with Australia in particular where the Critical Literacy movement had defined literacy very differently (see Misson and Morgan, 2006). Teachers in New Zealand and the USA are also comfortable with adding literacy to their job title; this reveals a very important point about the entire conceptualisation of the Literacy Strategy and the Framework for English.

So at both primary and secondary levels, the strategies did not carry the teachers with them, initial enthusiasm turned fairly quickly to disillusion and a mode of compliance not commitment. There really are lessons to be learned from this vast initiative, its 'impact' and its ineffectiveness. The authors in this volume make a careful and research-informed evaluation of the Literacy Strategy and offer insights and perspectives into its legacy. The literacy debate is far from over but we have learned a great deal about what the debate should really focus upon and we are very clear that learning or literacy are not 'a game'.

References

Barber, M. (2006) *The Learning Game: arguments for an Education Revolution*, London: Gollancz.

Barton, D. (1994) *Literacy: an introduction to the ecology of written language*, Oxford: Blackwell.

Beard, R. (1999) *National Literacy Strategy: review of research and other related evidence*, London: Department for Education and Employment.

Brooks, G. (1998) 'Trends in Standards of Literacy in the United Kingdom 1948–1996', *Topic*, 19, 1–10.

Brooks, G., Pugh, A.K. and Schagen, I. (1996) *Reading Performance at Nine*, Slough: National Foundation for Educational Research.

Bullock, A. (1975) *A Language for Life (The Bullock Report)*, London: HMSO.

Earl, L., Watson, N., Levin, B., Leithwood, K., Fullan, M. and Torrance, N. (2000) *Watching and Learning 1: First Report of the external evaluation of England's National Literacy and Numeracy Strategies*, London: Department for Education and Employment.

Earl, L., Watson, N., Levin, B., Leithwood, K., Fullan, M. and Torrance, N. (2001) *Watching and Learning 2: Second Report of the external evaluation of England's National Literacy and Numeracy Strategies*, London: Department for Education and Employment.

Earl, L., Watson, N., Levin, B., Leithwood, K., Fullan, M. and Torrance, N. (2003) *Watching and Learning 3: Final Report of the external evaluation of England's National Literacy and Numeracy Strategies*, London: Department for Education and Employment.

Goodwyn, A. (2003) 'Literacy or English: the struggle for the professional identity of English teachers in England', in *English Teachers at Work: narratives, counter-narratives and arguments*, Australian Association for the Teaching of English/Interface, Kent Town: Wakefield Press.

Goodwyn, A. (2010) *The Expert Teacher of English*, London: Routledge.

Goodwyn, A. and Findlay, K. (2002) 'Secondary Schools and the National Literacy Strategy', in *Improving Literacy at KS2 and KS3*, ed. Goodwyn, A., London: Paul Chapman, pp. 45–64.

Goodwyn, A. and Findlay, K. (2003a) 'Shaping Literacy in the Secondary School: policy, practice and agency in the age of the National Literacy Strategy', *British Journal of Educational Studies*, 51(1), 20–35.

Goodwyn, A. and Findlay, K. (2003b) 'Literature, Literacy and the Discourses of English Teaching: a case study', *L1-Educational Studies in Language and Literature*, 2(3), 231–8.

Holme, R. (2004) *Literacy: an introduction*, Edinburgh: Edinburgh University Press.

Misson, R. and Morgan, W. (2006) *Critical Literacy and the Aesthetic: transforming the English classroom*, Urbana, IL: National Council of Teachers of English (NCTE).

Stannard, J. and Huxford, L. (2007) *The Literacy Game: the story of the National Literacy Strategy*, London: Routledge.

Street, B. (1984) *Literacy in Theory and Practice*, Cambridge: Cambridge University Press.

Whitty, G. (2006) 'Teacher Professionalism in a New Era', paper presented at the first General Teaching Council for Northern Ireland Annual Lecture, Belfast, March.

Williams, P. (2008) *Independent Review of Mathematics Teaching in Early Years Settings and Primary Schools*, London: Department of Children and Family Services (DCFS).

Chapter 1

Beyond the heuristic of suspicion

The value of media literacy

Andrew Burn

Introduction: histories of media education in the UK

A backward glance at the construction of media education in the English curriculum reveals four patterns which make useful starting points for a consideration of what is happening now, and what might develop in the future.

These four patterns follow a common theme set by the first pattern, in which media education has been imagined as what I will call a 'heuristic of suspicion'. It has been the ill-tempered police officer of meaning, pushing teachers and students into a paranoid scrutiny of newspapers and television programmes to detect bias, misrepresentation and other distortions of some imagined 'truth'. Behind this uncongenial figure lies a tangled history of protectionist impulses, clearly identified by David Buckingham (2003). Buckingham points to the well-known influence of Leavis (Leavis and Thompson, 1933), whose approach to media education he characterises as cultural protectionism: an effort to protect children from the debasing effects of the mass media. He also identifies the no less rigorous efforts of Marxist ideology theorists to protect young people from the ideological effects of the media by teaching them strategies of interrogation intended to unmask the ideologies of the dominant groups in society and the media industries – strategies which, while their political intention might have been the polar opposite of Leavis's, look remarkably similar in their form and joyless denial of pleasure. The third form of protectionism Buckingham notes is moral protectionism, again based in reading strategies of suspicion, this time to expose the supposed immorality of media representations of, in particular, sex and violence. While this impulse is considerably stronger in the USA than in the UK (or indeed European media education in general), it is nevertheless a factor in the institutional regulation of media texts for young people, and in the value systems sometimes applied by fundamentalist religious groups to schools' choice of texts.

The second pattern discernible in curricular constructions of media in English is that it is often imagined as a genre of factual representation and communication: essentially, news media. It is as if the entire function of narrative texts and imaginative fiction is reserved for Literature. Two histories are noteworthy here.

One, again, may be Leavis, whose critical readings of media texts for school students never embraced the narrative structures of comic strips or the poetics of film, but rather made advertising their object of attack (Leavis notoriously invented many of the advertising texts he used, the better to exemplify their debased nature). The other history helps to explain how, regrettably, media literacy is again, at the present time, being seen as a matter of how citizens retrieve and critically appraise factual information. This is the history of the computer. As Lev Manovich has memorably described, the computer, from its inception in the form of Babbage's Analytical Engine in the 1830s, has developed as a processor of information, in contrast to the history of photography (also beginning in the 1830s with Daguerre's Daguerrotype), which is a history of cultural representations (Manovich, 1998). As these two technologies have become fused in the multimedia computer, what we may be seeing is the difficulty of information and communication technology (ICT) educators in understanding how the number-cruncher has become a tool of cultural production, while media and English teachers struggle with the implications of the cultural representations which have been their traditional stock-in-trade – films, poems, stories – becoming computable. It is partly for this reason that computer games, a cultural form that has always by definition been a set of computable representations, pose such interesting and challenging questions for media and English teachers as they consider how to teach such a form in the classroom (a question to which I will return below).

In the wider world of policy, politicians and bureaucrats have continued to be trapped by this division of 'media' into, effectively, fictions on the one hand and factual information on the other. In Europe at least, the 'fictions' have been largely the interest of film educators, who have considered how cinema narratives can be critically explored in schools in much the same appreciative mode as literature teachers deploy in their approach to literary fictions. Meanwhile, the policy makers have been largely preoccupied with how information is conveyed to citizens through electronic media, particularly online. In the UK, where the promotion of media literacy is a designated responsibility of the super-regulator OFCOM, this kind of literacy is seen mainly as a set of competences in handling factual information delivered by the Internet: how to access it, retrieve relevant information, be critically aware of its provenance and trustworthiness, adapt it for whatever purposes might be important to the user.

So, the general effect of this fact/fiction divide in the educational and policy arenas is to overemphasise both the importance and the risks of factual information in young people's lives, and to almost completely neglect the most important uses they actually make of the media: the music, dreams, fantasies, play, dramatic narratives, whimsical performances, album-making, aspirational self-representation, parodic invention and casual communication which make up most of their online lives.

The third pattern of the 'heuristic of suspicion' in the English curriculum is that is represents, essentially, an act of critical *reading*. Media within English has been located within the reading section of the curriculum, with no equivalent provision made in the writing section. In England, then, it has been mandatory since the inception of the National Curriculum to teach children to *read* the media (that is, critically interrogate it), but not to *write* it (that is, produce their own media texts) (QCA, 2007). There is a doubly suspicious stance here: a suspicion, again, of media texts, positioning them as objects of a critical gaze quite different from that envisaged for literature; but also a suspicion of young people's own media production work, implicitly devalued by comparison with creative writing. There have been, indeed, criticisms of student media productions within the media education community, castigating it as incompetent and derivative, reproducing the very ideologies that teachers seek to expose (see Buckingham, 2003, for an extended account of this). But such pessimistic attitudes have largely been replaced in more recent years by positive accounts of the value of production work, based in rationales of conceptual learning, creative transformation and cultural practices of media production increasingly typical of young people's informal media cultures (Potter, 2005; Jenkins, 2006; McDougall, 2006).

Finally, successive versions of the English curriculum have demonstrated a suspicion of semiotic modes beyond language. Recent versions recognise the growing argument for a multimodal approach to textuality and literacy (Kress and van Leeuwen, 2000; Jewitt and Kress, 2003); but the occasional reference to multimodal texts arguably produces only internal contradictions within what is effectively a conservative ring-fencing of language, buttressed by an increasingly unconvincing argument for its superiority over communicative modes. This argument takes curious turns. In 2004–5 a 'conversation' was held with stakeholders by the agency responsible for curriculum development over the period of New Labour's terms of office, the Qualifications and Curriculum Authority (QCA), about the future of the English curriculum. In its response document, the QCA argued, in reply to a number of submissions making the case for a version of the curriculum incorporating contemporary media texts, that:

> Alongside views that media and screen-based texts [can] have their place in English 21 there is the caveat that these should never be at the expense of our rich book-based literary heritage – a point more fully elaborated in terms of the purpose and value of engaging with verbal language: *the study of literature has one conspicuous advantage over the study of film and television media, in that it develops the skills of analysis, argument and discourse alongside language skills.*
>
> (QCA, 2005; emphasis added)

This kind of argument can be seen as a diluted residue of the Leavisian attack on popular culture. The authors of the curriculum here display a softened stance on the teaching of texts such as comics, films and television, allowing them a place as part of a wider cultural landscape, but there remains the firm belief that they need to be treated suspiciously, and to be seen as somehow thinner, more insubstantial, less nourishing than literature.

My intention here is to oppose this view, by argument and example. The argument is that there is no logical reason why the study of comic strip and animated film should not develop 'the skills of analysis, argument and discourse alongside language skills' just as effectively as the study of literature.

What, then, might the traditions, practices and theories of media education have to offer an English curriculum that might move it away from these limitations and distortions? I will frame my suggestions within the so-called 3-Cs model of media literacy (cultural, critical, creative). These Cs also inform the most recent version of the English framework in England; but the cultural, critical and creative elements there carry different meanings from those which inform media education. My proposals will build on a model developed in 2007 with James Durran (Burn and Durran, 2007), as part of an account of a decade of media education in the first specialist Media Arts college in England.

Culture: rethinking the divisions

The real debate about culture in the English curriculum is the tension between what the Cox Report (DES and the Welsh Office, 1989) labelled cultural heritage and cultural analysis. There is no explicit reference to this debate, however, in the curriculum. Culture there seems to mean 'multicultural', which, while it is a worthy aspiration to widen the selection of literature included in the curriculum, fails to account for the distinction between the literary canon and the popular cultural affiliations and experience of many of our students. How, then, might we rethink this distinction, and make something productive of the tensions that still exist?

My suggestion is to return to the definitions of culture offered by the influential cultural theorist Raymond Williams, whose work triggered the birth of Cultural Studies in Britain. Williams proposed three 'levels' of culture: the 'selective tradition'; the 'documentary tradition'; and the 'lived culture' (Williams, 1961). It was the third level, the proposal of a 'common culture' grounded in the everyday cultural practices of working-class people, which inspired Cultural Studies' subsequent attention to the politics of the popular, the structures of youth cultures, and the importance of audiences in the determination of meaning and value. The emphasis on lived culture remains a strength of media education, and no one would dispute its importance. Nevertheless, Cultural Studies (and media education) have largely ignored Williams's other two cultural levels. What would it mean to revisit them? Perhaps the first thing to say is that an attention to the 'selective tradition' need *not* represent a return to the narrow focus on heritage literature. Rather, the 'selective tradition' implies a critical focus on the mechanisms by which certain texts are privileged, conserved, sedimented into lasting traditions. This kind of critical attention to the social processes which determine (and contest) cultural value are surely the kind of processes which we would expect our students to learn to understand, and indeed to participate in.

Cultural value is a difficult area for media educators and for English teachers. Both are locked into forms of cultural distinction which they must defend, yet are unable to fully acknowledge or explain. The resistance of media teachers to the traditional values of elite culture is admirable, and the championing of popular culture in a curriculum which has little room for such material must be sustained. But it is absurd to be boxed into a position which is unable to recognise the intrinsic value of texts beyond the popular domain; or to consider the tastes and judgements which recognise (perhaps even construct) such value. Furthermore, it is clear that the texts of popular culture frequently undergo a revaluation by successive generations: yesterday's trash B-movie becomes today's cult classic; the arcade games of the 1970s are curated for exhibition in elite galleries; the pulp comic strips of the twentieth century acquire both economic and cultural value as the collectors' items of today.

But something similar happens in the construction of a literary canon. Through what processes of critical commentary, hagiography and 'bardolatry' was Shakespeare elevated into national poet? How are the popular oral cultures of medieval England conserved and instituted by the academy as valued literary works? How does the development of the European novel separate out 'literary fiction' from what becomes dismissively known as 'genre fiction'? How could a value judgement settle the score between the work of Isaac Asimov and William Golding? Philip K. Dick and George Orwell? Philip Pullman and J.K. Rowling? Emily Bronte and Catherine Cookson? Interestingly, the spurious work of cultural distinction continues from these literary sheep and goats into successive media adaptations. Orwell's work produces the art-house films of *1984* and *Animal Farm*; Philip K. Dick's stories morph into sci-fi classics starring Arnold Schwarzenegger and Harrison Ford, popular blockbusters which nevertheless trouble easy distinctions between popular and art-house cinema; J.K. Rowling's stories become Warner box office triumphs and computer games, while Philip Pullman's are first adapted for the stage of the National Theatre (though subsequently into film and a computer game). These processes of evaluation, exercises of taste, histories of shifting judgements usually appear in the classroom as inscrutable features of culture. Arguably, however, English and media teachers have a role, to open up these processes to scrutiny, beginning with a sensitive recognition of the cultural histories of the students themselves.

Williams's second category, the documentary tradition, suggests how culture at one level is a residue of a society which no longer exists; his examples are the art, literature and architecture of the ancient world. In media education, there is very little history, but rather a persistent focus on the new, which the advent of digital media and, recently, the participatory Internet has intensified into an obsessive neophilia. Williams's concern for cultural history reminds us that a proper interest in the contemporary moment can be balanced with an interest in the archaeologies of media texts, institutions and audiences. In one school where I am currently conducting research, for example, media teachers are helping students to explore the history of the camera from the camera obscura to the production of personal image-banks typical of modern digital cameras, mobile phones and online image-sharing communities.

English, by contrast, is very much preoccupied with literary history; though not necessarily in the way Williams imagines in his notion of the documentary record. The emphases are sometimes on the development of formal aesthetic features of literary texts, and on celebratory accounts of the lives of writers. However, something approaching an interest in literature as a documentary record of significant world events (the War poets, for example), social conditions (Dickens's reportage and social critique, perhaps) and the minutiae of social convention (Austen, Swift, Chaucer) can also often be the focus.

So we can see that, in English and in media classrooms, both cultural dispositions and cultural capital are imported into school from children's prior experience, and either legitimised or sidelined. The ideal might be that we build on these experiences, both valuing them and extending them into new areas. It is clear also that this is by no means an unconscious or purely instinctive process. Rather, it is a critical process, in which students become aware of cultural provenances, of the collision and negotiation of cultural tastes typical of human society, and of the aesthetic properties of material media. The critical aspect of this process is the subject of the next section.

Critical literacy: rhetoric and poetics

Media education has always been a form of critical practice, as in the forms of 'critical literacy' propounded today, which encourage students to question 'who constructs the texts whose representations are dominant in a particular culture at a particular time; how readers come to be complicit with the persuasive ideologies of texts; whose interests would be served by such representations and such readings' (Morgan, 1997).

This is a strength of media education. It can be seen as a rhetorical tradition, beginning with Aristotle's *Rhetoric*, and developing into the rhetorical studies of the modern day, which critically analyse political messages and the persuasive techniques they employ. For Aristotle, the art of rhetoric fell into three categories: *ethos* (the ethical context, emphasising the intentions of the speaker); *logos* (the substance of the spoken text); and *pathos* (the emotional engagement of the audience). I mention these ancient categories because they are still with us. The production regime in which a media text is generated, the structures of the text itself, and the reception regime in which audiences engage with the text – these three categories are fundamental to contemporary conceptions of the cultural exchange of meanings in Cultural Studies (du Gay *et al.*, 1997). They are also fundamental to the conceptual framework employed by media educators: the bedrock of the critical understanding students are expected to acquire.

There is a history of unease among media educators, however, about what happens when this critical approach becomes isolated from the pleasures of engaging with the media or the creative enjoyment of media production. At the level of public examinations in the UK (at GCSE and A level), conceptual and critical understanding is often assessed through written essays which analyse media texts or evaluate the students' own production work. It is all too easy for such work to become a decontextualised, dutiful rehearsal of what the student imagines the teacher or examiner wants to hear (Buckingham *et al.*, 2000). Part of the solution to this problem has often been seen as a closer integration between creative work and critical understanding. In the following example, for instance, 12-year-old students making a video game are asked to imagine themselves as games journalists writing a review of their own game:

Saturday 25th March, 2006

KIDS MAKE THEIR OWN GAME!

Students in Year 8 at Parkside Community College in Cambridge have formed a games company named PIG productions, in order to create a spectacular adventure game with an impeccable plot. PIG is an acronym for Parkside Interactive Games, and PIG's first game is currently in the making, by the name of Jimmy De Mora and the Dying World. Using Mission-Maker and just under 30 creative minds, students work in one of the English rooms at their school to design and make the game. . . .

The game is scheduled for release at all good game stores from May 2006, as the final touches are currently being made to the game. Lucky people who have had the opportunity to preview the game have never given it less than 4 stars, mainly for the plot.

The game follows secret agent Jimmy De Mora, who is living in a world that is deteriorating thanks to global warming, and is suddenly faced with the kidnapping of his daughter and sister. He has to rescue many prisoners, including much of his family, and seek a holy artefact for renewable energy. Some say the game is a cry for attention to the melting polar ice-caps, some say it's an exaggerated joke. Whatever is said, we can't wait to see how the final release is seen by the gaming world!

While this is a relatively light-hearted example, the students have been encouraged to consider various aspects of the games industry (studio production, games magazines, games retail outlets), game audiences and the political message of the game itself, as well as the possibility of different audience interpretations. This has been accomplished in the form of a written role-play, integrated into a suite of activities around the game production (writing walk-throughs; designing posters and game-box covers; designing and producing the game itself with an authoring software package), rather than an abstract activity divorced from the creative context.

Another example from classroom practice which demonstrates the importance of teaching and learning about media institutions is a Year 8 lesson taught by

James Durran of Parkside Community College, Cambridge. As well as its use in developing critical understandings of media institutions, it demonstrates how and why the same concepts can be applied to literary texts. It consists of an analysis of the game-box cover of *Harry Potter and the Chamber of Secrets* (Electronic Arts, 2002). First of all, this cover represents the media institutions involved in developing the Harry Potter franchise across different media, mainly by the inclusion of company logos. There are:

- EA – Electronic Arts, the games giant which publishes the game, and controls its production by a separate development company, KnowWonder, whose logo also appears.
- WB – Warner Brothers, which own the rights to the Harry Potter franchise, and make the films.
- ELSPA – the Entertainments Leisure Software Publishers Association, the UK umbrella organisation for the games industry, which has here applied the European industry's self-regulating age advice labelling scheme; in this case, giving the game a 3+ rating.

Inside the box and on the CD-ROM are other logos, representing institutions as different as *The Times Education Supplement*, which reviewed the game, and Dolby Sound, whose licensed technology produced the soundtrack of both game and film.

A critical reading of these logos by students, then, can show that texts such as Harry Potter do not exist in a vacuum, but are subject to a complex political economy. Global reach can only be achieved through the involvement of multinational companies such as Warner and EA; but such companies may also exert forms of control over content which smaller 'independent' companies may seek to resist. Games and films are subject to forms of regulation controlling the relation between their content and the age of their audience, with the mediating role of parents playing a role in the considerations here. Such forms of regulation are themselves a matter of social and political debate, involving (in this and similar instances) national regulators, the industry itself, parental groups and European and national politicians. The consumption of games is mediated by processes of review, both online by players and in more traditional forms of journalistic review. And finally, the textual structures of games, from their programmed narratives and play sequences to the sound they incorporate, are partly determined by specific technologies, each with their own history of development.

However, it is not only computer games that depend on this complex institutional involvement. The lesson that media education can offer English in this respect is that all texts have some kind of institutional context. There is very little history of attention to such contexts in the traditional pedagogies of English; though only a little reflection is needed to suggest its importance. The ability of technologies to make new meanings and social practices possible is evident from Caxton's printing press to today's social networking; the power of publishers over the utterances of authors was as evident to Thomas Chatterton and Dickens as it is to J.K. Rowling; the power of patronage may have passed, in the time between Shakespeare's work and Simon Armitage's, from monarchy and aristocracy to corporate and civic institution, but it still exists.

The other two key areas of critical understanding relate to text (Aristotle's *logos*), which I'll return to in the next section and audience. Again, media education has a robust tradition of critical attention to the nature of media audiences. While various versions of English promote the idea of writing for a 'real audience', the idea of actually studying audience behaviours, the social processes of textual reception and use, and the nature of interpretive communities rarely appears. Again, this kind of critical understanding is something media educators can bring to the table. It enables us to ask important questions: How do readers, spectators, players choose which texts to read, watch, play? What kinds of taste regimes operate; and are they influenced by peers, by families, by school, or indeed by the forms of comment and critique now evident in online social networks? What kinds of uses are texts put to? Do they function as 'cultural capital'? As mechanisms of pleasure? As philosophical stimuli? As catharsis? Political exchange? Expressions of conformity or dissent? Rehearsals for future life? Workshops for social dilemmas?

All the above questions and themes fall under the heading of the rhetorical aspect of critical literacy – and it is here that the traditions of media education are stronger than those of English, and able to robustly equip the literacy ship, as it were. I want to turn now to an aspect of critical literacy where English has the better-developed tradition – the poetics of textuality.

The media education approach to textuality has essentially been a semiotic one. Rooted in adaptations of 1960s and 1970s structuralist semiotics and narratology, most conspicuously those of the early Barthes, it has paid little attention to textual aesthetics. By contrast, English has always operated within an aesthetic tradition that can be traced back to Aristotle's *Poetics*, particularly in its conceptions of the formal properties of narrative structure, of tragic and comic drama, and of poetic metaphor and prosody. While English teachers know that such structures are only of interest in the service of meaning, it seems likely that one regrettable effect of the National Curriculum has been to reduce the teaching of literary texts again to decontextualised and fragmented fixations with such structures. Nevertheless, my point here is that the rhetorical and poetic aspects of critical literacy belong together. The problem has been that media education has been better at the former, English at the latter; and they need to come together.

What might this look like in practice? The following example will serve to develop a little further what I mean by a poetics of the media, and the aesthetic aspect of media texts. As with the Harry Potter example, the text in question is both a literary and a media text, so also serves as an example of the necessary entanglement of the two traditions for which I am arguing. The activity can be seen as a form of 'reverse-engineering': using an authoring technology to literally undo the fabric and structure of a filmic text to see how it is made. In this case, the video-editing software Adobe Premiere is used to disassemble fragments of Baz Luhrmann's *William Shakespeare's Romeo + Juliet* (1996), to explore how particular aesthetic effects are achieved. Furthermore, students are encouraged to creatively remake sections of the film, experimenting with different shot sequences and soundtracks. Before they begin the work, they work with the teacher to consider the function of different filmic structures: Figure 1.1 shows an exploration of different camera angles and shots, for example.

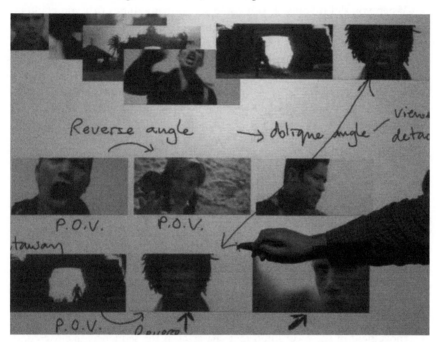

Figure 1.1 Whiteboard notations of different shot types, preparing students to create new film sequences using material from Baz Luhrmann's *William Shakespeare's Romeo + Juliet.*

While on the one hand, this kind of activity forms part of the conceptual framework of media education (understanding the 'language' of media texts), it is also a consideration of the aesthetic properties of the text. Aesthetic judgement, in the sense developed by Bourdieu (1985), is an expression of socially determined cultural taste, and this politics of culture is central to the work of media educators, who must conduct the negotiation of taste and judgement in their classrooms, encouraging students to reflect consciously on how such tastes are formed – a delicate and difficult business, as anyone who has worked with students to make music videos based on their own musical preferences will know. In the case of this filmic remaking, however, the focus is more closely on how particular aesthetic choices can be made using the materials of the text, and what the effects of these will be. This is closer to Aristotle's original notion of *aisthesis* as sense-perception than it is to the rarefied forms of aesthetic judgement characteristic of heritage literature or arts education. One student remarks, for instance, how he has learned: 'the use of being able to cut from shot to shot, instead of being, like, in a theatre and watching the whole thing on one screen constantly . . . how you can create emotions using particular techniques'. Another has learned to recognise montage – the juxtaposition of disparate images to make new meanings:

> When you did it yourself, you could see so many things that you could do with it, that you wouldn't have thought of doing . . . if you'd seen a picture of a clock, you wouldn't have put it maybe with, like, the police car, but when you can see it, and you can dissolve it into each other . . . and you can see it and how it changes it, how it makes it more interesting or do different things.

And another has found, through practical experiment, how the temporality of film can be stretched or elided:

> I don't think I shall be able to go to the cinema, or watch another movie, without thinking about all the different shots and sounds in a small scene again . . . I found the idea that you could make a shot with the camera much longer or shorter, or faster or slower . . . fascinating and clever. I thought the shot was however long you filmed it with the camera for.

Another student considers the narrative function of the camera as an eye, a proxy for a witness in the narrative, or for the spectator:

> Also, at that point when the camera tracks up, it is the first time there has been any significant movement in it. The camera has stayed still to reflect the movement of the most important character in the sequence: like Mercutio, the camera has witnessed everything, but has done nothing about it . . . The final shot is of a new character to the sequence: Samson. The camera is placed at an oblique angle to him. He is not an important character, he is at the side of the action. His emotion, his expression of fear and anxiety, needs to be acknowledged – not felt – by the audience. He simply watches – he does not act.

This kind of critical work, a fluid mix of technical production, aesthetic choices and critical reflection, is close to the kind of work students might undertake in painting pictures, choreographing dance, directing drama, writing poetry. It is situated in a 'media arts' model of media education; it exemplifies the kind of thing I am thinking of as a 'poetics' of media education. However, it would be a mistake to think that a poetics of this kind can float free from the political considerations of rhetoric: the two need to inform each other, as I have already argued.

Finally, these examples demonstrate a growing awareness of the 'grammar' of the moving image: how particular camera movements or edited sequences produce meaning as well as the particular images they shape. The value for students of understanding language grammar has been much debated in the history of English teaching; a recent book takes the arguments forward, considering how concepts of linguistic structure can be extended to wider semiotic frameworks, how they can be responsive to context and culture, and how they can be applied across different modes and media (Locke, 2010). There is no room to rehearse the arguments here; rather, I will outline briefly my own assumptions, derived from my classroom practice as a former teacher, and from my own research over the last decade or so.

First, the evidence seems to suggest that a conceptual grasp of the semiotic structures underlying a text is useful, if not necessary. Students can reach sophisticated understandings of texts without a technical understanding of its structure; and can, by the same token, make sophisticated texts of their own without such an understanding. But, if it can be achieved without slipping into empty formalism, decontextualised exercises and laborious naming of parts, it can aid analysis and creative production. This applies to the visual grammar (Kress and van Leeuwen, 1996) of comic strips and graphic novels, the 'kineikonic' grammar of the moving image (Burn and Parker, 2003) and the ludic grammar of computer games (Burn, 2010), as much as it does to the grammar of language.

Second, to explore the structures of meaning across a range of media forms such as these promises a richer, more complex, more robust understanding. A good recent example is a secondary Head of English who looks across book, film and game to enable his Year 8 students to gain a more sophisticated understanding of point of view and systems of address in narrative fiction (Partington, 2010).

Third, an understanding of textual structures – the mechanisms which serve both the rhetorical and poetic functions of books, poems, polemic tracts, films, television dramas, comics or role-playing games – needs to grow out of students' creative production of their own texts as well as analysis of other people's. One advantage of the remaking of *Romeo + Juliet* is that the students' grasp of dramatic gesture, character function, montage and camera movement is coming *both* from an analytical look at Luhrmann's text *and* the production of their own edited sequences. It is this essential link that recent versions of the National Curriculum framework for English fail to provide for. They go some way towards recognising the need for students to learn to *read* multimodal texts ('understand how meaning is created through the combination of words, images and sounds in multimodal texts', QCA, 2007); but the section of the framework which specifies what textual production is required refers only to *writing*. It remains mandatory, then, as I noted earlier, for students in England to study multimodal texts, but not to produce their own.

These examples suggest, then, that to be most effective, critical understanding needs to be integrated with creative production. But what exactly do we mean by creativity? How does it function as an aspect of media literacy? How might it represent common ground between media education and English?

Creativity: imagination, rational thought and textual production

Creativity in education is a much-debated idea. It is very differently conceived, not only by different academic traditions such as those of cognitive psychology, sociology or philosophy, but also by different stakeholders such as teachers, artists, workshop leaders, government think tanks and policy makers (Banaji and Burn, 2007).

My preferred approach to creativity draws on the work of the Russian psychologist, Lev Vygotsky, for whom the creativity of children was closely related to play (Vygotsky, 1931/1998). Vygotsky shows how children learn through play the meaning of symbolic substitution through imaginative treatment of physical objects, such as a child using a broomstick as an imaginary horse. These symbolic understandings become internalised and develop into the mental processes of creative thought. Vygotsky's argument is, however, that true creativity only develops when the imaginative transformations of play are connected with rational thought.

Here's an example. Figure 1.2 shows a comic strip superhero designed by a 12-year-old girl. It comes from a series of lessons in which students critically explore the idea of superheroes: what social and cultural meanings they carry; how the 'grammar' of their design works; what kinds of narrative surround them. Having learned to analyse commercial comics, the students are then asked to design their own superhero comic front cover. This character, Tigerwoman, has been chosen by its author to shift the gendered balance of the traditional superhero pantheon, producing a representation of powerful femininity. In this respect, it adopts traditional motifs of superhero iconography: the costumes, masks, urban scenarios, subordinate police forces, moonlit landscapes typical of the visual narratives of DC and Marvel comics, and of the animated and live action film and television spinoff franchises. In Vygotsky's terms, then, this girl has playfully adopted a range of cultural resources, and worked with what Vygotsky calls 'semiotic tools' to transform them into something new, something she has imagined. 'Semiotic tools' would here include not only the physical materials (paper, felt-tip pens), but also the visual 'lexis' and grammar she has deployed. At the same time, rational processes of representation can be seen: the gendered representation referred to above, and a causal narrative thread running through the visual composition. In these respects, this can be seen as a creative piece of work in Vygotsky's terms, a piece of work involving imaginative transformation and critical thought.

Figure 1.2 A 12-year-old girl's superhero design.

However, it can also be seen in terms of the cultural aspect of media literacy. The drawing makes considered, critical, pleasurable use of the resources of popular culture, partly in the service of an egalitarian message. Furthermore, the cultural work of the image can be related to the girl's own social identity. What it means to be female, to be a girl moving into womanhood, is a concrete, personal affair as well as a generalised political statement. The signifiers of femininity most salient to 'tween' girls are produced by this girl as attributes of her imaginary characters: painted nails, exposed midriffs, eye makeup, figure-hugging costumes. While she has not, in fact, experimented with these aspects of tweenhood, she cannot but be aware of other girls in her class who have. The possible routes through girlhood here are laden with moral and sexual ambivalence, opening up different routes to adulthood, but also to risk and name-calling.

Creativity, then, whether it is seen in poetry writing, comic-book design, filming and editing, or game production, is not a mysterious force of the Romantic imagination. Rather, it is a specific synthesis of thought and imagination, oscillating between the mind of the individual learner and the social context of the learning. Creative students imagine something new, but they use existing cultural resources, and they craft the imaginings according to a rational design. The teacher's job is to provide the resources and tools and to guide the process. Tools may here include material tools, whether they be felt-tips, cameras or digital-authoring software; but they will also include semiotic tools such as concepts of narrative or textual structure. Resources will include experience of other texts which have gone before, setting up the dialogic chain imagined by Bakhtin between the new utterance and the 'already-known, already-uttered' (Bakhtin, 1952/1981). They will also include some sense of who the new text is for – its audience. And the teacher needs to provide a sense of the contemporary moment – how this new text fits into the discursive landscape. Students bring a strong sense of this from their own experiences of literature and the media; but this sense needs to be recognised and made visible in the classroom. To hermetically seal creative production from the social contexts which inform it and can receive it makes no sense. At the same time, dialogism implies both an immersion in the contemporary moment, and a distance from it. The awareness of the utterances which go before produces a historical perspective, an ability to live in the cultural moment and stand outside it, looking at it from the point of view of earlier decades, societies, generations, the point of view implied by Raymond Williams's documentary level of culture. It is this kind of multi-dimensional creativity, criticality, cultural awareness that the model of literacy outlined in the final section attempts to provide.

Towards a cultural-semiotic model of literacy

The 3-Cs model of media literacy, then, suggests the need for media educators to interweave the cultural dispositions of their students with an expanding exploration of new cultural territory, in the context of playful, imaginative, creative production work. The balance is important, and is laid out in the 'cultural-semiotic' model of media literacy I developed some years ago with James Durran (Burn and Durran, 2007), whose classroom work is represented in the examples used in this chapter. This model (Table 1.1) connects Williams's three levels of culture (shown on the left), the popular 3-Cs structure, here conceived of as the social functions of media literacy (shown in the centre), and the semiotic work of media discourses, design, production and interpretation, derived from the work of Kress and van Leeuwen (2000) (shown on the right).

Table 1.1 A cultural-semiotic model of media literacy

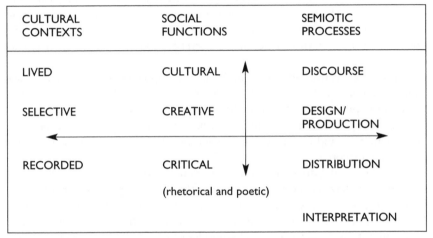

CULTURAL CONTEXTS	SOCIAL FUNCTIONS	SEMIOTIC PROCESSES
LIVED	CULTURAL	DISCOURSE
SELECTIVE	CREATIVE	DESIGN/ PRODUCTION
RECORDED	CRITICAL	DISTRIBUTION
	(rhetorical and poetic)	
		INTERPRETATION

It proposes, then, that media educators and English teachers move beyond a preoccupation with the contemporary moment of lived culture, though always returning to this moment as the space where meaning is made in the social realm for our students: where values are chosen, identities forged, pleasures enjoyed, representations understood. But at the same time, the contemporary moment is enriched by an interrogation of the past: of the cultures of parents and grand-parents, of media texts revalued through retro-culture, of the archaeology of media, the history of cinema, the origins of the camera, the birth and adolescence of video games.

The model proposes, as I have argued above, that the critical aspect of media literacy consists partly of the rhetorical analysis of media texts, institutions and audiences. On the one hand, this implies a critical distance from the lived culture: for students to explore the lived pleasures of popular culture, but at the same time stand outside it, historicise it, imagine it from other points of view, move beyond their own cultural values to explore those of other groups, other times, other generations. On the other hand, it implies critical understandings of the mechanics of rhetoric: of the grammatical devices of persuasion and argument, the syntax of ideology. In this respect, it connects with the semiotic model on the right of the diagram in Table 1.1. It proposes that, in order to achieve this critique, students need to understand the semiotic modes chosen in the process of design, the technologies of inscription deployed in the material construction of media texts, and the modes and media of distribution which bring these texts to their audiences.

At the same time, the model requires the poetics of the media I have explored in this chapter. This stance of appreciation aims to help students connect the aesthetic forms of the media, on the one hand, with their social meanings (the rhetorics); and on the other hand with their technologies of representation (the semiotics). It asks students to consider how the grammars of visual design, the moving image, computer game design, create these social meanings and the affective charge which invariably accompanies them. It asks them to analyse how these meanings and emotions are bound up in particular stylistic markers; and how these relate to their own aesthetic preferences and cultural values, as well as those of others.

Finally, the creative function of media literacy represents how the creative act connects also in two dimensions. It is indissolubly linked with the critical function (indeed, the production of new media texts can be the best way for students to grasp the rhetorics and poetics of the media); it is the means for the expression of aesthetic taste and for the self-representations through which social roles and identity are explored.

In the horizontal dimension, it represents the students' entry into the world of cultural production: a dialogic relation to the archaeology of past media texts, an interrogation of the selective tradition, an intervention in lived culture. Meanwhile, in relation to the semiotic dimension, creative production operates as an apprenticeship in the practical semiotics of the media: it enacts the critical understanding of textual structure and design, and the social interest invested in these structures.

Conclusion: beyond the old divides

English and Media Education belong together. They need each other – they serve as correctives to each other's prejudices, restrictions of scope, intellectual limitations. The examples and model offered in this chapter are intended to move beyond the sterile polarities constructed by mandatory curricula in the UK, to move beyond the opposed stances of suspicion and reverence applied respectively to media texts and literary texts. Literature is out of its jacket, marked with the signs of its economic and material production, bleeding into other media, subject to the online transformations of fans able to rewrite the hallowed word with no respect for textual boundaries. Conversely, films, television drama, comic books and computer games have grown their own respectable histories, canons and heroic author figures. They are collected, revered, curated, acknowledged by the institutions of high art which once reserved their attention for the traditional elite arts. In this world of cultural reversals, English and media teachers owe it to their students to make common cause: to embrace models of literacy which collapse the boundaries of elite and popular culture, of today's and yesterday's cultural moment, of the meaning and structure of texts, of the lexico-grammar of language and the equivalent structures in other media. Nothing will be lost, and there is much to gain.

References

Bakhtin, M.M. (1952/1981) *The Dialogic Imagination*, ed. M. Holquist, Austin: University of Texas Press.

Banaji, S. and Burn, A. (2007) *Rhetorics of Creativity*, Arts Council England, at www. creative-partnerships.com/literaturereviews

Bourdieu, P. (1985) *Distinction: A Social Critique of the Judgement of Taste*, London: Routledge.

Buckingham, D. (2003) *Media Education: Literacy, Learning and Contemporary Culture*, Cambridge: Polity.

Buckingham, D., Fraser, P. and Sefton-Green, J. (2000) 'Making the Grade – Evaluating Student Production in Media Studies', in Sefton Green, J. and Sinker, R. (eds) *Evaluating Creativity*, London: Routledge.

Burn, A. (2010) 'Rules of Grammar, Rules of Play: Games, Literacy, Literature', in Locke, T. (ed.) *Beyond the Grammar Wars: A Resource for Teachers and Students on Developing Language Knowledge in the English/Literacy Classroom*, London: Routledge.

Burn, A. and Durran, J. (2007) *Media Literacy in Schools: Practice, Production and Progression*, London: Paul Chapman.

Burn, A. and Parker, D. (2003) *Analysing Media Texts*, London: Continuum.

DES and the Welsh Office (1989) *English for Ages 5–16* (The Cox Report), London: HMSO and Department of Education and Science.

du Gay, P., Hall, S., Janes, L., Mackay, H. and Negus, K. (1997) *Doing Cultural Studies: The Story of the Sony Walkman*, Milton Keynes: Open University and Sage Publications.

Electronic Arts (2002) *Harry Potter and the Chamber of Secrets*, Knowwonder/Electronic Arts.

Jenkins, H. (2006) *Convergence Culture: Where Old and New Media Collide*, New York: New York University Press.

Jewitt, C. and Kress, G. (eds) (2003) *Multimodal Literacy*, New York: Peter Lang.

Kress, K. and van Leeuwen, T. (1996) *Reading Images: The Grammar of Visual Design*, London: Routledge.

Kress, G. and van Leeuwen, T. (2000) *Multimodal Discourse: The Modes and Media of Contemporary Communication*, London: Arnold.

Leavis, F. and Thompson, D. (1933) *Culture and Environment*, London: Chatto and Windus.

Locke, T. (2010) *Beyond the Grammar Wars: A Resource for Teachers and Students on Developing Language Knowledge in the English/Literacy Classroom*, London: Routledge.

McDougall, J. (2006) *The Media Teacher's Book*, London: Hodder Education.

Manovich, L. (1998) *The Language of New Media*, Cambridge, MA: MIT Press.

Morgan, Wendy (1997) *Critical Literacy in the Classroom: The Art of the Possible*, London: Routledge.

Partington, A. (2010) '*Content vs Concept*: Exploring the Use of Students' Cultural Experience in the Classroom and the Implications for a Model of Learning Progression in Literacy'. Unpublished dissertation, Institute of Education, University of London.

Potter, J. (2005) '"This Brings Back a Lot of Memories" – A Case Study in the Analysis of Digital Video Production by Young Learners', *Education, Communication & Information*, 5(1), 5–24.

QCA (2005) *English 21 Playback: A National Conversation on the Future of English*, London: Qualifications and Curriculum Authority.

QCA (2007) *The National Curriculum: English*, London: Qualifications and Curriculum Authority.

Vygotsky, L.S. (1931/1998) 'Imagination and Creativity in the Adolescent', in *The Collected Works of L.S. Vygotsky*, 5, 151–66.

Williams, R. (1961) *The Long Revolution*, London: Chatto and Windus.

Chapter 2

What happened to teachers' knowledge when they played 'The Literacy Game'?

Viv Ellis

In November 2009, I travelled to China for a conference on teacher development and school reform. The conference committee had invited five international guests: a former adviser on school standards to Tony Blair; an American expert on anti-racist education; a freelance consultant on sustainable development and food security; a Norwegian rhetorician and part-time magician; and me. I was the bottom of this eclectic bill – which was a shame as I had no hope of following the magician. The former school standards adviser was the headline act and his role, as he saw it, was to tell the Chinese audience about the miraculous transformation of the school system that had been effected in England and how it had been achieved. His PowerPoint presentation opened with a startling graph: a flat line beginning around 1950 and running perfectly horizontally until 1997 when standards in literacy started to rise exponentially. This transformation, he went on to explain, was a consequence of the National Literacy Strategy, a unique experiment in system-wide change that had tackled fifty years of stagnating standards in England's primary schools. The legend on the graph noted that it represented the proportion of England's 11-year-olds attaining Level 4 in end of Key Stage 2 tests.

Aside from showing that variety entertainment is alive and well in Shanghai, I begin with this story as it is a fairly typical 'victory narrative' account of the National Literacy Strategy and Framework for Teaching English at Key Stage 3, an account repeated in considerably more detail and at greater length by John Stannard and Laura Huxford in *The Literacy Game: The Story of the National Literacy Strategy* (2007). The narrative stresses the urgent moral and political imperatives, caricatures a failed 'progressivism' and *laissez-faire* attitude to English teaching, moves forward by way of selective citation of research and evidence and, occasionally, just gets really carried away by the historical (self-)importance of it all (hence the use of Key Stage 2 test results as a measure of standards since the 1950s). The genre is Romance: the ignorant are vanquished by our heroes on the noble white steed of New Labour.

Even for some in the academic community, the Strategies represented a 'new moral order' (Bourne, 2000) as key instruments of a wider social policy that sought better access to educational services – and consequently, it was assumed, greater social mobility for all young people, but especially those from economically poorer backgrounds.[1] To say that they were well intentioned sounds mealy-mouthed but I do not believe anyone doubts that both the National Literacy Strategy (DfES, 1998a) and the Framework for Teaching English (DfEE, 2001) were meant to do good. 'Education, education, education' was New Labour's self-proclaimed priority in its first term; its ambitions were high. And there were unprecedented levels of funding to support these reforms: £3.8 billion was invested in the Primary and Secondary National Strategies between 1998 and July 2010.[2] In these circumstances – high political risk and extraordinarily high levels of financial commitment – there could be no sense of failure, hence the Blair adviser's odd graph and the more careful, retrospective rationalisations of Stannard and Huxford, and others.

In this chapter, I am concerned with English and literacy teachers' professional knowledge and how it played out in classrooms, with children, during the time of the National Literacy Strategy and the Framework. I am therefore particularly concerned with how these initiatives were or were not taken up by teachers in the course of an activity that was already in motion before the advent of the Strategies – English teaching. To state the obvious, English teachers, as a profession, were already teaching prior to the Strategies, as much as leading Strategy figures may have preferred this not to be the case; English teachers were never going to be a 'blank slate'. And in the course of their practice, they drew on personal, local, national and international histories of English teaching activity, work that had influenced and been shaped by curriculum development, teacher training, action research, national curricula, subject associations, etc., over many decades. Rather than solely theoretical concerns with knowledge and with teachers as education workers, over the last few years I have been interested in finding out what happened to learning in classrooms and the ways in which the reforms of teacher knowledge (represented by the National Literacy Strategy and the Framework but also by Standards for teachers and the regulation of teacher training [e.g. DfES, 1998b]) permeated classrooms and figured in teachers' changing practices. Like other contributors to this volume, I would like to argue for a more nuanced and critical perspective on the Strategies than that necessarily advanced (given the politics) by those who led them. In doing so, I refer to Stannard and Huxford's (2007) account but also to the research and inspection evidence, and my own work as a researcher and teacher educator. Throughout, I also suggest that forty years of social science research into learning and human development might have offered some useful insights to anyone considering systemic change on such a scale.

Much of the criticism of the Strategies, it seems to me, especially early on, focused on whether certain approaches to literacy teaching were appropriate (e.g. the place of synthetic phonics in the teaching of reading; the use of genre theory in the teaching of writing) or whether grammatical definitions were correct in the documentation. Of course, there was also criticism of the coercion involved in the implementation of the National Literacy Strategy, particularly the degree to which some schools and teachers claimed to have been bullied. There were also arguments about the 'de-professionalisation' of teaching, focused on the restrictions on English teachers' individual autonomy – understood, most often, as their freedom to do as they pleased. In my view, these arguments about methods, linguistically correct terminology and the individual teacher's freedom, while important, were not the central issue. The central issues for me were how English teaching, collectively, was coming to be understood as a profession, and the profound shift in responsibility for developing professional knowledge, away from English teachers to central government, from education to a reduced version of politics.

In *The Literacy Game*, Stannard and Huxford acknowledge the political imperatives in play, the 'political timetable and the public promises on standards made by Government' (2007, p. 111). The only approach to tackling this political problem, in their view, was the 'big bang' theory: specify from the centre and require every teacher to follow the specifications. In contrasting the 'big bang' to 'slow change', the authors reveal the Strategies' infamous intolerance of criticism and the exercise of teachers' agency: 'slow changes can have negative impact because they generate uncertainty, and create scope for the unwilling to resist involvement' (ibid.). Ironically, generating uncertainty and creating resistance were outcomes of the 'big bang' approach anyway – as teachers genuinely tried to make sense of what they were presented with, their opportunities for understanding the new approaches to be mediated through talk were increasingly restricted. Videos were shown; overhead transparencies were projected; handouts were . . . handed out. Questions were closed down in a variety of ways; I personally experienced the 'we don't have time for questions; write them on a post-it note and stick it on the wall and, if we have time, we'll look at them at the end' approach. The questions usually were not dealt with and occasionally, if one dared to persist, like a local authority adviser friend of mine did, you were told to 'fuck off' by someone important during the coffee break.[3]

The Strategies' 'big bang theory' was based on the premise that teachers' behaviours needed to be changed and, possibly, just possibly, their minds would follow. The Strategies' interest was primarily in what teachers *did* in classrooms and not whether they understood what they were doing. In their book, Stannard and Huxford do link changing behaviour to changing minds even though it was just the first 'practical step' of behaviour they were interested in (2007, p. 113). But during the initial implementation phase, senior figures in the Strategy, in my hearing, spoke of 'changing behaviours *not* minds'.[4] Indeed, Stannard and Huxford quote approvingly from a paper by Michael Barber, Blair's first schools' adviser, who declaimed that 'winning hearts and minds is not the best first step in any process of urgent change' (Barber and Phillips, 2000, quoted in Stannard and Huxford, 2007, p. 114). So asking and answering questions, trying things out and adapting them, using uncertainty to come up with practical alternatives – all these were not just unnecessary but positively unwelcome responses from teachers. All that was required was compliant reproduction of routines from the training materials. In my view, it is this divorce between mind and behaviour that, for all the political rhetoric, led to uneven change and slow progress towards the political target (80 per cent of 11-year-olds attaining Level 4 in Key Stage 2 tests), growing unease among teachers and eventually more critical evaluations of the National Literacy Strategy by researchers from Canada's Ontario Institute for Studies in Education (Earl *et al.*, 2003).

Divorcing mind from behaviour is known as the Cartesian dualism, a phenomenon Sylvia Scribner called the 'metaphysical spectre', one that seemingly hangs over much contemporary policy. Speaking as a researcher, and drawing on the work of Lev Vygotsky and other psychologists, Scribner argued that:

> neither mind as such, nor behaviour as such, can be taken as the principal category of analysis in the social and psychological sciences. Rather, the theory proposes that the starting point and primary unit of analysis should be culturally organised human activities.
>
> (Scribner, 1985, p. 199)

In terms of education policy, as with learning in classrooms, the key point here is that change begins by understanding what people do and why. New ideas are introduced, mediated through practical interaction and dialogue, and new and qualitatively better forms of practice can and do emerge because practitioners *know* more. This process is not an unobtainable ideal, either: English teaching in England has a long tradition of curriculum development and organisational change based on just this model, whether the Schools' Council projects in the 1960s and 1970s, or the later National Oracy and National Writing projects. The way change works has not altered in the decades that followed; the way politics works has.

The kind of broader political imperatives driving the Strategies could be described as neoliberal concerns with social inclusion and social mobility. Whilst striving for these goals, New Labour's reforms of public services came to be characterised by their commitment to improving the existing political settlement through the creation of markets and the manipulation of market forces.[5] This modality of reform has come to be known as the New Public Management and, indeed, according to some (e.g. McLaughlin *et al.*, 2002), the UK could be seen as the 'birthplace' of New Public Management. Over time, New Public Management has been extended from its earlier concerns with marketing and other business functions to its current 'focus on governance in delivering public services' (ibid.). New Public Management approaches to governance seek to:

- take a 'hands-on' approach;
- specify outcomes;
- use Standards as performance criteria;
- de-centralise and privatise public services;
- introduce or improve competition between providers of those services;
- be parsimonious in allocating resources.

The emphases will differ between public services according to policy priority and what is politically expedient but these principles capture the essence of New Public Management. The National Literacy Strategy and the Framework were good examples of this type of reform at work in the education sector:[6] they were avowedly top-down and highly specified; outsourced for their implementation to private organisations on the basis of competitive tendering; and tied to performance targets that were, above all, politically important, particularly when politics is defined as the work of being re-elected. New Public Management's characteristic parsimony in allocating resources is less true with respect to the Strategy and Framework, particularly in its first phase. But the point was always, as Stannard and Huxford acknowledge, that the huge investment was a one-shot 'big bang' that needed to be so effective that further resourcing on the same scale would never be required again. 'Second' and further stages of implementation would only require monitoring of local developments to ensure they were compliant with the general specification; that is, the initial major investment would create an audit culture in which teachers would then self-consciously restrict the exercise of their agency.

So what happened to standards of teaching and learning in English over this period, as a consequence of the 'big bang' reforms? The post-1997 angle of growth on the Blair adviser's PowerPoint does not quite capture the scene and not only because his measure (Level 4) has only existed since 1989. Even if we use the government's own interpretation of standards as a yardstick, it is, to put it as positively as possible, a mixed picture. Two recently published reports have helped to clarify the situation. The first is a five-year review of inspection evidence by the government's own inspectors, Ofsted (Office for Standards in Education, Children's Services and Skills), and the second is the final report and recommendations of the independently funded Cambridge Primary Review. In Ofsted's report, *English at the Crossroads* (2009), standards are observed to have risen only slowly and unevenly. There continues to be a gap between the high and low achievers; girls continue to do better than boys; white working-class boys on free school meals continue to perform the worst, in so far as the testing regime captures these things. Too few schools have taken advantage of any later flexibility in the Strategies that has been allowed over the last few years. In particular, encouragement of independent learning, the reading of whole books and wider reading and, particularly, the teaching of writing are all found wanting. Students are taught *about* writing, says Ofsted; they are not taught how to write. Dull lessons are observed where children copy laboriously from the board. Lessons are stuck in a formula with too much teacher-talk. The children themselves tell inspectors they are bored. The sense from Ofsted's review is that where good English teaching is happening it is in spite of the Strategies and not because of them. And all this is from the government's own inspectors.

The Cambridge Primary Review finds that primary schools and teachers are generally in 'good heart' but that the quality of educational processes in classrooms is limited by a 'restricted, restrictive and misleading' concept of standards

(Alexander, 2009). Indeed, although there has been some upward movement in levels of attainment in national tests, the authors of the Review found 'little or no evidence' that the introduction of the tests themselves (as a key driver of the performance management and accountability) had driven up standards. Indeed, the work of Peter Tymms and others has methodologically questioned the use of national curriculum test results as benchmarks in measuring progress, given their intrinsic unreliability for such a purpose (e.g. Tymms, 2004). In its recommendations, the Cambridge Review report asserts the need for 'a pedagogy of evidence and principle, not prescription. . . . The principle that it is not for government or government agencies to tell teachers how to teach, abandoned in 1997, should be reinstated' (Alexander, 2009).

Although Ofsted's report is critical of the current state of teaching and learning in English, framed by the implementation of the Strategies over the last thirteen years, the report's recommendations are in turn shaped by the same assumptions. For Ofsted, the central task for government is to consider ways in which good practice can be identified and disseminated more widely and to publicise what successful schools have done. Ofsted's report allows no space for the development of English teaching from within and no concern for the profession's own views about directions the subject and its pedagogies might take. What is on offer is a slightly more relaxed form of managerialism that still relies on the core assumptions of delivering public services more efficiently by laterally transferring centrally recommended practices from one setting to another. Thus *what works* is identified in terms always and already defined by policy priorities and measured against what the politician has promised the electorate. Alexander's report rightly captures the nature of the problem: there has been a withering away of teachers' capacity to access and develop their professional knowledge and a shift in responsibilities for knowledge-creation away from schools and teachers to bureaucracy and the *realpolitik.*

Distinctive or specialised knowledge is a characteristic of professional groups – bestowing status and conferring both rights and responsibilities. The sociologist Julia Evetts has distinguished between two ideal-types of professionalism in what she refers to as 'knowledge-based work' such as teaching (Evetts, 2009, p. 263): 'organisational professionalism' and 'occupational professionalism'. Organisational professionalism is associated with standardised procedures enacted within a discourse of control characterised by hierarchical structures of authority and external forms of regulation and accountability (such as target-setting and inspection). Occupational professionalism is associated with discretion, judgement and local control of the work enacted within – and constituting – diverse professional discourses of collegial authority and trust, and regulated in ethical terms by occupational associations. To oversimplify, organisational professionals get told what to do and how to do it whereas occupational professionals have to figure these things out for themselves. The rise of New Public Management as a modality of public service reform has led to profound consequences for professionals and professionality, according to Evetts.

For knowledge-based workers such as teachers, the extended form of occupational professionalism places much greater responsibilities upon them for interpreting complex social situations such as classrooms and schools and coming up with novel solutions to problems and with new ideas for the development of practice. Drawing on Vygotsky's (1986, 1978) ideas about the imagination and learning, I use the phrase *professional creativity* to describe this capacity and form of agency (Ellis, in press). Creativity, in this interpretation, is a combination of perception (and analysis) and innovation (or production) at the level of concepts. In other words, it is about engaging with one's social situation and responding to it with new ideas. Perception and analysis (learning to see, to notice, in your classroom) were not capacities that the Strategies sought to develop among English teachers. New ideas were introduced ('rolled out'), on the basis of principles that did not require understanding and, in this way, the capacity of teachers to access and to develop their professional knowledge was marginalised. So, to adopt Evetts's ideal-types, I am arguing that there has been a shift from occupational forms of professionalism to organisational forms under which English teachers have simply been conceived of as a delivery mechanism for centrally scripted teaching routines from the political sphere. My concern is not so much the loss of any individual autonomy for teachers but for what this shift can mean for children learning in classrooms (teachers' explicitly *professional* responsibilities).

To illustrate how these approaches to re-conceiving professionality and teachers' professional knowledge impacted on classrooms and young people's learning, I turn to the English department at Gilbert High School, an urban, multicultural comprehensive secondary school in a West Midlands borough. I want to argue that the case of Gilbert High is prototypical (Langemeyer and Nissen, 2005) in relation to many departments in secondary schools in England in the early part of the twenty-first century; that is, the way the introduction of the Framework for Teaching English played out in this school describes a recognisable pattern leading to similar outcomes under similar conditions. I am not arguing that what happened at this school is universally true and I do accept that some English departments in England responded positively to the Framework and were supported by informed local authority consultants. But the case of Gilbert High, for me, is prototypical of what happened to teachers' knowledge when they were pressurised, coerced or 'big-banged' into 'delivering' the Strategy. This English department is somewhat unusual in that most of its teachers have taught English locally for twenty years or more; the head of English has taught at Gilbert High for twenty-one years, originally as a part-time English and Special Needs teacher. Most teachers in the department had also been part of one of the major national curriculum development projects of the 1980s and 1990s such as the National Oracy Project or the Language in the National Curriculum project. Unsurprisingly, this group of teachers were acknowledged to be expert practitioners and were often called upon by the local authority adviser to offer help to other schools. They spoke confidently about their practice and gained pleasure and derived momentum from a conscious awareness of their own expertise. I have known the school and many of its teachers for several years, having worked with them on teacher education and research.

In late 2004, I received a surprising call from the head of English that was, to all intents and purposes, a cry for help – surprising above all in that I knew this person to be both a highly expert English teacher and a very confident individual. About the same time I was developing a pilot research and development project in teacher education, one in which student teacher learning would be reconceptualised within a new design for organisational learning focused, in secondary schools, on subject departments (cf. Ellis, 2007). As I felt that I might learn something useful from finding out more about the problems she was recounting, I agreed to visit the school, conscious, I have to say, that I might be of no use or might even make matters worse.

During the visit, I learned that concerns had started to grow during the summer of 2004 when the school received its Key Stage 3 test results and shortly after in the first term of the 2004–5 school year when a cohort of Year 6 pupils from partner primary schools transferred to Gilbert High. The 2004 test results were not as good as previous years and the local authority's Key Stage 3 English consultants (the former highly regarded adviser having recently taken early retirement) had visited the school to monitor the implementation of the Framework. As part of the Strategy's usual approach of 'challenge and support', the head of English was put under pressure to set students in groups and to abandon the department's 'mixed ability' policy; to adopt a literal interpretation of recommended Framework methods; and to draw more heavily on numerical student data in planning teaching. These approaches were presented as more likely to 'meet the individual needs' of 'at risk' students who were 'entitled' to 'access the Key Stage 3 curriculum'. The pressure to adopt these approaches came from the local authority consultants and also from the school's newly appointed head teacher, wary of Ofsted and somewhat curious anyway about the English department's ways of working. The discourse of 'needs'/'at risk'/'entitlement to access' was becoming increasingly widespread and was – given that teachers do want to do the best by their students – at least partly persuasive.

At the same time, the new Year 7 cohort was about to start and information received from the primary schools (who had been working with the National Literacy Strategy for the last five years or so) suggested that an unusually high proportion of the students had serious literacy difficulties. Many students from one primary school, in particular, were reported as having grapho-phonic decoding problems. Given the pressure from the local authority consultants and the head teacher, and the promise of additional support from the consultants in the new ways of working, the Gilbert High School English department reluctantly decided to abandon mixed ability teaching and to work with children in sets, adopting a literal interpretation of the Framework for Teaching English, as advised.

By the time the head of English phoned me in late 2004, the department had been working for about three months with 56 Year 7 students, divided into two 'bottom sets', all of whom had attained below level 3 in end of Key Stage 2 tests.

The teachers had been drawing extensively on the Framework, mediated by the local authority consultants. The class teachers reported increasingly poor student behaviour, little progress in learning, unusually hostile relationships with and between the students with the teachers experiencing a mix of emotions such as guilt, anger, anxiety and confusion. After talking things through with the head of English, we agreed that the school would become part of the pilot I was working on, to allow me to access funding and resources and to situate the work within what would become a practice-developing piece of research.

I visited the school again with a group of six student teachers in January 2005 and we observed lessons and talked to all members of the English department. We also conducted reading and writing miscue analyses with each of the Year 7 students and interviewed them about their attitudes to reading, writing, English lessons and school. Prior to our visit, we had also asked the English department to provide us with a writing sample for each of the students as well as some brief background information – e.g. any information they had been sent by the primary schools, attendance figures, and so on.

During our visit, teachers had planned the two lessons observed to address the word and sentence level objectives for Year 7 in the Framework for Teaching English. In one lesson, the teacher was trying to explain the complex sentence and how it differed from simple and compound sentences. Teacher-talk dominated the lesson, apart from occasional, resistant interjections from the students. In the other lesson, the teacher was going through spelling rules, again very much from the front and, at one point, the children were asked to copy *onomatopoeia* from the board. Onomatopoeia was one way, they were told, to work out how to spell a word. Copying onomatopoeia from the board took some time, as you might imagine, and much of the lesson was taken up with ensuring accuracy and neatness in the students' writing. I personally found observing the lessons exceptionally awkward as I was aware of the real expertise of the teachers I was observing and I was shocked, to be blunt, that they were teaching in this way. I was also surprised at the writing samples the teachers had prepared, not so much at the quality of the writing but at the way the writing had been elicited: the students had been given a textbook task, a cartoon strip of a man coming out of a cake shop and slipping on a banana skin which they were then asked to write as a story. Figure 2.1 overleaf shows what Karl wrote; the activity was called 'What happened next?'

What was most surprising about the writing samples was, first, the task the children had been given, as I had never seen these teachers resort to textbook activities of this sort before. In fact, the department had been extraordinarily proud of never using textbooks, even though their photocopying budget suffered from this approach. The stories the children produced in response to this task had little meaning other than as a 'writing sample'. Second, the way the teachers spoke about the children's writing was also noticeably different. Dialect forms and phonetic spellings such as *sis* ('The man sis [*sees*] a cake in the window') were now spoken of as aberrations and markers of substandard performance rather than (as previously in the department) as nonetheless systematic and as a potential

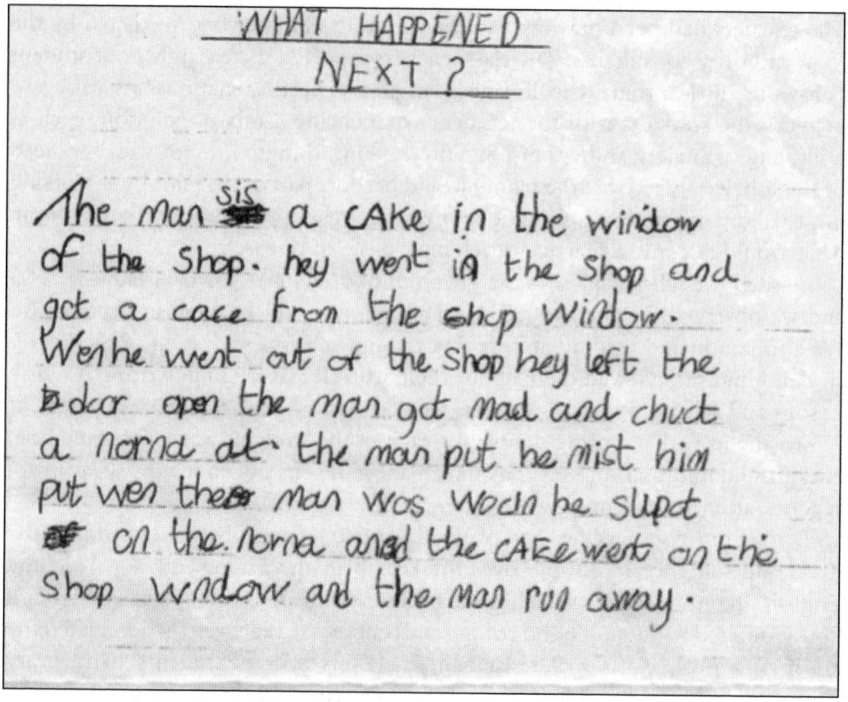

> WHAT HAPPENED
> NEXT ?
>
> The man sis a cAKe in the window of the Shop. hey went in the Shop and got a cace from the shop Window. Wen he went out of the Shop hey left the door open the man got mad and chuct a norma at the man put he mist him put wen theer man wos wocln he slupt on the norma and the cAKe went on the Shop wndow and the man run away.

Figure 2.1 Karl's 'writing sample'.

way-in to developing new varieties of written language. Moreover, the teachers did not now seem to recognise what the children were already doing in the writing they had produced; the way Karl, for example, was already using complex sentences to show how something was done ('Wen he went out of the shop hey left the door open') even though his punctuation was not always helpful. The way these teachers spoke about what their students could do was qualitatively different from their former ways of thinking.

Over the next two months, I visited the English department and spoke with the teachers on another two occasions, to feed back the outcomes of the miscue analyses, interviews and observations and to begin planning some new teaching sequences. Given my knowledge of the department and its teachers, I approached the work with some trepidation but quite quickly, to my relief, I found myself simply helping to remind them what they already knew and had been doing successfully for years. The results of the miscue analyses showed a very mixed picture and grapho-phonics was not the only or principal concern, by any means. The teachers already knew that the two classes, even though 'bottom sets', were not homogenous entities. They knew that understanding and exploring the students' own language with them allowed some purchase on the new varieties they were being asked to learn. They knew that complexity in syntax is not something that has to be explicitly taught before it appears, either in speech or in writing. So in the planning of the new teaching sequences, I actively encouraged them to draw on their previously successful experience, on their knowledge and expertise in teaching students from the communities the school had served over many years. In their renewed planning, they focused above all in engaging the students in making meaning – in having something to say to someone about something, and being interested in how it was said. They decided to get the students to work on written narrative – initially through telling stories and anecdotes; then making puppets for a puppet show to visualise and verbalise characterisation and dialogue; listening to stories read aloud and watching film clips that subverted traditional fairy stories to raise knowledge of the genre to the surface; then, writing their own fairy story, drawing on the characters and situations invented in their puppet shows and, in particular, crafting the stories so that the way they were told was just as important as the plot. This latter stage was time-consuming and, like much of the sequence, messy, with few episodes of whole-class teaching. The teachers quite quickly reported greater satisfaction and a better atmosphere in the classrooms, despite the length of time it took to clear up after lessons. Karl, for example, usually disengaged in English lessons, had become engrossed in the characters and situations he had invented and in the telling of his story. Figure 2.2 shows Karl's fairy story, alongside the face of his ogre puppet.

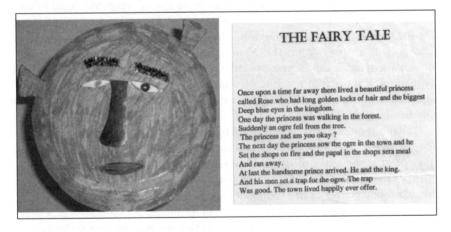

Figure 2.2 Karl's story.

At the end of the six-week sequence, the student teachers and I visited again, spoke to the teachers and the students, collected more writing (we had both the initial samples and the new stories assessed by teachers in another school) and, together, we started to think about what the experience meant for the beginning and experienced teachers and for the students. In conversation about Karl's fairy story, the teachers (student and experienced) could see how its meaning arose out of its location in a specific genre and how Karl's understanding of that genre was reflected in his construction of sentences and choice of words and that his understanding of that genre had been stimulated practically, through the making of a puppet, and in drama, rather than through drilling in generic structures. They noticed how Karl was manipulating length and type of sentence to mimic the rhythms of oral storytelling (for example, the placing of the short sentence, 'The trap was good'). And they could also see that the process of crafting and actively working on the telling had been supported by the use of a word processor – Karl deliberately staged line endings, for example. The Gilbert High English department also reinforced to the student teachers the responsibilities that these stories now placed on them – to engage with the meanings made by students like Karl and to offer feedback, suggesting where changes might improve the intended effect but also appreciatively, as readers. For the student teachers, the contrast between their first and final visits to the school exemplified a shift from what George Hillocks called a 'presentational' writing pedagogy to an 'environmental' one (Hillocks, 1984), from teachers specifying structures to imitate from the front of the classroom to teachers contriving opportunities for students to learn to write that drew on a variety of cultural resources. They were also able to see clear improvements in the quality of the writing through the assessments of our independent teacher colleagues.

For the English department and for me, however, the changes observed reflected a return on the part of the teachers to their deep professional knowledge after the superficially appropriated and poorly mediated intervention of the Framework for Teaching English. These Year 7 students, like Karl, were not abstract entities for whom the National Strategy Framework could provide deliverable remedies on a year-by-year or term-by-term basis. In this way, the problem was understood as one of accessing and developing the professional knowledge of the Gilbert High School English teachers in relation to the *actual* children in their classrooms.

Talking about knowledge in relation to school teaching can be a risky business. On the one hand, knowledge can become *thing-ified* – as a list of ingredients in a recipe or as some sort of viscous fluid that needs 'topping-up' in container-like brains. On the other, you can come across as someone who has swallowed a load of philosophy textbooks in a vainglorious search for justified, true belief. Neither position is particularly useful when working out how to improve a complex practice such as school-teaching. But the last forty years has seen strong interest in understanding knowledge in practice, from many social science perspectives, none of which seem to have been influential on recent policy making. The anthropological perspective, referred to earlier through the work of Scribner, has helped us to understand how knowledge is embedded in rituals and artefacts within specific communities. Sometimes, this approach – focused on 'situated cognition' – shows how knowledge is 'stretched over' people, their resources and their environments, to use Jean Lave's – a cognitive anthropologist – memorable phrase (Lave, 1988). The anthropological or ethnographic perspective has argued for a broader understanding of expertise and has shown that knowledgeable people do not always have their knowledge recognised and exploited. Scribner's example was that of workers in a dairy warehouse who were expert in picking and packing the various dairy products for distribution and delivery but who were subject to the rigid controls and specifications of office staff, none of whom actually *knew* the work. The argument has always been, from an educational perspective: just think how more effective the work/learning – and engaged the workers/students – would be if their knowledge and expertise was allowed to feed back into the enterprise. Actively rejecting the existing professional knowledge of the English teachers at Gilbert High School and attempting to replace it with a constant recipe for instruction from the political sphere had profoundly negative consequences for their students.

Cultural-historical activity theory (CHAT), a Vygotskian framework for understanding learning, change and development, also has much to offer any consideration of knowledge in processes of change. A CHAT perspective, as its name suggests, is interested in the cultural and historical evolution of practice, in how what goes on in specific settings (the 'situated' activity) is related to the historical channels (or 'traditions') of cultural practices. That is, how what goes on in one English classroom relates to – draws on and also helps to shape – what goes on and what has gone on in other English classrooms. The link between these different levels of activity and practice lies, from a CHAT perspective, in the 'tools' that are used – material or psychological (concepts or signs). CHAT is particularly interested in how people pick up and use conceptual tools when they work together on the same object or societally significant problem. The Finnish psychologist Yrjo Engeström has developed a 'third generation of activity theory' which uses, in participatory ways, a triangular device shown in Figure 2.3.

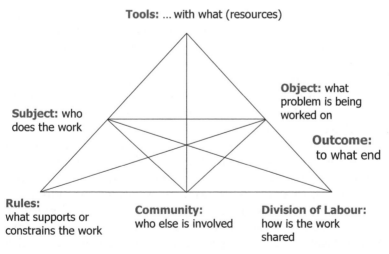

Figure 2.3 The structure of a human activity system, adapted from Engeström (1987).

The triangle represents an activity system – the joint work of a group of people sharing a potentially similar *object*, organised by certain social *rules*, conventions and *divisions of labour*. *Subject* means the group of people, who may or may not be co-present – in our case, English teachers; *tools* represent the conceptual resources they are using to work on (potentially) the same *object* and towards similar *outcomes*. In this case, the object of English teachers' work with students in classrooms might be the learning of subject English with the outcome of students as better readers and writers and talkers. It is also important to note that, in CHAT, object has a slightly archaic meaning: something that is intellectually and culturally interesting, motivating and desirable, and that can be interpreted differently. People working together through multiple interpretations of an object potentially allows for that object to be transformed or 'expanded' and this expansion can in turn lead to the identification of new tools and new ways of socially organising a practice – to qualitative improvements in that practice. Engeström (e.g. 1987; Engeström *et al.*, 1999) has given us many examples of this sort of 'expansive learning' in a number of professional settings and I have used similar methodologies with secondary English teachers (e.g. Ellis, 2010, 2008). This line of thinking about human activity also recognises that we each participate in multiple and potentially contradictory activity systems, so that the English teacher may also figure in a school's curriculum management activity system, a local branch of a subject teaching association, as well as the English department.

CHAT is a useful device for understanding how activity systems have evolved and how practice has come to be the way it is. With reference to the Gilbert High English department, it seemed to me that the conceptual tools offered by the Framework for Teaching English were not being picked up and appropriated in meaningful ways by the teachers and that, moreover, there was a sense that the tools offered (in the documentation and resources and in the local authority consultants' talk) were not fit for purpose in that they remained largely decontextualised and abstract, and unresponsive to the particular situation. This is not to say that the conceptual tools offered by the Strategies, and for which *post hoc* research rationalisations were provided, would always and ever be useless but that the models of teacher development and organisational learning underpinning the Strategies ('big bang', 'behaviours not minds', etc.) were impoverished. So in the case of Gilbert High, the tools (objectives-led teaching; synthetic phonics; syntax; etc.) offered by the Framework for teachers to use in working on their student's learning, 'slipped' around the activity system and simply became *rules*, norms of behaviour or social conventions that were visible and relatively easy to police by the consultants and inspectors. In my own research (e.g. Ellis, 2010), I have observed English teachers' superficial appropriations of the tool of *genre* in their teaching of writing, so that 'writing frames' become highly detailed plans given, as a rule, to every student in a class regardless of need.

A third perspective, theories of practice in the sociology of science, can also help to illuminate the importance of knowledge in professions such as school-teaching. Karen Knorr-Cetina, for example, studied the work of laboratory scientists and identified the importance of the emotional or affective dimensions of knowledge. Knorr-Cetina showed how, although some professional work is inevitably routine, the non-routine aspects of the work – when we confront unusual or unexpected problems, when we have to use our powers of perception and analysis to diagnose, to assess, to identify, to understand or to *relate to someone* – lead to a form of 'creative and constructive practice' that is distinctively professional (Knorr-Cetina, 2001, p. 175). Knowledge is important in Knorr-Cetina's analysis because it is the basis for social processes of 'engrossment and excitement' – people become professionals and define professionalism because they are interested in and enjoy developing what they know. Knowledge is not, for laboratory scientists or any other professionals, a list of answers, correct definitions and 'best-practice' routines, but arises out of a process of creative enquiry and transformation similar to CHAT's understanding of 'expansive learning'. It is this process of working on what Knorr-Cetina calls 'epistemic objects' that captures professionals' interests, lends direction and momentum to their work, and gives them pleasure because, unlike the 'closed boxes' of non-professional work, epistemic objects are intriguing, having 'the capacity to unfold indefinitely' (ibid., p. 181).

Characterising professional knowledge as something teachers are *necessarily* engrossed and excited by was clearly not a view the architects of the Strategies shared. Teacher knowledge always appeared to be a bit loose and woolly for Stannard and Huxford, shaped in 'fairly inadequate' ways by university departments of education and inevitably unable to pass muster against the rigour of the real experts, the educational psychologists (by which I think they must mean the experimental variety) (Stannard and Huxford, 2007, p. 10). The Strategies' aim was for English teachers to become passive recipients of 'evidence' from elsewhere; their reformed role was merely to do as they were told, with a later promise of 'flexibility' within the existing design. But the sustaining and motivating affordances for teachers of developing their professional knowledge (meaning knowledge that is both distinctive, collective and the basis for social action) were not important at all in 'the literacy game'. Increasing understanding, sharpening powers of perception and engaging in processes of enquiry and transformation were not the object of the National Literacy Strategy and the Framework, as the English teachers at Gilbert High found out. To that extent, for the profession, the Strategies had a profoundly negative effect.

If a reader of *The Literacy Game* expects to read a careful evaluation of the National Literacy Strategy, with acknowledgement of its flaws and honest self-criticism, they will surely be disappointed. Stannard and Huxford's eventual conclusions are un-apologetically hard line: if politicians wish to learn from the Strategies, they say, the message is to 'define clear, precise messages, common practices' and implement them 'persistently' (Stannard and Huxford, 2007,

p. 198). Schools should be rigorously monitored and inspected to ensure compliance; politicians should 'strengthen accountability all around and leave no doubt for schools about their priorities' (ibid.). It is a sour-faced message sung to a miserable old tune and the somewhat battle-scarred-sounding singers appear to have learned very little about systemic change in education, developing curriculum and pedagogy, and improving the knowledge-creating capacities of the English-teaching profession. As I have argued, to an extent, this is an understandable response from those most closely associated with what was, above all else, a political project, when politics had become reduced by short-termism and the endless game of being re-elected. But it is also a scathing indictment of the National Literacy Strategy as an educational reform, as a means of developing English and literacy teaching and as a programme of teacher development. Its failures, as I have argued, arise from its unwillingness to take teachers' knowledge seriously, to understand how the processes of knowledge-creation are essential attributes of any profession, enriching and developing practice, and sustaining and motivating practitioners in strengthening the profession from within.

So, what did happen to teachers' knowledge when they played 'the literacy game'? I have argued that English teachers' professional knowledge – the collective, conceptual inheritance that has evolved over many decades through the creative interventions of individuals and groups – was explicitly rejected as unsatisfactory in the design of the National Literacy Strategy and Framework for Teaching English. In its place, a set of recommended classroom routines explicitly related to targets derived from the political sphere was introduced, often with inadequate support and few opportunities for proper mediation. Rather than being an unintended consequence of patchy or poor quality implementation, the problems that were experienced by teachers and their students – and are reflected in the extremely mixed picture of improvement painted by the government's own data – were *built into the design* of the reforms and the understandings of teacher learning and development that underpinned them. The legacy of the National Literacy Strategy and the Framework could well be a reduction in English teachers' capacities to access and to develop their professional knowledge as a result of understanding their professional responsibilities differently. The risk is that the profession now judges itself by the efficiency of its 'delivery' – an entirely bureaucratic virtue – rather than by its contribution to the future of the knowledge-base and its responsiveness to changing and diverse populations of children.

In this chapter, I have been arguing from a position that emphasises teachers' essentially professional responsibilities in improving their own knowledge and practice, and that it is these very responsibilities that distinguish professional activity. I have suggested that it is in the stimulation and strengthening of English teachers' professional creativity – their capacity to improvise teaching in the classroom-moment on the basis of deep and developing knowledge of subject and students – that the best hope for positive change lies. And all the time there must be the recognition that to generate and to sustain real change, teachers, as professionals, must not only be engaged but engrossed and excited by the prospect. At the level of principle, this position is neither sentimental nor romantic but a fundamental basis for effective, value-for-money policy in the reform of public services such as education.

Notes

1   The work of British sociologist Basil Bernstein was often appropriated in support of the National Literacy Strategy's emphasis on explicit or 'visible' pedagogies for working-class children, as it had been in Australia in the 1990s (cf. Burgess *et al.*, 2010).

2   £3,835,707,000 was invested in the Primary and Secondary National Strategies between 1998 and 2010. In responding to the freedom of information (FOI) request, officials argued that it was impossible to disaggregate figures for literacy and English programmes from the wider Strategies throughout this period, although they were able to say that £1.1 billion was spent on primary literacy and secondary English programmes between 2005 and 2008. Freedom of Information Act request number 2010/0066245: Viv Ellis to the Department for Education, UK Government, August 2010.

3   The words are those used – perhaps exceptionally in this instance (I do not know) – but the incident is illustrative of the degree to which the Strategy was seen as non-negotiable.

4   At Strategy events for those involved in initial teacher education – the only sector for which the Framework was made statutory – Stannard and others repeatedly emphasised the reforms' urgency by focusing on the need to change teachers' behaviours quickly.

5   Ken Jones points out that the reforms were of course characterised by multiple influences – such as international comparisons (e.g. on the basis of OECD data) – but also by New Labour's desire to be seen to set itself against the ways in which previous, post-war Labour governments had run the public services (see Jones, 2003).

6   The Strategies were also accompanied by enhanced state control over all aspects of the education system: the invention of new agencies (e.g. Ofqual – the Office for Qualifications and Examinations Regulation); new professional qualifications (such as those for head teachers) and Standards; and the exclusion or marginalisation of former players such as local education authority advisers and teacher training institutions.

References

Alexander, R. (ed.) (2009) *Children, their World, their Education. Final report and recommendations of the Cambridge Primary Review*, London: Routledge.

Bourne, J. (2000) 'New Imaginings of Reading for a New Moral Order: A review of the production, transmission and acquisition of a new pedagogic discourse in the UK', *Linguistics and Education* 11, 1: 31–45.

Burgess, T., Ellis, V. and Roberts, S. (2010) '"How One *Learns* to Discourse": Writing and abstraction in the work of James Moffett and James Britton', *Changing English: Studies in Culture and Education* 17, 3: 261–74.

DfEE (Department for Education and Employment) (2001) *Framework for Teaching English in Years 7, 8 and 9 (Key Stage 3 National Strategy)*, London: DfEE.

DfES (Department for Education and Skills) (1998a) *The National Literacy Strategy: Framework for Teaching*, London: DfES.

DfES (1998b) *Teaching: High Status, High Standards. Requirements for Course of Initial Teacher Training* (Circular 4/98), London: DfES.

Earl, L., Watson, N., Levin, B., Leithwood, K., Fullan, M. and Torrance, N. (2003) *Watching and Learning 3: Final report of the OISE/UT evaluation of the implementation of the National Literacy and Numeracy Strategies*. Prepared for the Department for Education and Skills, England. Toronto: OISE/University of Toronto.

Ellis, V. (2007) 'More than "Soldiering On": Realising the potential of teacher education to rethink English in schools', in Ellis, V., Fox, C. and Street, B. (eds) *Rethinking English in Schools: A new and constructive stage*, London: Continuum.

Ellis, V. (2008) 'Exploring the Contradictions in Learning to Teach: The potential of Developmental Work Research', *Changing English: Studies in Culture and Education* 16, 1: 53–63.

Ellis, V. (2010) 'Studying the Process of Change: The double stimulation strategy in research on teacher learning', in Ellis, V., Edwards, A. and Smagorinsky, P. (eds) *Cultural Historical Perspectives on Teacher Education and Development: Learning teaching*, London: Routledge.

Ellis, V. (in press) 'Re-energising Professional Creativity: Seeing knowledge and history in practice', *Mind, Culture, and Activity*.

Engeström, Y. (1987) *Learning by expanding: An activity–theoretical approach to developmental research*, Helsinki: Orienta-Konsultit.

Engeström, Y., Miettinen, R. and Punamaki, R.-L. (eds) (1999) *Perspectives on Activity Theory*, Cambridge: Cambridge University Press.

Evetts, J. (2009) 'New Professionalism and New Public Management: Changes, continuities and consequences', *Comparative Sociology* 8: 247–66.

Hillocks, G. (1984) 'What Works in Teaching Composition: A meta-analysis of experimental treatment studies', *American Journal of Education* 93, 1: 133–70.

Jones, K. (2003) *Education in Britain: 1944 to the present*, Oxford: Polity Press.

Knorr-Cetina, K. (2001) 'Objectual Practice', in Schatzki, T.R., Knorr-Cetina, K. and von Savigny, E. (eds) *The Practice Turn in Contemporary Theory*, London: Routledge.

Langemeyer, I. and Nissen, M. (2005) 'Activity Theory', in Somekh, B. and Lewin, C. (eds) *Research Methods in the Social Sciences*, London: Sage.

Lave, J. (1988) *Cognition in Practice*, Cambridge: Cambridge University Press.

McLaughlin, K., Osborne, S.P. and Ferlie, W. (2002) *New Public Management: Current trends and future prospects*, London: Routledge.

Ofsted (2009) *English at the Crossroads. An evaluation of English in primary and secondary schools 2005–2008*, London: Ofsted.

Scribner, S. (1985) 'Vygotsky's Uses of History', in Wertsch, J.V. (ed.) *Culture, Communication, and Cognition: Vygotskian perspectives*, Cambridge: Cambridge University Press.

Stannard, J. and Huxford, L. (2007) *The Literacy Game: The story of the National Literacy Strategy*, with a Foreword by Barber, M., London: Routledge.

Tymms, P. (2004) 'Are Standards Rising in English Primary Schools?' *British Educational Research Journal* 30, 4: 477–94.

Vygotsky, L.S. (1978) *Mind in Society: The development of higher psychological processes*, M. Cole, V. John-Steiner, S. Scribner and E. Souberman (eds), Cambridge, MA: Harvard University Press.

Vygotsky, L.S. (1986) *Thought and Language*, A. Kozulin (ed. and trans.), Cambridge, MA: MIT Press.

Chapter 3

Policing grammar

The place of grammar in literacy policy

Debra Myhill and Susan Jones

Introduction

The contested place of grammar in a literacy curriculum is a peculiarly anglophone phenomenon: throughout most countries in Europe, for example, it is accepted as wholly natural that students should learn the grammar of their own language. But as a phenomenon, the debate about the role of grammar in English rehearsed in England is also common to the United States, Canada, Australia and New Zealand. In all five countries, the teaching of formal grammar was abandoned in the second half of the twentieth century, largely rejected by English teachers and educationalists as serving no educational value. English grammar, as taught prior to the 1960s, was largely a matter of syntactical analysis and identification of 'parts of speech', and the implication was that such grammatical knowledge would lead to students who wrote and spoke Standard English correctly. Thus grammar teaching was predominantly conceptualised as obedience to rules and the avoidance of error. However, a swelling tide of disenchantment with grammar arose in the late 1950s and 1960s. In 1962, Gurrey attributed the decline in grammar teaching to 'the lack of agreement on all salient points [which] has unsettled the belief of many older teachers that it is of value, and has led many of the younger ones to deny its usefulness' (1962: 7). English teachers, supported by research evidence which suggested there was no beneficial impact of grammar teaching on students' language use, believed their role was to enable and empower communication and self-expression, not to act as gatekeepers to language standards. Indeed, Randy Bomer, a former president of the US professional association for English teaching, the National Council of Teachers of English (NCTE), argued as recently as 2006 that 'most English teachers do not see themselves as grammar police, on the lookout for mistakes and intolerant of diverse ways of speaking' (NCTE 2006).

In this chapter, we will explore briefly the historical debate about grammar teaching, and provide a concise overview of the political and professional discourses about grammar and grammar teaching which predated the advent of the National Literacy Strategy (NLS). We will then outline in more detail the re-emergence of grammar in the National Curriculum and in the National Strategy, and the way grammar policy has been realised in classroom practice. Finally, we will offer a theorised position of a place for grammar in both literacy policy and literacy practice.

Grammar in the curriculum: a retrospective

The trajectory of grammar as part of an English curriculum has been heavily influenced and shaped by the parallel trajectory of subject English. Given its current status as a 'core' subject in the curriculum, it is hard to imagine that it is a relatively new subject, only having emerged as a university subject towards the end of the nineteenth century. Prior to that, English existed only as the study of Anglo-Saxon; and grammar as part of university study alongside rhetoric and dialectic. English as a university subject, as Eagleton (1991) describes it, grew as a counter-current to prevailing masculine hegemonies and was initially seen as 'a fatal emasculating force' (1991: 8) within universities (because it was commonly studied by women), but was then followed by an academic reconstruction, 'a reconstitution of the subject as the very essence of the English national spirit, the cultural arm of colonialism' (1991: 8). In the early twentieth century, English as a subject was trying to claim its place in the school curriculum: the Newbolt Report (Board of Education 1921) displaced Classics from the heart of the school curriculum, replacing it with study of the mother tongue, on the basis that there had been 'an underestimate of the importance of the English language and literature' (Board of Education 1921: 4). But Newbolt dismissed grammar on the basis that it was impossible 'to teach English grammar in the schools for the simple reason that no-one knows exactly what it is' (Board of Education 1921: 289). On the other hand, Newbolt believed that accessing the nation's cultural heritage through language and literature could provide children with a moral education and a sense of national identity: subject English was 'the channel for formative culture for all English people, and the medium of the creative art by which all English writers of distinction, whether poets, historians, philosophers or men of science, have secured for us the power of realising some part of their own experience of life' (Board of Education 1921: 12). In many ways, Newbolt's report presaged the ascendancy of literature as the cornerstone of the English curriculum, literature which opened up children's understanding of themselves and their world and which was more liberating and emancipatory than the dull routine of grammar drills and error correction.

In tandem with the emergence of subject English and the emphasis on English literature was an absence of serious academic study of grammar and language in English universities. Hudson and Walmsley (2005) offer an overview of the fluctuating status of grammar in the curriculum, and argue a link between the lack of research in linguistics in universities and the demise of grammar in schools. Whilst elsewhere in Europe and America, modern linguistics was flourishing (for example, Jespersen [1905] in Denmark; Fries [1951] in the USA; and Funke [1950] in Germany), very little was happening in England. In England, school grammar was informed by Latin grammar, not the understandings of modern linguistics, and through the first sixty years of the twentieth century, there developed 'an ever-widening gap in England between the practice of professional grammarians on the one hand, and the lay public and practice in schools on the other' (Hudson and Walmsley 2005: 595). And, as a consequence, English teachers became increasingly disenchanted with the apparent pointlessness of parsing and sentence analysis. The view expressed by Dixon (1975) that 'when we taught traditional grammar we could not, as research showed, claim to affect language in operation. In fact, grammar teachers, both past and present, have been among those most guilty of imposing a body of knowledge which never became a guide to action or a point of reference' (1975: 55) captures the zeitgeist of this period.

The Bullock Report (DES 1975) also rejected traditional grammar teaching which 'identified a set of correct forms and prescribed that these should be taught' (DES 1975: 169) and which 'put the emphasis less on knowing what to say than on knowing what to avoid' (DES 1975: 170). However, Bullock did assert the importance of more explicit teaching about language in the face of what he saw as an indulgent emphasis on creative writing in which writers were given very little instruction or feedback. So, at the point of the development of the National Curriculum in the late 1980s, there was very much a professional consensus, endorsed by literacy policy, that grammar teaching was a redundant enterprise.

Grammar in the National Curriculum

The introduction of the National Curriculum for England and Wales in 1990 will almost certainly be remembered as a key point in Britain's educational history. As a statutory instrument, enshrined in law, *English in the National Curriculum* (DES 1990) was the first mandatory outline of what should be taught in English, literacy policy with the full weight of the law behind it. It was a controversial curriculum, not just in terms of its decisions on grammar and Standard English, but also in terms of its emphasis upon the English literary heritage and its advocacy of a canon of approved texts. The period 1988–94, culminating in the boycott of the Key Stage 3 National Tests for English, is arguably one of the most critical periods in history for foregrounding fierce debates about subject English, and language and grammar were right at the heart of these debates.

The National Curriculum was preceded by two significant reports, the Kingman Report (DES 1988) and the Cox Report (DES 1989). The Kingman Report was commissioned by the Conservative government to investigate a model which could be used for training teachers in how language works, to consider how explicit language teaching should be, and what students needed to know about language. Kingman was a mathematician and it was expected that the report would endorse traditional teaching of grammar, based on a Latinate model, in line with Tory 'back-to-basics' education policy. But the Kingman Report was a compromise and to an extent pleased no one. It adopted a balanced approach, refusing to 'plead for a return to old-fashioned grammar teaching and learning by rote' and accepting that Latinate grammars constructed 'a rigid prescriptive code rather than a dynamic description of language in use' (1988: para. 1.11). At the same time, it was un-afraid to challenge prevailing professional orthodoxies that 'any notion of correct or incorrect use of language is an affront to personal liberty' (1988: para. 1.11). Its rejection of traditional grammar teaching, arguing that 'old-fashioned formal teaching of grammar had a negligible, or, because it replaced some instruction or practice in composition, even a harmful effect on the development of original writing' (1988: para. 2.27) was deeply disappointing to right-wing policy makers, including Margaret Thatcher, who believed that Kingman had been overly persuaded by the teachers and educationalists on the committee. Instead of representing anti-progressive and traditional views of English, Kingman followed the spirit of the Bullock Report, and recommended that children were explicitly taught about language. The language model proposed by Kingman had four components: the forms of the language; communication and comprehension; acquisition and development; and historical and geographical variation. But educationalists and linguists were not satisfied that the report offered a coherent linguistic model or a clear identity for subject English. Knott (1988) who was a Kingman Committee member, argued that the report had 'a rotten core' (1988: 16) because it had not established a coherent case for teaching knowledge about language; Knight (1988) maintained that the report was fundamentally flawed because it failed to engage meaningfully with the purposes for subject English; and Cameron and Bourne (1988) critiqued the inherent nostalgia and quest for nationhood enshrined by the report. Despite this widespread dissatisfaction with the report, Kingman's arguments for the place of teaching about language are very evident in the first version of English in the National Curriculum (DES 1990).

Almost immediately after the publication of the Kingman Report, the then education secretary, Kenneth Baker, established a working party, chaired by Brian Cox, to draw up proposals for English in a National Curriculum. Cox's (1991) own account of this period is illuminating, not least for throwing into sharp relief the vagaries of educational policy making! Baker set out to ensure that the Cox Working Group was comprised of traditionalists to avoid the influence that more progressive views appeared to have had on Kingman. But Baker seems to have based his judgements on superficial impressions rather than careful research. Cox gained his credibility as Chair of the group on the basis of his chief editorship of the Black Papers, right-wing critiques of progressive education policy, but he had also been running a ten-year campaign promoting creative writing, the very incarnation of progressive English teaching. According to Cox, although Baker was criticised for choosing members to reflect conservative ideologies, 'neither Baker nor Rumbold knew very much about the complex debate that [had] been going on at least since Rousseau about progressive education' (Cox 1991: 6). Significantly for the development of grammar policy, the Cox Committee included two well-respected linguists, Katherine Perera and Michael Stubbs, who were influential in shaping the report to take account of modern linguistic understandings. The Cox Report drew on the thinking of both Bullock and Kingman, and once again, rejected formal de-contextualised grammar teaching in favour of knowledge about language. On Standard English, Cox adopted a stance of linguistic equality, wholly at odds with policy makers' wishes, and maintained that 'on purely linguistic grounds, [Standard English] is not inherently superior to other non-standard dialects of English, but it clearly has social prestige' (DES 1989: 5.42). Reflecting on the dilemmas faced in drawing up the report, Cox notes the difficulties inherent in discussing grammar, noting that 'if we said we were in favour of the teaching of grammar, some teachers would think we were advocating a return to old-fashioned exercises in parsing and clause analysis' (1991: 34), whilst policy makers would read the phrase grammar teaching only in terms of formal learning and the standards debate. The Cox Report was received very unfavourably by right-wing politicians and the right-wing press, who felt it did not go far enough in insisting on the use of Standard English and in addressing 'incorrect' English usage in writing. Broadly speaking, the report was welcomed by teachers and educationalists, though by no means with warm unanimity. Stubbs (1989) outlines how the report is framed by competing discourses and ideologies which centre around grammar, and the way in which grammar is used symbolically to represent wider social values, particularly discipline, authority and hierarchy (Stubbs 1989: 239); as Cameron and Bourne (1988: 150) observed, 'a return to traditional grammar marks a return to the associated values'. Yet given the political climate in which it was written, the Cox Report managed to promote a descriptive view of grammar, in stark contra-distinction to political will, and to sow the seeds for an English curriculum based on language awareness, rather than language rules.

Cox (1991: 11) records that Kenneth Baker 'very much disliked the Report' and tells how Margaret Thatcher insisted on the deletion of 'where appropriate' from the requirement to use Standard English. There is no doubt that from a political perspective, neither the Kingman Report nor the Cox Report endorsed the 'back-to-basics' educational principles that policy makers espoused, and on the issue of grammar, both reports, with their rejection of traditional grammar teaching, were profoundly disappointing. Despite this, the first version of English in the National Curriculum (DES 1990) reflects much of the substance of both Cox and Kingman, and through its emphasis upon knowledge about language, rather than grammar, set in train a new interest in language. It was, of course, a hugely controversial curriculum, neither satisfying the liberal views of the profession nor the right-wing anti-progressive views of the government. It reignited the debate about grammar teaching, which had been dormant for thirty years, and provoked not simply political versus professional debate, but also debate within the profession. Cameron (1997) critiqued the way policy makers conceived of grammar both as 'a form of moral discipline' (1997: 229) and as 'an arbitrary assortment of technical terms' (1997: 230); in other words, grammar was a wholly remedial activity setting right both the linguistic and the moral peccadilloes of the nation's children. But she also criticised professional associations, such as the National Association for the Teaching of English (NATE) for opposing grammar from the same stance, and for being unable to offer an alternative and constructive place for grammar in an English curriculum. Cameron, along with other linguists such as Carter (1990) and Hudson (2004), challenged both policy makers and teachers by claiming a place for grammar on its own terms: knowing about one's own language and the metalanguage used to describe is a worthy object of study, just as is the study of science or poetry. But they drew on academic understanding of linguistics which was not shared by policy makers. Cox (1995: 13) noted that some members of the National Curriculum Council and the School Evaluation and Assessment Council were either ignorant of or unsympathetic towards linguistics research, and equally the vast majority of English teachers, coming into the profession predominantly via an English literature degree route, were also unfamiliar with modern thinking in linguistics. Cameron's rationale for a pedagogy for grammar teaching is based upon the key principle that 'knowing grammar is knowing *how* more than knowing *what*' (1997: 236) – the investigation and analysis of language is more important than the labelling and the terminology which are simply the tools to facilitate this.

For a teaching profession faced for the first time with a statutory curriculum and with statutory tests which held them accountable for the performance of their students, this was a period of substantial change. In an attempt to address the profession's anxiety about grammar and language teaching, a three-year project *Language in the National Curriculum* (LINC) was established by the Department for Education and Skills (DES), under the leadership of Ronald Carter, to support the teaching of the Knowledge about Language component of the curriculum. The training was large scale, involving teachers in the English department of every school in England and Wales. The LINC materials were educationally based on the thinking of Britton (who had been on the Bullock Committee) and emphasised the importance of addressing context, purpose and audience in language use. The materials also drew on the linguistic influence of Halliday, whose work on grammar placed meaning at the centre of attention. However, the LINC materials were never officially published and were rejected by the government: this was almost certainly because, yet again, the attitude to grammar they represented was liberal, contextual and descriptive and provided no endorsement of the teaching of rules and the correction of error, so beloved of the political right-wing.

There is little doubt, however, that this first version of the National Curriculum was a significant marker for things to come: it was the foundation stone on which literacy policy has been shaped ever since. There have been three revisions of this first English curriculum (1995, 1999, 2007), each a fairly deliberate attempt by policy makers to funnel the English teaching profession into a more standards-driven agenda. Each version of English in the National Curriculum plays around with phrasing and structure, and each gives subtly different emphases to different things, but in essence there have been no major changes over the lifespan of

Table 3.1 Comparing the 1995 and 2007 National Curriculum specifications for grammar in writing

1995 Key Stage 3 and 4	2007 Key Stage 4

Writing

1995 Key Stage 3 and 4	2007 Key Stage 4
Pupils should be encouraged to be confident in the use of formal and informal written standard English, using the grammatical, lexical and orthographical features of standard English.	• use clearly demarcated paragraphs to develop and organise meaning • use a wide variety of sentence structures to support the purpose of the task, giving clarity and emphasis and creating specific effects, and to extend, link and develop ideas • draw on their reading and knowledge of linguistic and literary forms when composing their writing.
Pupils should be encouraged to broaden their understanding of the principles of sentence grammar and be taught to organise whole texts effectively.	
Pupils should be given opportunities to analyse their own writing, reflecting on the meaning and clarity of individual sentences, using appropriate terminology, and so be given opportunities to learn about:	**Technical accuracy** • use the grammatical features of written standard English accurately to structure a wide range of sentence types for particular purposes and effect • use the full range of punctuation marks accurately and for deliberate effect.
• Discourse structure – the structure of whole texts; paragraph structure; how different types of paragraphs are formed; openings and closings in different kinds of writing;	
• Phrase, clause and sentence structure – the use of complex grammatical structures and the linking of structures through appropriate connectives, the use of main and subordinate clauses and phrases;	
• Words – components including stem, prefix, suffix, inflection, grammatical functions of nouns, verbs, adjectives, adverbs, pronouns, prepositions, conjunctions and demonstratives;	
• Punctuation – the use of the full range of punctuation marks, including full stops, questions and exclamation marks, commas, semi-colons, colons, inverted commas, apostrophes, brackets, dashes and hyphens.	

the National Curriculum. Within these various revisions, grammar remains largely conceptualised as a means to secure accuracy in written and spoken English, and to re-affirm the place of Standard English. However, the most recent versions (DfEE 1999; DCSF 2007) are less emphatic about Standard English and make some attempt to link grammar to meaning and effect. One way to see these changes is to compare the Writing Programme of Study in the 1995 and 2007 versions (see Table 3.1). The 1995 revision was an attempt to put right the liberal tendencies of the first version; this is the only version of the National Curriculum which sets out in detail a specific range of grammatical terminology to be taught. In contrast, the 2007 iteration is much less prescriptive about required terminology, although the focus on accuracy and Standard English is still evident.

Of course, across this time frame, the Conservative government which founded the National Curriculum was replaced by a Labour government. Perhaps the most surprising outcome of this is how little difference a change in government made to the National Curriculum.

Changing political landscapes

One reason, perhaps, why the arrival of a Labour government made relatively little difference to English in the National Curriculum may be because the focus for literacy policy shifted from the National Curriculum to the NLS for primary schools, and shortly after to the Framework for English for Key Stage 3. Tony Blair's establishment of the Standards and Effectiveness Unit, under the aegis of Michel Barber, signalled the dawn of a period of highly centralised policy making for literacy and more control both of curriculum content and teaching methods than at any time in history (for an excellent policy analysis of the NLS, see Moss 2009). This period also witnessed a silent shift of curriculum control from the Qualifications and Curriculum Authority (QCA) to the National Strategy team.

QCA continued, nonetheless, to produce a series of documents addressing grammar. The first, *The Grammar Papers* (QCA 1998), was written in recognition that grammar was a topic over which 'positions have often become unnecessarily polarised' in the hope that they would 'promote and inform wider professional discussion of grammar teaching' (1998: 3). The six papers in this booklet range from a historical overview of grammar and linguistics, an outline of grammar in the National Curriculum and how it might be taught, a report on teachers' grammatical subject knowledge, and a review of research on grammar teaching. The latter concludes that 'discrete teaching of parts of speech and parsing in de-contextualised exercise form is not a particularly effective activity' and that 'traditional formal grammar, as was commonly taught in Britain until the 1950s has proved unproductive' (QCA 1998: 55), thus reiterating the conclusions of Bullock, Kingman and Cox. It does suggest that there may be benefits derived from grammar knowledge in terms of students' awareness of how language works, which 'may in turn increase their sense of control over their writing' (QCA

1998: 55) but at the same time observes that there is no evidence of transfer of grammatical knowledge into writing competence. *The Grammar Papers* booklet was followed a year later by *Not Whether but How* (QCA 1999), a title which could be interpreted as a somewhat premature end to the grammar debate. It offers case studies and practical examples of ways in which grammar can be embedded constructively within the curriculum. The first chapters offer theoretical arguments for the role of grammar, including a contribution from Ronald Carter, the director of the LINC project, and George Keith, the initiator and developer of the English Language A level. My (Debra Myhill) own contribution drew on the findings of the Technical Accuracy Project (the worst-named project ever for a study of grammar!) which had analysed GCSE scripts, not for patterns of error but for patterns of usage and signs of development. Perera (1984) had conducted a detailed analysis of primary children's spoken and written language, and argued that teachers needed to know the typical trajectories of linguistic development, so their interventions could be more purposeful. The Technical Accuracy Project had aimed to achieve similar understanding at secondary level. Rereading my contribution with the wisdom of ten years' further research in this area and with all the privileges of hindsight, the emphasis on meaningful teaching of grammar to support students' 'developing ability to craft writing consciously', and a concern 'that *coverage* of the grammar does not obscure the *understanding* that should accompany it' (QCA 1999: 13) remains central to my own philosophy. I might, however, alter the title to 'What *teachers* need to know about grammar?' as my more recent research signals that teachers' linguistic knowledge is a key factor in supporting young writers' development.

Four years later, and paralleling the growing professional and political interest in talk, a third publication, *New Perspectives on Spoken English* (QCA 2003) was produced, comprising a set of discussion papers about spoken language, with contributions from some of the most significant figures in the field (Ronald Carter, Robin Alexander, Deborah Cameron, Neil Mercer, for example). Carter's chapter explores the grammar of talk, arguing that grammar knowledge should extend beyond the written sentence, and all the contributions are framed by contemporary understanding of language as socially situated. This is a significant document as it gives particular emphasis to the grammar of spoken language, something which had previously been largely ignored, other than in reference to Standard English.

Common to all three publications is a view of grammar which eschews traditional prescriptivism and rejects the drilling and exercises characteristic of traditional grammar teaching in favour of more purposeful and context-related approaches to grammar. Ironically, it may be that the shifting sands of power from QCA to the National Strategies offered QCA more freedom to engage in a more open-minded way with the complexity of the grammar debate. It is doubly ironic, therefore, that these publications were in effect eclipsed by the mass of training and publications which accompanied the implementation of the National Strategies.

Grammar in the National Strategy

The introduction of the NLS in primary schools in 1998 and its secondary companion, the Key Stage 3 Framework for English, in 2001 represented the most detailed outline of subject English and its learning outcomes ever written. Both were intended to reflect the National Curriculum, though oddly the first version of the NLS omitted Speaking and Listening completely from its specification. Both documents specified in very precise terms what teachers should address, including considerable reference to grammar and grammar terminology. As well as outlining teaching objectives by year group and under domain headings (such as Reading), the objectives were structured under headings of Word, Sentence and Text. This, in itself, leads to a very language-oriented way of thinking about literacy, and drew attention to issues of spelling and vocabulary at word level, to sentence structure and punctuation at sentence level, and to paragraphing and text structure at text level. One positive effect of this is that it expands grammatical thinking beyond the syntax of the sentence and includes both morphology at word level and broader issues of textual cohesion and coherence. Adopting a more critical stance, however, it did also mean that consideration of grammar and language could be narrowed to a level in which meaning was ignored. A word can usefully be analysed at word level for its morphological structure and spelling, but any decision about word choice and effect is simultaneously a word, sentence and text level choice. Selecting effective vocabulary is about understanding the rhetorical goal of the text overall and the nature of the impact desired, and then weaving that thinking through decisions made at word and sentence level. So, for example, in a horror story, a writer might choose to create fear through establishing imagery of darkness throughout the text, perhaps through darkness metaphors, through synonyms for darkness, or through repetition of a particular phrase or image. There is no such thing as a 'good' word until you have a sentence and a text to evaluate it within; just as there is no such thing as a 'good' sentence until it is placed within the rhythm of a paragraph and a text.

The first versions of the NLS and the secondary Framework generated considerable controversy about grammar. In particular, like the Kingman Report, they were critiqued for not having a coherent linguistic underpinning, and worse for promoting incorrect grammar. Hudson and Walmsley (2005) recall an 'official government-sponsored glossary of metalanguage' which 'a number of linguists were allowed to revise to remove gross errors' (2005: 615). Commentators discovered errors and inconsistencies in the NLS, the Framework and the supporting documentation (Sealey 1999; Cajkler 1999, 2002, 2004). Cajkler (2004) notes the paradox of policy which has accepted that grammar teaching is valuable, in the face of very little empirical evidence to confirm this, and the publication of support documents which are full of definitional errors, leaving teachers 'with a mixed bag of inconsistent imprecise materials' (2004: 12). Wyse (2001) challenged the research evidence that led policy makers to conclude that teaching grammar would improve writing, a view which underpins the *Grammar for Writing* (DfEE 2000) support materials. But it is also important to acknowledge that the grammar represented in the National Strategy is a far cry from the grammar exercises and drills and emphasis on 'bad' grammar that had been the initial impetus behind changing literacy policy from 1988 onwards. As Hudson and Walmsley note, in the National Curriculum and the National Strategy, 'prescription is dead – non-standard varieties are tolerated, as are informal registers; variety is accepted, but different varieties are suited to different occasions so the focus is now on the matching of variety to context' (2005: 615). For all its shortcomings, the National Strategy has offered a new representation of grammar, one which sees the potentiality of grammar for analysis and critique, and which sees the possibilities of making links between language awareness and language competence, and which is in line with modern linguistics in its attitude to language variety.

So how is grammar represented in the National Strategy? Like the National Curriculum, the primary and secondary versions have undergone several iterations, and it is useful to compare the first with the latest versions. It is hard to single out 'grammar' as it is not treated as a discrete area of knowledge and is embedded throughout the curriculum – there are many teaching objectives which do not refer directly to grammar but which could use grammar as a tool for discussion and analysis. For example, in the Renewed Framework for English (DCSF 2008), the most recent secondary strategy, one of the Speaking and Listening objectives for Year 10 is to 'Analyse, compare and contrast features of speech in a range of contexts and relate to their own speech', which could be approached with or without grammar knowledge. The first version of the NLS (DfEE 1998) has much in common with the 1995 iteration of English in the National Curriculum: it makes many explicit references to grammar and grammar terminology, and has a specific sub-section called Grammatical Awareness under Sentence level work. In Year 4, Term 2, for example, the teaching objectives under Grammatical Awareness are:

1   To revise and extend work on adjectives from Y3 Term 2 and link to work on expressive and figurative language in stories and poetry:
   - Constructing adjectival phrases
   - Examining comparative and superlative adjectives
   - Comparing adjectives on a scale of intensity
   - Relating them to suffixes which indicate degrees of intensity
   - Relating them to adverbs which indicate degrees of intensity and through investigating words which can be intensified in these ways and words which cannot.

(DfEE 1998: 40)

In the 2008 learning objectives for literacy of the Primary National Strategy, there is no section on Grammatical Awareness, and the parallel Year 4 sentence level and punctuation learning objectives are much less specific, foregrounding the purpose of the learning, and referring to the grammar terminology in brackets thus:

- Clarify meaning and point of view by using varied sentence structure (phrases, clauses and adverbials)
- Use commas to mark clauses, and use the apostrophe for possession.

(DCSF 2008)

At secondary level, the Renewed Framework (DCSF 2008) extends beyond KS3 into KS4, offering teaching objectives for all five years of compulsory secondary education. Table 3.2 shows a comparison of one strand, focusing on sentence structure and punctuation, in the original framework (DfES 2001) and the most recent (DCSF 2008). Again, what is very evident from this is how specific and itemised the earlier version was compared with the current version. The 2001 version names a host of grammar terms whereas the 2008 version only names clauses and sentences; the 2001 presents teaching objectives at a detailed level whereas the 2008 version summarises the teaching goals for sentence variety and punctuation in one sentence. The emphasis on meaningful attention to grammar seems more prominent in 2008, with its reference to 'appropriate detail', 'the relationship between ideas', 'create effects according to task, purpose and reader', and 'clarify meaning'; in 2001 this is limited to 'suit purpose'. However, the references to managing tense so 'that meaning is clear' and to 'remedy ambiguity' in sentences seems to be pointing rather more towards a notion of accuracy, rather than impact and effect.

Overall, reviewing the changes in the various iterations of both the National Curriculum and the National Strategy, it does appear that policy on grammar has moved from one which focuses close attention on grammatical terminology to one which is more actively encouraging attention to grammar as a meaning-making resource and a tool for learning about language in action. Equally, however, despite the general adoption of a non-prescriptivist stance to language in linguistic terms, there remains an underlying unresolved tension around Standard English and what 'technical accuracy' actually means. The place of grammar in literacy policy remains muddled and poorly conceptualised.

The National Strategy: grammar in practice

There is little doubt, then, that the broad intention behind the specification of grammar in the most recent versions of the National Curriculum and the National Strategy is to approach grammar as a meaning-making resource for analysing and creating text. But, probably contrary to policy makers' beliefs, enshrining something in policy does not guarantee that this is realised in practice. There remain many issues about how and why grammar is taught. Some of these issues arise from the training materials provided to support teaching. The *Grammar for*

Table 3.2 Comparing the specification for grammar in the 2001 and 2008 versions of the Framework for English

Key Stage 3 Framework for English DfEE 2001	Renewed English Framework DCSF 2008
Sentence construction and Punctuation (Year 7) Pupils should be taught to:	Varying sentences and punctuation for clarity and effect (Year 7: 8.2)
Extend their use and control of complex sentences by: – Recognising and using subordinate clauses – Exploring the functions of subordinate clauses e.g. relative clauses such as 'which I bought' or adverbial clauses such as 'having finished his lunch' – Deploying subordinate clauses in a variety of positions within the sentence	Vary sentence length and structure in order to provide appropriate detail, make clear the relationship between ideas, and create effects according to task, purpose and reader
Expand nouns and noun phrases e.g. by using a prepositional phrase	
Use punctuation to clarify meaning, particularly at the boundaries between sentences and clauses	Use punctuation accurately to clarify meaning and create effects in clauses, sentences and when writing speech
Keep tense usage consistent, and manage changes of tense so that meaning is clear	
Use the active or the passive voice to suit purpose	
Recognise and remedy ambiguity in sentences e.g. unclear use of pronouns	
Use speech punctuation accurately to integrate speech into larger sentences	

Writing (DfEE 2000) materials, for example, clearly try to demonstrate purposeful embedded grammar teaching, but this is not always what is actually demonstrated. In one video episode, a teacher is modelling writing and eliciting from the class a discussion about how the story creates tension: the teacher probes their responses and tries to support the children in justifying the answers. But too much of the teaching is devoted to identifying word classes or sentence types and then claiming that the 'adverb' creates tension, or the short sentence 'makes it scary'. There is almost no attention to the meanings of the words themselves, and the worry would be that young writers are left with the idea that it is good to use an adverb to create tension. In both primary and secondary school, the emphasis on adjectives as 'describing' words is commonplace and children are being encouraged to write wholly artificial noun phrases with three or four pre-modifying adjectives. This is actively endorsed in *Literacy Progress Unit: Sentences* (DfEE 2001) where writers are encouraged to develop noun phrases such as:

The small scrumptious slowly melting tomato pizza.

My tiny appetising fiercely bubbling ham pizza.

(DfEE 2001: 168)

Instead of thinking about description and about the image or mood they wish to convey, students are playing word games with adjectives in a meaningless way. The same is true of complex sentences, where students are being given targets to use more complex sentences, as though a complex sentence has merit in its own right. In our research (Myhill 2008, 2009), we have repeatedly recorded students expressing their need to use complex sentences, but with no understanding of what complex sentences might achieve in terms of effects in their writing. The important point here is that the grammatical feature itself is becoming the object of study, rather than the grammatical feature being a tool for showing how language works, or discussing different possibilities for expressing intended meanings. Wray *et al.*'s (2000) study of effective teachers of literacy also found that less effective teachers foregrounded the grammar point 'without providing children with a clear context in which these features served a function' (Wray *et al.*, 2000: 81).

Another aspect of grammar at policy level is that policy documents have never prescribed why or how grammar should be taught, simply what should be taught. This has given teachers great freedom in choosing when is an appropriate time to draw attention to a particular grammatical point, and in what contexts they would like to teach it. But this raises another important issue: the vast majority of teachers now teaching English are from the generation of students who were never taught grammar themselves, and there is often a lack of confidence in linguistic subject knowledge. The challenge of mastering grammar knowledge has been noted by many, including Cajkler and Hislam (2002), Cameron (1997) and Myhill (2010). In our current study of grammar teaching, one strong finding is teachers' fear and anxiety about grammar, and in particular about making mistakes with learners in the classroom. One teacher said 'I still panic a little bit about getting it right', whilst another noted her fear of 'nouns, verbs, prepositions, complex sentences, compound, you know, all the terminology that's really scary'. Another teacher recalled conversations about grammar within the English department and how she never admitted she did not understand: 'I keep it to myself because I feel a bit ashamed.' Teachers who are confident and capable teachers of literature frequently feel inadequate when faced with grammar, often having to check their understanding before teaching – 'I had to sneak round and remind myself what modal verbs were' – to avoid embarrassment. The consequence of this is that making connections between grammar terms and how meaning is constructed is difficult for teachers who are struggling with the foundational linguistic knowledge. As Andrews (2005: 75) noted, it is more likely 'that a teacher with a rich knowledge of grammatical constructions and a more general awareness of the forms and varieties of the language will be in a better position to help young writers'. Lack of confidence in linguistic subject knowledge is a serious barrier to the realisation of grammar policy and to the creative, meaningful teaching of grammar.

Grammar policy for a new millennium

This chapter has indicated a turbulent and ambivalent history of grammar in literacy policy, which is by no means resolved at the current time. It is a topic beset by ideology, by polemic and by prejudice, and these discourses act as barriers to genuine policy development. Neither politicians nor professionals are as yet clear in articulating either a purposeful policy for grammar in the curriculum or clear pedagogical practices for meaningful teaching of grammar. Is this time to call it a day on grammar?

We would suggest that grammar policy in the twenty-first century must address, as a matter of priority, the following three areas.

1. Establishing a clear conceptualisation of a pedagogic rationale for the teaching of grammar
A pedagogic rationale for the teaching of grammar would be founded upon modern linguistics and would explicitly adopt a descriptive perspective, which recognised language diversity, and the value of home dialects, but which also recognised that Standard English remains the language of power, and therefore supported children in bidialectalism, the ability to switch language codes for different contexts. It would eschew narrow conceptualisations of grammar as concerned solely with the removal of error, and would instead articulate a rationale for grammar based on the benefits of language awareness which offers learners 'conscious control and conscious choice over language which enables them both to *see through* language in a systematic way and to use language more discriminatingly' (Carter 1990: 119). It might suggest that there is no such thing as teaching grammar, only the teaching of speaking and listening, reading and writing, where grammar is a resource for analysis, critique and reflection.

2. Devoting committed attention to the development of teachers' linguistic subject knowledge
Mr Disgusted of Tunbridge Wells and the right-wing press seem to take a delight in pillorying English teachers for their lack of confidence in grammar, without

acknowledging the absurdity of expecting teachers who were not taught grammar at school and who took English literature degrees to be competent linguists. Any policy development for grammar teaching needs to include sustained consideration of teachers' professional development needs. One-off courses or self-study guides in grammar are rarely sufficient: for teachers or trainee teachers 'can't just mug up their grammar from a book; if they are to teach it actively they will have to learn it actively, be given opportunities to ask questions and to argue. It's a classroom project not a homework project' (Cameron 1997: 237). Professional development needs to allow opportunities for initial introductions to linguistic concepts and later opportunities to revisit and refresh this learning. It should also include linguistic investigations of text which encourage confidence in making independent connections between linguistic terms and their use in multiple contexts.

3. Enabling collaborative development of effective pedagogies for the teaching of grammar

We do not yet know enough about effective pedagogies for grammar teaching. Our own research is showing strong positive benefits on writing when grammar points are embedded meaningfully in the scheme of work and when grammar is only addressed where it has relevance to the writing task in hand. But it is also raising questions about which groups of learners benefit most (our study suggests it is able writers); about the infinitely varied way in which teachers use teaching materials; and about the impact of teacher subject knowledge on student outcomes. Classrooms are complex environments, and teaching is a highly complex activity. We need to create opportunities for researchers, linguists, advisers and teachers to collaborate in the development of a pedagogy for grammar teaching which is not uni-dimensional but multidimensional, and rooted in critical practice.

If future literacy policy on grammar addresses these three areas, we generate a fertile ground for developing a literacy curriculum in which the study of English language and literature are genuinely mutually complementary. Moreover, it would establish a professional environment in which policing grammar became less important than shared development of practice, and one perhaps where, as Cox argued, there was space for 'professionalism to gain control of all classrooms' (1991: 13).

References

Andrews, R. 2005 Knowledge about the Teaching of Sentence Grammar: The state of play. *English Teaching: Practice and Critique* 4 (3): 69–76.

Board of Education 1921 *The Teaching of English in England (The Newbolt Report)*. London: HMSO.

Cajkler, W. 1999 Misconceptions in the NLS: National Literacy Strategy or no linguistic sense? *Use of English* 50 (3): 214–27.

Cajkler, W. 2002 Literacy across the Curriculum at KS3: More muddle and confusion. *Use of English* 53 (2): 151–64.

Cajkler, W. 2004 How a Dead Butler was Killed: The way English National Strategies maim grammatical parts. *Language and Education* 18 (1): 1–16.

Cajkler, W. and Hislam, J. 2002 Trainee Teachers' Grammatical Knowledge: The tension between public expectations and individual competence. *Language Awareness* 11: 161–77.

Cameron, D. 1997 Sparing the Rod: What teachers need to know about grammar. *Changing English: Studies in Reading and Culture* 4 (2): 229–39.

Cameron, D. and Bourne, J. 1988 No Common Ground: Kingman, grammar and the nation. *Language and Education* 2 (3): 147–60.

Carter, R. (ed.) 1990 *Knowledge about Language*. London: Hodder and Stoughton.

Cox, B. 1991 *Cox on Cox: An English curriculum for the 1990s*. London: Hodder and Stoughton.

Cox, B. 1995 *Cox on the Battle for the English Curriculum*. London: Hodder and Stoughton.

DCSF 2007 *English in the National Curriculum*, http://curriculum.qcda.gov.uk/key-stages-3-and-4/subjects/key-stage-4/english/index.aspx Accessed 10 February 2010.

DCSF 2008 Secondary English, http://nationalstrategies.standards.dcsf.gov.uk/secondary/english Accessed 10 February 2010.

DES 1975 *A Language for Life (The Bullock Report)*. London: HMSO.

DES 1988 *Report of the Committee of Enquiry into the Teaching of the English Language (The Kingman Report)*. London: HMSO.

DES 1989 *English for Ages 5–16 (The Cox Report)*. London: HMSO.

DES 1990 *English in the National Curriculum*. London: HMSO.

DfE 1995 *English in the National Curriculum*. London: HMSO.

DfEE 1998 *The National Literacy Strategy: Framework for Teaching*. London: DfEE.

DfEE 1999 *The National Curriculum for England, English Key Stages 1–4*. London: DfEE.

DfEE 2000 The National Literacy Strategy: Grammar for Writing. London: DfEE.

DfEE 2001 *Literacy Progress Unit: Sentences*. London: DfEE.

DfES 2001 *Framework for Teaching English: Years 7, 8 and 9*. London: DfES.

Dixon, J. 1975 *Growth Through English*. Sheffield: NATE.

Eagleton, T. 1991 The Enemy Within. *English in Education* 25 (3): 3–9.

Fries, C. 1951 *The Structure of English: An introduction to the construction of English sentences*. London: Longman.

Funke, O. 1950 *Englische Sprachkunde: Ein Überblick ab 1935*. Bern: Francke.

Gurrey, P. 1962 *Teaching English Grammar*. London: Longman.

Hudson, R. 2004 Why Education needs Linguistics. *Journal of Linguistics* 40 (1): 105–30.

Hudson, R. and Walmsley, J. 2005 The English Patient: English grammar and teaching in the twentieth century. *Journal of Linguistics* 41 (3): 593–622.

Jespersen, O. 1905 *Growth and Structure of the English Language*. Leipzig: B.G. Tuebner.

Knight, R. 1988 Reading the Kingman Report. *Use of English* 40 (1): 7–17.

Knott, R. 1988 Heart of Darkness: The making of the Kingman Report. *English in Education* 22 (3): 4–18.

Moss, G. 2009 The Politics of Literacy in the Context of Large-scale Education Reform. *Research Papers in Education* 24 (2): 155–74.

Myhill, D.A. 2008 Towards a Linguistic Model of Sentence Development in Writing. *Language and Education* 22 (5): 271–88.

Myhill, D.A. 2009 Becoming a Designer: Trajectories of linguistic development, in R. Beard, D. Myhill, J. Riley and M. Nystrand (eds) *The Sage Handbook of Writing Development*. London: Sage, pp. 402–14.

Myhill, D.A. 2010 Changing Classroom Pedagogies, in A. Denham and K. Lobeck (eds) *Linguistics at School: Language awareness in primary and secondary education*. Cambridge: Cambridge University Press, pp. 92–106.

NCTE 2006 Beyond Grammar Drills: How language works in learning to write. *The Council Chronicle Online*. http://www.ncte.org/magazine/archives/125935 Retrieved 10 February 2010.

Perera, K. 1984 *Children's Writing and Reading: Analysing classroom language*. Oxford: Blackwell.

QCA 1998 *The Grammar Papers*. London: QCA.

QCA 1999 *Not Whether but How*. London: QCA.

QCA 2003 *Perspectives on Spoken English*. London: QCA.

Sealey, A. 1999 Teaching Primary School Children about the English Language: A critique of current policy documents. *Language Awareness* 8 (2): 84–97.

Stubbs, M. 1989. The State of English in the English State: Reflections on the Cox Report. *Language and Education* 3 (4): 235–50.

Wray, D., Medwell, J., Fox, R. and Poulson, L. 2000 The Teaching Practices of Effective Teachers of Literacy. *Educational Review* 52 (1): 75–84.

Wyse, D. 2001 Grammar for Writing (sic)? A critical review of empirical evidence. British Journal of Educational Studies 49 (4): 411–27.

Chapter 4

The origins, evaluations and implications of the National Literacy Strategy in England

Roger Beard

Introduction

With the National Strategies in England scheduled to end in 2011, it is timely to take stock of the National Literacy Strategy (NLS), which ran for five years from 1998 before becoming part of the broader National Primary Strategy (NPS) (DfES, 2003). Taking stock can allow the impact of the NLS to be discussed in the context of its origins and, in particular, the research that has informed it, throughout its duration. Such a discussion may also illustrate the complex relationships between research, policy and practice. This kind of discussion may also indicate the implications of the NLS for programmes of educational change, not only in the UK but in other parts of the world. Soon after its launch, the NLS was described (together with the companion National Numeracy Strategy (NNS), which is not being discussed here) by a world authority on educational change as the most ambitious large-scale strategy of educational reform witnessed since the 1960s (Fullan, 2000, p. 1).

The NLS in England was set up by the incoming government of 1997 to raise standards of literacy in English primary (elementary) schools (5–11-year-olds) over a five- to ten-year period. It built upon some initiatives taken in the final year of the outgoing government of 1992–7, further adding to centralised government responses to some major concerns about pupil (student) attainment, teaching approaches and the professional development of teachers that had been identified in research and in school inspection during the previous ten years or so.

Although non-statutory, many elements of the NLS have been widely adopted in English primary schools. The effect appears to have been a substantial increase in pupil attainment in primary school children, as measured in the results from national tests that are annually administered to 11-year-olds. At the same time, the NLS has presented substantial demands on teachers, by introducing new teaching approaches and by making considerable demands on their subject knowledge. Its initial impact was deemed to be so successful that elements have been extended into secondary schools. A number of critiques have also resulted, including the following: (i) the increase in standards has been largely illusory because of teachers 'teaching to the test'; (ii) attention to other areas of the statutory curriculum has been eroded; (iii) the Strategy has neglected oracy; and (iv) independent reading has been inadequately promoted. These issues will be addressed later in this chapter.

The sense of timeliness in taking stock is underpinned by the recognition of a strong international trend towards frequent and wide-ranging reform, covering the governance, management, organisation, content and assessment of learning (Le Métais, 2003). The significance of this trend is of particular interest in comparisons between the outcomes from the Performance in International Reading Literacy (PIRLS) in 2006 and 2001 (Twist et al., 2003, 2007). The largest changes were in the increases in overall pupil performance in the Russian Federation, Hong Kong, Singapore and Slovenia, four countries that have been subject to large-scale structural and/or curricular reform. The challenge for educators is how to engage with such reforming trends while giving due consideration to the full extent of the relevant evidence base, even though this evidence may sometimes be at odds with personal beliefs and values.

This chapter explores the evidence base in relation to the origins, evaluations and implications of this unprecedented attempt to change the ways reading and writing are taught in English primary schools. The chapter will also illustrate the challenges incurred in balancing the substance of attempted change with the levers through which change may be effected, so that the means do not distort the ends. Where such distortion occurs, it is important not to lose sight of the key issues in relation to the teaching and learning of literacy that lie at the heart of the Strategy.

The origins of the NLS

The origins of the NLS may be better understood by taking account of the increasing centralisation of education policy by the UK government from the late 1980s: in curriculum content; in national testing; in inspections of schools; and, finally, in guidance on how to teach. Each of these four strands of centralisation has evolved from four different quasi-autonomous central government organisations – all of which have different degrees of delegated powers. Each strand of centralisation has made a distinctive contribution to the critical mass of central policy, but each has also brought with it the potential to undermine or distort the impact of one or more of the others. It needs also to be noted that each centralising strand has itself undergone radical transformation, thus adding to the demands on the professionals whose implementation of policy rests on their understanding of the implications for practice.

A national curriculum

The first centralising strand was the introduction of a national curriculum in all four UK countries in 1989. In England (DES, 1989), several epistemological decisions were taken by the body delegated to oversee the national curriculum, then called the National Curriculum Council, which were to have long-term impact. While the first national curriculum for English provided for the equitable division of its programmes of study between the three elements of Speaking and Listening, Reading and Writing, it appeared far less informed by psychological research in language and literacy. This imbalance may help explain why, in the 43 pages of the 1989 national curriculum for English for primary schools, there was only one mention of phonics, the teaching method that helps children to build their understanding of phoneme–grapheme correspondences (Beard and Willcocks, 2002). This parsimonious reference seemed to fly in the face of a major research synthesis on early reading in the USA (Adams, 1990).

The first version of the curriculum also seemed insufficiently informed by the experimental research in writing that was undertaken in the 1980s, particularly in the composing of writing (in accessing and structuring content in different discourse structures) and the implications for teaching that related to it (e.g. Bereiter and Scardamalia, 1987; Hillocks, 1986, 1995). As with the teaching of phonics, this apparent neglect may have distorted the national curriculum and subsequently placed at risk the implementation of the NLS, on which the national curriculum was built.

After several evaluations, the national curriculum was revised (DfE, 1995) after a review chaired by a senior civil servant (Dearing, 1994). In the revised version, 'key skills' for reading in the early years (5–7-year-olds) were spelled out in greater detail including reference to the importance of 'phonological awareness' and the learning of 'relationships between print symbols and sound patterns', although there was still no explicit reference to phonemes. Reference to phonemes was eventually included in a further minor revision of the national curriculum in 1999, a year after the teaching of phonemic segmentation and blending was mentioned in the National Literacy Strategy guidance for teachers. Similarly, in writing, there were greater details in the 1995 curriculum of purposes and audiences for writing, although still very few details of composing strategies in relation to content and discourse knowledge. Such inconsistencies raise important issues about how securely teachers were placed to teach the revised versions of the national curriculum and in time implement the NLS guidance.

National testing

The second centralising initiative was an annual programme of national testing for 7, 11 and 14-year-old pupils that began in 1991. Arrangements assumed a higher profile in England because of the annual publication by newspapers of league tables based on the performances of individual schools. The assessment system was originally based on discrete groups of specific criteria, which were equated to different levels of attainment, from level one (the lowest) to level eight, in a rather formulaic way. Following the revision of the national curriculum in 1994–5, however, broad 'level descriptions' have been used, on a 'best fit' basis.

There has also been a more subtle – some would say insidious – change. When the tests were first developed, the 'typical' (modal) attainment for 11-year-olds was level four. Since then, the government body delegated to oversee curriculum and assessment has equated level four with the notion of 'national expectation', as a part of a broader target-setting culture that central governments of both main political parties have adopted. The target-setting culture and its possibly distorting influence are discussed in more detail later. (For a historical review of national testing in the UK, see Shorrocks-Taylor, 1999.)

The implications of the testing programme for assessment practices were all the stronger because national testing was centrally located at the heart of the education system, alongside curriculum content. This centrality was probably endorsed by policy makers because the results from the administration of the first tests in 1995 raised serious concerns: only 49 per cent of pupils achieved level four in English and only 47 per cent in mathematics. More importantly, the high-stakes culture created by the testing regime – centred on the school league tables – has represented a serious risk of distorting the teaching and learning potential of the national curriculum and, when it was eventually introduced, the NLS.

School inspections

The third centralising initiative is that, since 1992, the 19,000 publicly funded English primary schools have also been subjected to a programme of school inspections, initially every four years, coordinated by a central government Office for Standards in Education (OFSTED).[1]

Before 1992, schools were inspected by Her Majesty's Inspectorate (HMI), although the small size of the inspectorate (about 300) meant that individual schools were only fully inspected on an average of once every 30 years or so. The new national database of inspection evidence was increasingly used to produce annual reviews and other subject-specific publications. The role of a reduced HMI included monitoring the training of inspectors and school inspections and undertaking special investigations, for instance a longitudinal evaluation of the NLS (HMI, 1999, 2002).

There has again been the potential for the inspection programme – in conjunction with the testing regime – to distort the impact of one or more of the other strands of centralisation. An inspection of an individual school takes account of the school's national test results and draws on data that compare these results with those from schools with similar socio-economic catchments. The inspections can thus inadvertently distort schools' priorities and curriculum provision in ways that were not intended when the inspection programme was set up.

The National Literacy Strategy

The fourth centralising initiative was the National Literacy Strategy, although it lacked the statutory status of the other three. The Strategy was the result of the work of a Literacy Task Force that had been set up by the Shadow Secretary of State for Education and Employment, David Blunkett, in May 1996. The Task Force, led by Professor Michael Barber, from the University of London Institute of Education, published a preliminary consultation report in February 1997 and a final report in August 1997 (LTF, 1997a and b). In its second report the Task Force set out the details of a 'steady, consistent strategy' for raising standards of literacy which could be sustained over a long period of time and be made a central priority for the education service as a whole.

The main aspects of the Strategy were as follows:

(i)   An initial national target that, by 2002, 80 per cent of 11-year-olds should reach the standard 'expected' for their age in English (national curriculum level four). In the event, the target was reached in reading but not in writing. At the time when this chapter is being written, the proportion of 11-year-old students attaining level four in English is now 81 per cent, being higher in reading (86 per cent) than in writing (67 per cent) and in girls (85 per cent) than in boys (76 per cent).

(ii) *A Framework for Teaching*, an A4-sized ring binder (DfEE, 1998a) which sets out termly teaching objectives for the 5–11 age range, based on the national curriculum, providing a practical structure of time and class management for a daily literacy hour. The *Framework* was 'renewed' in 2006, to set out twelve strands of English and rewritten in a new, electronic format which allows for customized planning, teaching and assessment, with links to a range of resources.

(iii) A programme of professional development for all primary school teachers, centred on a *Literacy Training Pack* (DfEE, 1998b).

(iv) Funding to support the establishment of a 'field force' of local authority literacy consultants, who were in turn trained and supported by a national team of experienced professionals under the leadership of a national director, John Stannard, whose account of his role was published in Stannard and Huxford (2007).

The original *Framework* included bullet point reminders that, as well as the literacy hour, additional time may also be needed for: reading to the class (e.g. in end of day sessions); pupils' own independent reading (for interest and pleasure) and extended writing (especially for older pupils). However, the relegation of these key issues to three bullet points in a substantial A4-sized ring binder ran the risk that their significance and implications would be overlooked or undervalued in schools, even though dialogues about literacy teaching in the local training and in-school development were able to pick up on these points.

Predisposing factors: pedagogy and attainment

During 1998, I was commissioned by the director of the NLS to write an independent review of the research and other related evidence that had influenced the National Literacy Strategy (Beard, 1999). In a subsequent paper, I distinguished between the 'predisposing' and the 'precipitating' influences on the NLS (Beard, 2000a). The former could be taken as indicating that literacy teaching in England was in need of radical change: the teaching of early literacy had become largely individualised and appeared to be out of line with the practices suggested by school effectiveness research; the teaching of early reading often largely comprised hearing children read books in an order suggested by commercial publishers; the teaching of writing relied heavily on de-contextualised exercises; accumulating inspection evidence suggested that there was often relatively little 'teaching' per se. The use of 'shared' (whole-class) and 'guided' (group) teaching of reading and writing were not common, despite the apparently widespread espousal of Vygotsky's theories in teacher education.

Furthermore, standards in literacy among English primary school children had appeared to remain largely stable between 1948 and 1996 (Brooks, 1998). When compared with other countries, English reading standards seemed similar to those in a 'middle' group of countries in performance tables. In the middle and upper parts of the range of scores, children from England performed as well as those in countries much higher in the rank order. However, England had a long 'tail' of underachievement (Brooks et al., 1996). According to the Literacy Task Force, the existence of this tail, in particular, seemed to suggest the use of the direct, 'interactive' teaching approaches that were being used with 'at risk' pupils in the USA and Australia and which are discussed further below (LTF, 1997a and b).

Precipitating factors: LIFT and the NLP

If these were the influences that 'predisposed' the Literacy Task Force towards the possible structure of a National Literacy Strategy, then the 'precipitating' influence were the Literacy Initiative for Teachers (LIFT) and the National Literacy Project (NLP). The LIFT project was developed in London in the mid-1990s and was independently evaluated by a team from the University of London Institute of Education (Sylva et al., 1999; Hurry et al., 1999). The researchers note in their final reports the influence of LIFT on the subsequent national initiatives. LIFT comprised a programme for children in Reception and Year 1 classes that included a relatively higher level of direct teacher instruction than was common at that time (see for example Donaldson, 1993). Children in the LIFT classes made significantly more progress in reading than children in the comparison classes. Interestingly, although the LIFT classrooms were managed in a more obviously teacher-led way than those in the comparison classes, this also had an impact on the way children spent their time, engaging in more literacy-focused activities. This involved not only whole-class teaching but an orchestration of group work, in teacher supervised groups (as in guided reading) and high level independent work. There is also warning (subsequently prophetic in LIFT's transmogrification into the NLS) from one of the LIFT-related papers of a need to strengthen the explicit phonics side of the curriculum, which might even produce even better results (Hurry *et al.*, 1999).

The NLP was set up by the previous government in its final year of office (1996) in 18 English local education authorities. The NLP reflected several of the main elements of the LIFT project as well as taking account of the implications of the school effectiveness research discussed below and the overseas literacy research with 'at risk' pupils. Its aims included improving standards of literacy in participating primary schools in line with national expectations and developing detailed, practical guidance on teaching methods and activities.

Participating schools implemented two key structures, a *Framework for Teaching* and the literacy hour. These were earlier versions of what were subsequently to be included in the NLS. The *Framework* recommended the use of teaching methods that were new to the UK, particularly shared and guided reading and writing and also more systematic phonics (through the word-level work, which also included spelling and vocabulary) than was common in school, according to inspection and research evidence (see also Beard, 2000b).

The NLP was led by a senior member of Her Majesty's Inspectorate, John Stannard, who was to go on to lead the NLS. He saw the *Framework* as providing schools with a means of shifting the emphasis in planning for the revised National Curriculum for English (DfE, 1995) from 'what' to 'how'. This was done by using 'text, sentence and word level' provision to provide coverage, balance and progression in literacy teaching. However, he also saw the purpose of the *Framework for Teaching* as presenting teachers not with increased prescription but with a wide range of new and challenging decisions about tasks, activities and methods (Stannard, 1997). Nevertheless, the literacy hour represented a new level of prescription for primary school teachers in England.

The daily hour of time for dedicated literacy teaching was derived from the Final Report of the review of the national curriculum (Dearing, 1994, p. 30).[2] The literacy hour was central to the NLP and was to become equally central to the NLS. The recommended structure of the hour was as follows: approximately 15 minutes of whole-class 'text-level' work (shared reading or writing); approximately 15 minutes of whole-class 'word-level' work (vocabulary, phonics and spelling); approximately 20 minutes of differentiated group work; and a whole-class plenary session.

The NLP was independently evaluated by the National Foundation for Educational Research (NFER) using data from 250 schools. The standardised test results (using the *Primary Reading* and *Progress in English* tests) revealed a significant and substantial improvement over the 18-month period. Final test scores had improved by approximately six standardised score points for 7–9-year-olds and for 9–11-year-olds, equivalent to 8 to 12 months progress over and above what is expected in these ages. Girls had higher average scores than boys and made more progress during the project. Children eligible for free school meals, those with special educational needs and those learning English as an additional language had lower scores, but all these groups also made statistically significant progress. All ethnic groups benefited equally (Sainsbury *et al.*, 1998). While the evaluation findings from the NLP were impressive, caveats need to be added: the schools where the NLP was implemented were generally in disadvantaged areas where there were arguably greater possibilities for improvement in educational attainment. In addition, the data on writing were far more limited and less holistic than the data on reading, being largely limited to accuracy.

In the light of the emerging success of the NLP, the Literacy Task Force took the decision to recommend the use of the literacy hour and a slightly amended form of the *Framework for Teaching* across the whole of England from 1998 onwards. The LTF recommendation was that every primary school should adopt the *Framework* unless it could demonstrate through its action plan, schemes of work and test performances that its own approach was at least as effective as that of the use of the literacy hour (LTF, 1997b).

The Literacy Task Force saw the literacy hour as reflecting some of the main attributes of school and classroom effectiveness. The issue of effectiveness had attracted increasing attention after the publication of a major study a decade earlier (Mortimore *et al.*, 1988; see also Mortimore, 1991) and the LTF (1997b) took particular note of the implications of the meta-analyses by Scheerens (1992) and Creemers (1994). School effectiveness is generally gauged by the further progress which pupils make than might be expected from consideration of the school's intake. The LTF (1997b) drew attention to the gains from 'structured teaching' (including making clear what has to be learnt; dividing material into manageable units; teaching in a well-considered sequence; encouraging pupils to use hunches and prompts; regular testing for progress; immediate feedback) and 'effective learning time' (see also Teddlie and Reynolds, 1999). Other cited sources included Wasik and Slavin (1993), who report that dramatic improvements in student attainment are achievable within the context of a fully implemented, comprehensive strategy (see also Slavin, 1997), and Crevola and Hill (1998). In line with the implications of these studies, the NLS also included a substantial professional development programme, based on five days work in each primary school in England, using a centrally provided package of textual and video materials. To support implementation in the schools in their areas of England, over 300 'literacy consultants' (advisory teachers) were recruited, mostly from schools.[3]

This immediate 'roll-out' raised important issues, as a gradual extension of the NLP to different parts of England might have been expected, according to preparedness. One of the Literacy Task Force members (Reynolds, 1998) published a paper to argue that, although the NLS appeared to have high validity, its implementation risked low reliability in such a sudden extension. The response of Michael Barber, who became head of the new Standards and Effectiveness Unit in the incoming government of 1997, was that a 'learn as we go' approach would be taken and that extra resources would be devoted to dealing with weaknesses identified in implementation (Barber, 1999). Implementation weaknesses soon appeared, although the initial outcomes from the NLS were generally

perceived as sufficiently positive by policy makers for the NLS to be
the first three years of secondary schools in 2001 (for an indepe
the relevant research, see Harrison, 2002).

The short-term 'internal evaluation' of the NLS

The NLS was 'internally' evaluated (i.e. from within the UK) by Her Majesty's
Inspectorate, who surveyed practice in a national sample of 300 schools over a
four-year period and provided regular interim reports as well as a final one (HMI,
2002). The first interim publication (HMI, 1999) reported that the literacy hour
was adopted in virtually all 300 schools. Shared reading was apparently well
understood and successfully introduced in most of these schools. The first interim
evaluation also reported some recurrent weaknesses in less effective schools:

- the purposes of, and the teacher's role in, guided reading were not always
  understood;
- in the teaching of the literacy hour, word-level work, especially phonics, was
  not taught systematically or given the required emphasis (confirming the
  earlier caveat of Hurry *et al.*, 1999);
- the head teacher's leadership was sometimes unconvincing;
- there were sometimes substantial weaknesses in communication between the
  Strategy and individual schools, which hampered the support which could
  be given.

These findings were largely corroborated by a research council-funded project led
by Ros Fisher (2002) focusing on the use of the literacy hour in 20 classrooms
in rural schools. Fisher reports changes in planning and teaching but argues that
some of the changes were less marked than teachers thought. She also points out
some of the factors, other than technical features of teaching, that bear upon
classroom success, including teachers' views about literacy and literacy learning,
classroom interaction and pupil learning style.

The major issue of writing

It was, however, the teaching of writing that caused greatest concern, so much
so that, in 2000, HMI published a discussion paper that central government would
be unlikely to achieve its 80 per cent target because of the 'under-achievement'
in writing and especially in boys. The paper was indicatively titled *The Teaching
of Writing in Primary Schools: Could do better.* The issue is well illustrated in the
2000 national test results (see Figure 4.1 overleaf).

HMI (2000) suggest that a number of factors may have contributed to the
underachievement, including the following:

- the legacy of reliance on de-contextualised exercises;
- insufficient teaching of writing;

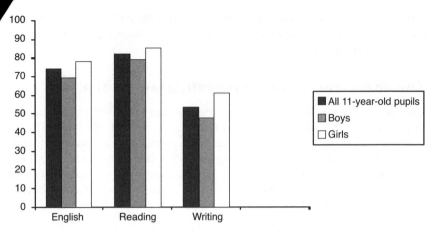

Figure 4.1 Percentage of pupils attaining level four or above in 2000.

- pupils practising writing rather than being taught how to improve it;
- a lack of balance between the teaching of writing and reading;
- insufficient transfer of literacy learning into other subjects.

As was mentioned earlier, the problem may also be related to curriculum provision being insufficiently informed by psychological research findings on writing. The findings draw attention to the importance of content knowledge, as well as purpose and audience, and of the role of various facilitative procedures to support composition. Without such provision, the teaching of writing may comprise little more than setting tasks and marking outcomes (Hillocks, 1986; see also Hillocks, 2003).

Central government responses to the evaluation findings

In line with the 'learn as we go' approach in the implementation of the NLS, resources were devoted in 1999 to additional training in areas of provision where there were identified weaknesses. In particular, these comprised further guidance materials on progression in phonics, developing early writing for 5–7-year-olds, grammar for writing for 7–11-year-olds, and assistance for 5–6- and 7–8-year-old pupils who need additional support in literacy learning. None of these were specifically evaluated and it is difficult to gauge their success. One exception to this was provision of materials and approaches to assist 9–10-year-old pupils who need additional support in literacy learning, the *Further Literacy Support* (FLS) programme, an intervention programme introduced in 2003 to assist 9–10-year-olds whose attainment is below the national standard (but who do not have 'special needs'). The main features of FLS were 12 weeks of additional support in the spring term of Year 5 for approximately 20 per cent of an average class (about six children). The children are taught in withdrawal groups by a teaching assistant, using scripted materials.

The effectiveness of this 'supplemental' programme was investigated through an externally commissioned, independent national evaluation study, using standardised tests and teacher assessments of children's attainment (Beard *et al.*, 2004a; see also Beard *et al.*, 2004b). The literature suggests that little research has been done on the effectiveness of supplemental programmes for this age-range (McIntyre *et al.*, 2005). Test scores (using the NFER *Literacy Impact* tests) and teacher assessments from the national evaluation of FLS indicated short-term catch-up in reading by the target group of over 1,000 children and subsequent sustained movement similar to other 9–10-year-old pupils over two terms. Similar, but not statistically significant, catch-up was found in writing. National test data, from a year after the programme ended, indicate that over 90 per cent of the target children did meet or exceed 'national expectations' in reading at age 11 and 84 per cent in English overall. As bringing children up to age-related attainment at age 11 was the primary purpose of the FLS programme, these data are an important measure of its success.

The longer-term 'internal evaluation' of the NLS

The HMI concluded its four-year evaluation of the NLS in 2002. The final report included the following conclusions. There had been clear improvements in teaching in the 300 schools, the *Framework for Teaching* having given greater focus to literacy teaching. There had been increases in direct teaching, a clearer structure, higher expectations of pupils and greater progression and continuity.

There were also continuing concerns, again reflecting what Reynolds (1998) had prophetically called 'unreliable implementation':

- the teaching of phonics was still insufficiently systematic;
- guided reading was still not well taught in many schools;
- day-to-day assessment was not being sufficiently linked to progress;
- the NLS was insufficiently embedded in the National Curriculum;
- head teachers were not always providing appropriate leadership and management and this was weak in 10 per cent of schools.

Overall, however, HMI suggest that teachers now needed to develop a more questioning and reflective approach to the next stage of implementation. Similar conclusions can be found in the 'external evaluation' of the NLS.

The 'external evaluation' of the NLS

In parallel with the HMI evaluation, central government commissioned an external evaluation (i.e. from outside the UK) of the NLS, and its companion National

Numeracy Strategy, from the Ontario Institute for Studies in Education (OISE). Again, there were interim reports in line with the 'learn as we go' approach. The final report records the following successes in the NLS (Earl *et al.*, 2003):

- the breadth of influence of the NLS on teaching and learning;
- its adaptation within a coherent vision (as shown in 'Progression in Phonics'; 'Developing Early Writing'; 'Grammar for Writing'; 'Additional/Early/ Further Literacy Support');
- its value for money;
- its policy coherence over time;
- the balance of 'pressure and support'.

The final point is of particular interest. It suggests that one possible distortion, created by the inspection and testing programme on what schools do, has been partly exonerated, in the eyes of the external evaluators, in promoting educational change. The OISE evaluation also raises some questions and challenges for the NLS which are discussed in the section below on some specific lessons for other large-scale reform.

Other independent, longitudinal evaluative work on the NLS

Other independent, longitudinal evaluative work on the NLS has been done at the London School of Economics (Machin and McNally, 2008) which has found that the NLS produced 'good value for money' improvements in pupils' literacy at age 11, using pupils in Wales as a control group. The authors found that the policy initiative significantly raised reading scores at a relatively low cost and have used statistical modelling to project the findings to pupils' increased employment prospects and earnings in adulthood. Machin and McNally conclude that the literacy hour fares well when compared to other policies in terms of cost effectiveness and that the findings are of strong significance when placed into the wider education debate about what works best in schools for improving pupil performance, especially if public policy is aimed at changing the content and structure of teaching to significantly raise pupil achievement.

Another study with longitudinal elements but using qualitative data was undertaken by Webb and Vulliamy (2006, 2007). Fieldwork was conducted in a sample of 50 schools, replicating a study conducted a decade previously in the same schools. The findings suggest that there had been more changes in teaching styles and in classroom organisation in the 7–11 age-range in the previous five years than in the previous two decades. Such changes include a dramatic increase in whole-class teaching, the use of learning objectives shared with pupils and changes in pupil seating arrangements. Through compliance with centrally imposed changes in pedagogy, teachers' experiences have led them to change some of their professional values concerning desirable pedagogy. Supporting interview transcripts include the following:

I think that the Literacy Strategy and the Numeracy Strategy changed everybody's views . . . I am saying 'everybody's', but it certainly changed mine, it really did change mine – my views as a teacher and how to teach the subjects – because I think that if we are all honest we weren't teaching literacy as it should have been taught.

(Deputy head, October 2003)

Going back a few years I didn't know what I was teaching, the kids didn't know what they were learning and at the end of the lesson we didn't know whether we'd learnt it and nobody bothered to find out whether we'd learnt it. Now I know what I'm teaching, they know what they're learning and at the end of the lesson I'm going to know whether they've learnt it and what's more important they're going to know whether they've learnt it – and that's what's improved teaching.

(Year 3 teacher, July 2005)

Despite criticisms of over-prescription, Webb and Vulliamy demonstrate widespread endorsement by teachers and head teachers of the changes in teaching methods developed through the national literacy and numeracy strategies. The study also contains a caveat that, if the pressures of testing and performance tables are maintained, these will continue to constrain creativity in primary classroom practice and prevent the development of a confident new professionalism by primary teachers.

Some specific lessons from the NLS for other large-scale reform: OISE

Recognition of such issues may be of assistance in considering the implications of the NLS for programmes of educational change in other parts of the world. As was mentioned earlier, a study of a major initiative like the NLS/NPS also illustrates the challenges incurred in balancing the substance of attempted change with the levers through which change may be effected. The challenges of addressing this balance are evident in the recommendations contained in the OISE evaluation report (Earl *et al.*, 2003).

Build deep teacher understanding

The OISE study highlights the fundamental issue of teacher subject knowledge in major educational programmes of this kind. For instance, the NLS consultants were asked to rate how far teachers have the subject knowledge needed to implement the Strategy well and teachers were asked the same question. The results are shown in Figure 4.2 overleaf.

The Ontario report notes that this finding raises a key issue in the professional development of teachers, and in learning theory as a whole, that can be traced

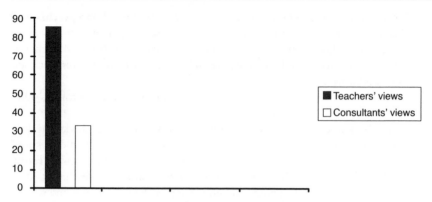

Figure 4.2 Teachers' and consultants' views on whether teachers 'have the subject knowledge needed to implement the Strategy well'.

back to Socrates: of teachers 'not knowing what they do not know'. As has been indicated earlier, for historical reasons in England there were key areas where the subject knowledge of teachers appeared insecure at the time when the NLS was implemented, especially in the teaching of phonics and writing. Future strategies of this kind are likely to benefit from the strategic planning of professional capacity-building in the context of existing practice.

Deflect attention from preoccupation with single achievement scores

This area seems to have been one of the most evident examples of unintended consequences of the target-setting component of the NLS. The OISE evaluation argues that teachers' preoccupations with single achievement scores has risked distorting the implementation of the more substantial aspects of teaching and learning that are embraced by the Strategy. It is difficult to see how this issue can be fully resolved while the publication of school league tables continues on an annual basis.

Consider how the strategy can be sustained

The indications are that there was large-scale adoption of the literacy hour and general compliance with the Strategy, even though it lacked the statutory status of the national curriculum content, national testing and school inspections. The OISE evaluation report argues that this degree of compliance may in turn result in a culture of dependence and a lack of awareness of how educational provision can improve further. This argument has subsequently been endorsed by Ofsted (2009) who, in a review of English teaching, suggest that if standards are to rise further, all schools need to reflect on what works generally and how this can be adapted to their own classrooms, with teaching being flexible and responsive to pupils' particular needs, rather than being based on preconceived views of what constituted a good lesson.

Develop greater 'assessment literacy' in schools

The OISE report suggests that one of the key elements in developing this sense of ownership is greater use of 'assessment literacy' in schools. A preoccupation with the test-related performances that are associated with national strategies can be more positively directed including greater use of test and assessment data for formative purposes: in specifying and critically analysing what children need to learn next, rather than just in recording what children have achieved. This may be especially important in the development of children's writing, which involves many subtleties and nuances (Beard, 2005; Beard *et al.*, 2009; Beard and Burrell, 2010).

Extend the strategy to parents, families and the public

Another unanticipated outcome from 'high-stakes' and high-profile school-based national initiatives is that they deflect attention from families and communities, whose culture and childcare practices also contribute significantly to children's attainment. There remains a continuing challenge for policy makers, to avoid the defeatist myth that schools make no difference, without bouncing to the other extreme that they make all the difference. How to build on initiatives like the NLS, to develop productive and sustainable educational collaborations with home and communities, remains a major issue.

Some more recent developments

In the light of the above recommendations, it is interesting to note a number of developments that have been added to the Strategy in recent years. In 2003 the NLS and the NNS became part of a National Primary Strategy, with encouragement for teachers to maintain a broader curriculum and to give greater attention to creativity, assessment for learning, and health and physical education, with additional guidance being provided for the development of speaking and listening (DfES, 2003). At the same time, there have been further initiatives to address areas of long-standing concern in English literacy education. The teaching of phonics has become the focus of a national enquiry, with schools being asked to introduce greater synthetic phonics (phonemic blending) (Rose, 2006). The renewed *Primary Framework for Literacy and Mathematics* (DfES, 2006) includes greater details on synthetic phonics but less prescribed detail overall.

Some generic lessons from the NLS for other large-scale reform: Moss

Moss (2009) has recently used a research council-funded study to try to identify the lessons that can be learnt from the NLS about literacy policy and its role in large-scale education reform programmes. She describes one of New Labour's promises to the electorate in 1997 as indicating that state-funded education could be 'fixed' and turned into a high-quality delivery system from which all would benefit; it could be fixed by direct intervention from politicians committed to overhauling the public sector and applying new principles which would see standards rise. The NLS was the main vehicle for change, whilst the target for achievement in literacy became one of the most public and obvious measures of the government's success in reforming education.

Moss concludes that, over the decade that followed New Labour's election, early optimism about what government could achieve was tempered by the twists and turn of events, which saw the education performance data plateau just short of the government's targets. She also describes the NLS as 'morphing' into the Primary National Strategy, as it gradually moved from the centre of political action to a more peripheral position. Moss argues that, within government itself, the NLS's progress has acted as an important catalyst for reflection on what works in public sector reform more generally and the challenges those running such programmes face.

Recurrent criticisms of the NLS

While the OISE study (Earl *et al.*, 2003) is helpful in taking stock of generic issues, a limitation of the broad remit of that evaluation is that it has not provided for a way of taking stock of the Strategy's legacy in relation to specific issues in the teaching and learning of reading and writing. In order to take this further, it may be helpful to return to some of the recurrent criticisms of the NLS referred to earlier.

It is often argued that the increase in standards has been largely illusory because of teachers 'teaching to the test'. This argument is understandable, given the 'high-stakes testing' that is now established in England. However, there are some less widely aired qualifications in this line of argument.

First, extensive national test preparation is apparently now very common in England in the final year of primary education. Yet it is apparently more effective in reading than in writing. The reasons for this warrant investigation. While national tests are by their nature external and unseen, the effectiveness of advance preparation would appear to be more likely in the encoding communicative act that is writing, rather than in the decoding communicative act that is reading. It is, after all, possible to 'rehearse' paragraph links and sentence starters and to store technical vocabulary ready for use in writing. Yet, although such preparation for written tests and examinations has been endemic in education for decades, sometimes euphemistically called 'exam technique', it is not so evidently possible in relation to decoding and comprehending unseen text.

Second, if the implementation of the NLS has generated 'illusory' attainment gains in terms of national test scores, why is it that significant gains in reading have also been found in the evaluation of the NLP and FLS, which have used a range of other standardised tests, for which specific test preparation was not possible? Such a portfolio of pupil gain data seems to be unprecedented in English primary education (for a discussion of some less successful precedents, see Beard, 2002). Could it not be that the strategic use of shared, guided and independent teaching literacy in the NLS might not have had some effect, perhaps manifesting an empirical line back to the LIFT project over a decade ago?

The possibility that the Strategy risked eroding the remainder of the statutory curriculum, especially in other subject areas, may initially appear rather odd, given the non-statutory status of the NLS. It may appear even odder, given that the 2003 initiative brought the literacy and numeracy strategies and much of the rest of the primary curriculum together in a single conceptual framework (DfES, 2003). However, if such erosion were likely, then the availability of an inspection system, often also subject to criticism, may be seen both as a positive counterbalancing lever, to ensure pupil entitlement to the statutory curriculum and also to provide a source of exemplary practice. For instance in the Ofsted report on *The Curriculum in Successful Primary Schools* (2002), it is reported that

> such [successful] schools had embraced the National Literacy and Numeracy Strategies positively . . . [and] recognised that these initiatives would be the key to achieving the highest standards in English and mathematics and that they could also have a positive impact on teaching and standards in other subjects . . . The teachers were adept . . . at making good use of links across subjects which strengthened the relevance and coherence of the curriculum for pupils and ensured that pupils applied the knowledge and skills learned in one subject to others.
>
> (Ofsted, 2002, p. 7)

It is perhaps inevitable that the neglect of oracy would be an issue raised in the context of a literacy initiative, even though the 1990s national test data did not indicate the relatively low attainment in speaking and listening that were reported for reading and writing. Several early studies of the implementation of the NLS (e.g. Hargreaves *et al.*, 2003; Skidmore *et al.*, 2003; Smith *et al.*, 2004) report that, despite the aspirations of the NLS to engender greater use of 'interactive' teaching, teacher–pupil dialogue in both the shared and the guided sessions of the literacy hour was teacher-dominated, usually often comprising questions to which the teacher already knew the answer.

This is far from a new finding in educational research, going back many years to the work of Flanders (1962) in the USA and Barnes *et al.* (1969) in the UK, for example. However, given the extensive NLS training materials that exemplified interactive teaching, such findings may perhaps be more reasonably seen as raising fidelity issues. More importantly, the literacy learning variable is sometimes overlooked in such studies: silent reading may not show up on codings of speech but it may be a major variable in the comprehension and fluency (NICHHD, 2000). Nevertheless, the renewed *Primary Framework for Literacy and Mathematics*

(DfES, 2006) has four strands for Speaking and Listening, which provide more specific guidance than the national curriculum. The relevant strands of *Assessing Pupils' Progress* initiative (DCSF, 2009) add to this provision for oracy, further underpinning more formative 'assessment for learning' systemic elements.

If the NLS lacked adequate promotion of voluntary, independent reading, it was not because it was omitted from the original *Framework* (which had a reminder of additional time for reading to the class and pupils' own independent reading) but perhaps because it lacked the exemplification and detailed guidance that it might have warranted. The original *Review of Research and Other Related Evidence* clearly evidenced the fact that, for many years, children's literature had been an area of substantial strength in British education (Beard, 1999). The *Review* also drew upon the national survey of children's voluntary reading by Coles and Hall (1999) to argue that provision of literature in schools needs to be informed by what they choose to read in their leisure time. Particular mention was made of the conspicuous structures and forms of poetry that arouse interest and invite investigation. This need to think through, and then beyond, the Strategy was subsequently endorsed by an Ofsted report on *Reading for Pleasure and Purpose*:

> The last few years have seen a marked improvement in the reading standards achieved by thousands of children across the country. That has been a genuine success story. In the effective schools, pupils had opportunities that extended well beyond the typical literacy hour, to practise and to improve their reading skills. Reading had a high profile in the curriculum with time given to it in addition to literacy lessons, such as using the library and the reading of a class novel.
>
> (Ofsted, 2004, p. 24)

Conclusion

This chapter has attempted to take stock of the National Literacy Strategy in England by discussing its development in the context of the research that has contributed to it. In my own view, the accumulated research base of the late 1990s provided substantial evidence to support the case for raising literacy standards in the United Kingdom and for modifying the ways in which reading and writing were taught in many primary schools (Beard, 2002; see also Beard, 1993, and Beard and Oakhill, 1994, for an indication of the professional debates of the time). This chapter has shown how, if large-scale educational reform is used to bring about such changes, research has a crucial role to play in providing an evidence base for policy, in evaluating implementation and in informing implications.

But large-scale educational reform invariably creates debate: opinions proliferate; attitudes entrench. It is hoped that this chapter has shown how research can lift such debate above an exchange of situated viewpoints by providing validly conceptualised, reliably collected and rigorously analysed evidence. The OISE evaluation report judges that the NLS was 'well-grounded in research (at least compared with most other change efforts)' (Earl *et al.*, 2003, p. 140). The *Final Report* of the recently published *Cambridge Primary Review* (*CPR*) has taken a rather different view, in a 'policy milestone' note: that the NLS was less well-founded empirically and was less successful than the National Numeracy Strategy (Alexander, 2009, p. 44). Readers may wish to judge for themselves how this chapter corroborates or contradicts this view (also see, for example, Brown, *et al.*, 2003). Readers may also note how few of the references in this chapter are cited in the *CPR*, in which a substantial number of relevant peer-reviewed publications have apparently been overlooked (see also Beard, 2010).

In judging the success of the NLS, complex questions remain about the extent of schools' fidelity in implementing the recommended practices, whether its effectiveness was compromised by local factors and whether the productive changes in practice that it promoted can be sustained. Also, any success in raising literacy standards, whatever the criteria used, will reflect the sustained hard work of thousands of teachers and children. With reference to the NLS, such success also needs to be weighed against an increase in central government investment in primary education: in training materials; in-service programmes; and the appointment of several hundred literacy consultants.

The possibility that research has been judiciously applied in ways that have bolstered national attainment – mediated by the promotion of more productive pedagogical approaches – is of particular interest, coming as it does after a time when educational research in the UK has been subjected to substantial criticisms (e.g. Hargreaves, 1996; Tooley and Darby, 1998; Woodhead, 1998; see also Beard, 2000b, 2003; Wyse, 2003). The legacy of the NLS may in time confirm that, if research evidence is critically considered and the implications sensitively implemented, then it can contribute significantly to raising educational standards and, indirectly, to improving the life-chances of thousands of children.

Acknowledgements

An earlier version of this chapter was published in Greek in E. Matsagouras (ed.) (2007) *School Literacy*. Athens: Grigoris Publications. ISBN 978–960–333–518–4. I am very grateful to Pete Dudley, National Director, National Strategies, Primary; and Alan Howe, Senior Director, National Strategies, Secondary, for their comments on a subsequent version. Responsibility for the final version is entirely my own.

Notes

1 Inspections initially lasted a week and normally covered the following: the standards achieved; teaching quality; curricular and extra-curricular activities; student care; partnership with parents and the school's leadership and management. Subsequently, inspections have been shorter with similarly shorter periods of notice and also incorporating greater provision of self-evaluation.

2 Assuming a 36-week teaching year, to allow a margin for the induction of new pupils, assessment work, school events and educational visits, the Dearing Report

recommended that 180 hours of English be taught directly for 5–7-year-olds, an hour a day in the 36 weeks referred to above. A related recommendation was that another 36 hours were to be taught through other subjects. For 7–11-year-olds the figures were 162 and 18 respectively.

3   The influence of these personnel, should not be underestimated. They wrote guidance and training materials, ensured consistency of 'delivery' through national and regional training the trainer events, visited local authorities and supported local developments, quality-assured the work of local consultants, and ran briefings for primary head teachers and others.

References

Adams, M.J. (1990) *Beginning to Read: Thinking and Learning about Print*, Cambridge, MA: MIT Press.

Alexander, R.J. (ed.) (2009) *Children, their World, their Education: Final report and recommendations of the Cambridge Primary Review*, London: Routledge.

Barber, M. (1999) Presentation at the United Kingdom Reading Association Annual Conference, Chester, July.

Barnes, D., Britton, J. and Rosen, H. (1969) *Language, the Learner and the School*, Harmondsworth: Penguin.

Beard, R. (ed.) (1993) *Teaching Literacy: Balancing Perspectives*, London: Hodder and Stoughton.

Beard, R. (1999) *National Literacy Strategy: Review of Research and Other Related Evidence*, London: Department for Education and Employment.

Beard, R. (2000a) 'Research and the National Literacy Strategy', *Oxford Review of Education*, 26, 3 and 4, 421–36.

Beard, R. (2000b) 'Long Overdue? Another Look at the National Literacy Strategy', *Journal of Research in Reading*, 23, 3, 245–55.

Beard, R. (2002) 'As the Research Predicted? Examining the Success of the National Literacy Strategy', in R. Fisher, M. Lewis and G. Brooks (eds) *Raising Standards in Literacy*, pp. 38–54, London: Routledge.

Beard, R. (2003) 'Not the Whole Story of the National Literacy Strategy: A Response to Dominic Wyse', *British Educational Research Journal*, 26, 6, 917–28.

Beard, R. (2005) 'Teaching Writing: Using Research to Inform Practice', in G. Rijlaarsdam, H. Van den Bergh and M. Couzijn (eds) *Research in Effective Learning and Teaching of Writing*, Amsterdam: Kluwer.

Beard, R. (2010) 'Review of *Children, their World, their Education: Final report and recommendations of the Cambridge Primary Review* (edited by Robin Alexander)', *Cambridge Journal of Education*, 44, 3, 315.

Beard, R. and Oakhill, J. (1994) *Reading by Apprenticeship?* Slough: National Foundation for Educational Research.

Beard, R. and Willcocks, J. (2002) 'The National Literacy Strategy in England: Changing Phonics Teaching?' in D. Schallert, C.M. Fairbanks, J. Worthy, B. Maloch and J.V. Hoffman (eds) *51st Yearbook of the National Reading Conference*, pp. 94–105, Madison, WI: National Reading Conference.

Beard, R. and Burrell, A. (2010) 'Investigating Narrative Writing by 9–11 Year Olds', *Journal of Research in Reading*, 33, 1, 77–93.

Beard, R., Pell, G., Shorrocks-Taylor, D. and Swinnerton, B., with Sawyer, V., Willcocks, J. and Yeomans, D. (2004a) *National Evaluation of the National Literacy Strategy Further Literacy Support Programme: Final Report*, London: Department of Education and Skills.

Beard, R., Shorrocks-Taylor, D. and Pell, G. (2004b) 'Evaluating Further Literacy Support', *Literacy Today*, 38.

Beard, R., Myhill, D., Riley, J. and Nystrand, M. (eds) (2009) *Handbook of Writing Research*, London: Sage.

Bereiter, C. and Scardamalia, M. (1987) *The Psychology of Written Composition*, Hillsdale, NJ: Lawrence Erlbaum.

Brooks, G. (1998) 'Trends in Standards of Literacy in the United Kingdom 1948–1996', *Topic*, 19, 1–10.

Brooks, G., Pugh, A.K. and Schagen, I. (1996) *Reading Performance at Nine*, Slough: National Foundation for Educational Research.

Brown, M., Askew, M., Millett, A. and Rhodes, V. (2003) 'The Key Role of Educational Research in the Development and Evaluation of the National Numeracy Strategy', *British Educational Research Journal*, 29, 5, 655–72.

Coles, M. and Hall, C. (1999) *Children's Reading Choices*, London: Routledge.

Creemers, B.P.M. (1994) *The Effective Classroom*, London: Cassell.

Crevola, C.A. and Hill, P.W. (1998) 'Evaluation of a Whole-School Approach to Prevention and Intervention in Early Literacy', *Journal of Education for Students Placed At Risk*, 3, 2, 133–57.

Dearing, R. (1994) *The National Curriculum and its Assessment: Final Report*, London: School Curriculum and Assessment Authority.

Department of Education and Science (DES) (1989) *English in the National Curriculum*, London: Her Majesty's Stationery Office.

Department for Education (DfE) (1995) *English in the National Curriculum*, London: Her Majesty's Stationery Office.

Department for Education and Employment (DfEE) (1998a) *The National Literacy Strategy: Framework for Teaching*, London: DfEE.

Department for Education and Employment (1998b) *The National Literacy Strategy: Literacy Training Pack*, London: DfEE.

Department of Education and Skills (DfES) (2003) *Excellence and Enjoyment: A Strategy for Primary Schools*, London: DfES.

Department for Education and Skills (2006) *Primary Framework for Literacy and Mathematics*, London: DfES.

Department for Children, Schools and Families (DCSF) (2009) *Getting to Grips with Assessing Pupils' Progress*, London: DCSF.

Donaldson, M. (1993) 'Sense and Sensibility: Some Thoughts on the Teaching of Literacy', in R. Beard (ed.) *Teaching Literacy: Balancing Perspectives*, pp. 35–60, London: Hodder and Stoughton.

Earl, L., Watson, N., Levin, B., Leithwood, K., Fullan, M. and Torrance, N. (2003) *Watching and Learning 3: Final Report of the external evaluation of England's National Literacy and Numeracy Strategies*, London: Department for Education and Employment.

Fisher, R. (2002) *Inside the Literacy Hour*, London: RoutledgeFalmer.

Flanders, N.A. (1962) 'Using Interaction Analysis in the Inservice Training of Teachers', *Journal of Experimental Education*, 30, 4, 3316.

Fullan, M. (2000) 'The Return of Large-scale Reform', *Journal of Educational Change*, 1, 5–28.

Hargreaves, D.H. (1996) *Teaching as a Research-based Profession: Possibilities and Prospects*, London: Teacher Training Agency.

Hargreaves, L., Moyles, J., Merry, R., Paterson, F., Pell, A. and Esarte-Sarries, V. (2003) 'How Do Primary School Teachers Define and Implement 'Interactive Teaching' in the National Literacy Strategy in England?' *Research Papers in Education*, 18, 3, 217–36.

Harrison, C. (2002) *The National Strategy for English at Key Stage 3: Roots and Research*, London: Department for Education and Skills.

Her Majesty's Inspectorate (HMI) (1999) *The National Literacy Strategy: An Evaluation by HMI*, London: Office for Standards in Education.

Her Majesty's Inspectorate (2000) *The Teaching of Writing in Primary Schools: Could Do Better*, London: Office for Standards in Education.

Her Majesty's Inspectorate (2002) *The National Literacy Strategy: The First Four Years*, London: Office for Standards in Education.

Hillocks, G. (1986) *Research on Written Composition*, Urbana, IL: National Conference on Research in English/ERIC Clearinghouse on Reading and Communication Skills.

Hillocks, G. (1995) *Teaching Writing as Reflective Practice*, New York: Teachers College Press.

Hillocks, G. (2003) *Reconceptualizing Writing Curricula: What We Know and Can Use*. Online. http://www.ioe.ac.uk/study/departments/ecpe/24541.html (accessed 31 August 2010).

Hurry, J., Sylva, K. and Riley, J. (1999) 'Evaluation of a Focused Literacy Teaching Programme in Reception and Year 1 Classes: Child Outcomes', *British Educational Research Journal*, 25, 5, 637–49.

Le Métais, J. (2003) *International Trends in Primary Education: INCA Thematic Study No. 9*. Online. http://www.inca.org.uk/pdf/thematic_study_9.pdf (accessed 31 August 2010).

Literacy Task Force (LTF) (1997a) *A Reading Revolution: How We Can Teach Every Child to Read Well*, London: Literacy Task Force c/o University of London, Institute of Education.

Literacy Task Force (1997b) *The Implementation of the National Literacy Strategy*, London: Department for Education and Employment.

Machin, S. and McNally, S. (2008) 'The Literacy Hour', *Journal of Public Economics*, 92, 5–6, 1441–62.

McIntyre, E., Jones, D., Powers, S., Newsome, F., Petrosko, J., Powell, R. and Bright, K. (2005) 'Supplemental Instruction in Early Reading: Does It Matter for Struggling Readers?' *Journal of Educational Research*, 99, 2, 99–107.

Mortimore, P. (1991) 'The Nature and Findings of School Effectiveness Research in the Primary Sector', in S. Riddell and S. Brown (eds) *School Effectiveness Research: Its Messages for School Improvement*, London: Her Majesty's Stationery Office.

Mortimore, P., Sammons, P., Stoll, L., Lewis, D. and Ecob, R. (1988) *School Matters: The Junior Years*, Wells: Open Books.

Moss, G. (2009) 'The Politics of Literacy in the Context of Large-scale Education Reform', *Research Papers in Education*, 24, 2, 155–74.

National Institute of Child Health and Human Development (NICHHD) (2000) *Teaching Children To Read: An Evidence-Based Assessment of the Scientific Research Literature on*

Reading and Its Implications for Reading Instruction (Report of the National Reading Panel), Washington, DC: Government Printing Office.

Office for Standards in Education (Ofsted) (2002) *The Curriculum in Successful Primary Schools*, London: Ofsted.

Office for Standards in Education (2004) *Reading for Pleasure and Purpose*, London: Ofsted.

Office for Standards in Education (2009) *English at the Crossroads*, London: Ofsted.

Reynolds, D. (1998) 'Schooling for Literacy: A Review of Research on Teacher Effectiveness and School Effectiveness and its Implications for Contemporary Educational Policies', *Educational Review*, 50, 2, 147–62.

Rose, J. (2006) *Independent Review of the Teaching of Early Reading*, London: Department for Education and Skills.

Sainsbury, M., Schagen, I., Whetton, C., with Hagues, N. and Minnis, M. (1998) *Evaluation of the National Literacy Strategy: Summary Report*, Slough: National Foundation for Educational Research.

Scheerens, J. (1992) *Effective Schooling: Research, Theory and Practice*, London: Cassell.

Shorrocks-Taylor, D. (1999) *National Testing: Past, Present and Future*, Leicester: British Psychological Society.

Skidmore, D., Perez-Parent, M. and Arnfield, S. (2003) '*Teacher–Pupil Dialogue in the Guided Reading Session*', *Reading: Literacy and Language*, 37, 2, 47–53.

Slavin, R.E. (1997) 'Success for All: Policy Implications for British Education', paper presented at the Literacy Task Force Conference, London, 27 February.

Smith, F., Hardman, F., Wall, K. and Mroz, M. (2004) 'Interactive Whole Class Teaching in the National Literacy and Numeracy Strategies', *British Educational Research Journal*, 30, 3, 395–411.

Stannard, J. (1997) 'Raising Standards Through the National Literacy Project', paper presented at the Literacy Task Force Conference, London, 27 February.

Stannard J. and Huxford, L. (2007) *The Literacy Game: The Story of the National Literacy Strategy*, London: Routledge.

Sylva, K., Hurry, J., Mirelman, H., Burrell, A. and Riley, J. (1999) 'Evaluation of a Focused Literacy Teaching Programme in Year 1 Reception Classes: Classroom Observations', *British Educational Research Journal*, 25, 5, 617–35.

Teddlie, C. and Reynolds, D. (eds) (1999) *The International Handbook of School Effectiveness Research*, Lewes: Falmer Press.

Tooley, J. and Darby, D. (1998) *Educational Research: A Critique*, London: Office for Standards in Education.

Twist. L., Sainsbury, M., Woodthorpe, A. and Whetton, C. (2003) *Reading All Over the World: Progress in International Reading Literacy Study: National Report for England 2003*, Slough: National Foundation for Educational Research.

Twist, L., Schagen, I. and Hodgson, C. (2007) *Readers and Reading: The National Report for England 2006* (Progress in International Reading Literacy Study), Slough: National Foundation for Educational Research.

Wasik, B.A. and Slavin, R.E. (1993) 'Preventing Reading Failure with One-to-One Tutoring: A Review of Five Programmes', *Reading Research Quarterly*, 28, 178–200.

Webb, R. and Vulliamy, G. (2006) *The Impact of New Labour's Education Policies on Primary School Teachers' Work*, London: Association of Teachers and Lecturers.

Webb, R. and Vulliamy, G. (2007) 'Coming Full Circle: The Impact of New Labour's Education Policies on Primary School Teachers' Work', *Oxford Review of Education*, 33, 561–80.

Woodhead, C. (1998) 'Academia Gone to Seed', *New Statesman*, 20 March.

Wyse, D. (2003) 'The National Literacy Strategy: A Critical Review of Empirical Evidence', *British Educational Research Journal*, 26, 6, 903–16.

Chapter 5

New Zealand's literacy strategy

A lengthening tail and wagging dogs

Stephanie Dix, Gail Cawkwell and Terry Locke

Introduction

It is now over ten years since the March 1999 publication of the *Report of the Literacy Taskforce*, commissioned by the same National-led government that had initiated a raft of curriculum and qualifications reforms in New Zealand in the 1990s. The report was subtitled: 'Advice to the Government on achieving its goal that: "By 2005, every child turning nine will be able to read, write, and do maths for success"' (Ministry of Education (MOE) 1999: 2). Like literacy strategies in other settings, its goal was ambitious and susceptible to varying definitions and, of course, occasioned by various claims of crisis. In New Zealand's case, the cause for concern was the verdict of successive international literacy surveys from 1990 onwards indicating a wide gap between the highest and lowest levels of reading achievement and significant differences in performance in all areas between particular groups of children, in particular Maori and Pasifika children, boys, and children from low socio-economic schools.

The National Literacy Strategy as implemented in New Zealand was really a set of evolving strategies that were rolled out to teachers in primary and intermediate schools as a series of distinct measures. In this sense, the Strategy was in marked contrast to the National Literacy Strategy in England which was a single, coherent and comprehensive measure aimed at a radical transformation of the educational landscape. However, like its English counterpart, the measures associated with the National Literacy Strategy in New Zealand were certainly aimed at changing teaching practices and, of course, outcomes for New Zealand students.

This chapter begins by indicating the kinds of social changes occurring in New Zealand after the election of a Labour Government in 1984 and into the first decade of the new millennium. We describe the various measures implemented or planned for implementation (including the introduction of national standards) since 1990 that we can collectively call the New Zealand Literacy Strategy, highlighting differences from the NLS in England. We discuss the aimed-for transformation, critique it and review the extent to which outcomes for New Zealand students have improved as a result of NLS measures. In doing so, we indicate some of the continuing debates surrounding the implementation of these measures.

Crisis, what crisis?

The National-led coalition government announced its goal in October 1998 that 'by 2005, every child turning nine will be able to read, write, and do maths for success'. In the same month, the Minister of Education appointed both a Literacy Taskforce and a Literacy Experts Group. The former was tasked with providing 'advice about achieving the goal from their perspectives as principals, teachers and advisers', while the latter was tasked with providing advice 'from a theoretical and academic perspective' (Douglas 2002: 22).

What prompted this policy initiative was a sense of crisis, brought about by New Zealand's declining performance in international literacy surveys and fuelled by media headlines suggesting that New Zealand's reputation as the nirvana of literacy instructional excellence had been severely dented and decrying the abandonment of 'phonics' in favour of 'whole language' (Limbrick 2000). In a 1970–71 International Association for the Evaluation of Educational Achievement (IEA) survey involving 15 countries, New Zealand's 9 and 14-year-olds came out top in reading achievement. There were other indicators and endorsements also that New Zealand was a world-beater in literacy instruction (see Wilkinson 1998).

In 1990–91, New Zealand participated in a second IEA survey, this time involving 32 countries (see Wagemaker 1992). While its students still performed highly – 14-year-olds were ranked fourth in overall achievement and 9-year-olds were ranked sixth – a number of worrying trends emerged. Compared with 1970–71, the 1990–91 survey showed a widening *variation* in achievement. In fact, New Zealand's 14-year-olds showed the widest spread of scores of any participating country. What an analysis of the scores revealed was both a *gender gap* and a *home language gap*. At the 9-year-old level, for example, boys' literacy levels were well below those of girls in all measures, though the gaps were smaller for 14-year-olds. As reported by Wilkinson (1998), the *'home language gap* was found in all reading literacy domains . . . Internationally, New Zealand students showed . . . the largest home language gap at both age levels among all countries participating in the IEA survey' (p. 147). Such results were corroborated nearer to home in the 1996 results of the National Education Monitoring Project (NEMP) on reading and speaking, which identified 20 per cent of students as below expected levels of band achievement, a gap between Maori and non-Maori achievement and a *home language gap* (Flockton and Crooks 1997).

The knee-jerk response to these gaps was to explain them in terms of classroom practice and more generally in terms of failings in New Zealand's much vaunted approach to literacy instruction (even though this had appeared to stand the country in good stead in the 1970s).[1] Other commentators, however, have attributed such gaps to factors outside the classroom (e.g. Wilkinson 1998; Limbrick 2000; Elley 2004). The most salient of these are changes in New Zealand's demographic. Right now, this country is home to over 200 different ethnic groups. In recent years, New Zealand's Maori, Asian and Pacific populations have been growing faster than the 'European or other' population. Table 5.1 reflects dramatic changes in New Zealand's ethnic make-up. The Asian population in New Zealand has doubled since 1991, driven largely by migration, while the growth of Maori and Pasifika populations compared to the European one has been largely driven by births (higher fertility rates and a young age structure). Another indicator of New Zealand's increasing ethnic diversity is reflected in 2001 census data, which showed that 1 in 5 children below the age of 5 was identified as belonging to at least two ethnic groups. In 1986, this had been 1 in 10 (see Statistics New Zealand 2008; Ministry of Social Development 2009). In short, New Zealand classrooms have become markedly more culturally and linguistically diverse.

Table 5.1 The changing ethnic face of New Zealand

Ethnicity	% of population by year*			
	1996	2001	2006	2026
European or other ethnicity	82.4	79.2	76.8	69
Maori	15.4	15.1	14.9	17
Pasifika	6.1	6.7	7.2	10
Asian	5.3	7.0	9.7	16
Middle Eastern/Latin American/African	0.5	0.7	0.9	1

Note: * Percentages add up to more than 100 per cent because census questionnaires allow respondents to identify with more than one ethnicity.

Other extraneous factors relate to socio-economic conditions. Limbrick (2000) pointed to a 'greater polarisation of wealth and living conditions' (p. 6) as having an impact on the educational opportunities of many of this country's young. A 2008 article in *The Press* asserted that 'the income gap between families of unqualified and qualified parents has more than doubled over 25 years' (Anon., 2008: ¶2; see also Cotterell *et al.*, 2008). In addition, Limbrick (2000) identified factors in the educational sector with the potential of having a detrimental effect on practices within classrooms: changes in the administration of New Zealand schools in the direction of self-management; a major curriculum shake-up (for a discussion of the impact of this on primary teachers, see Locke *et al.*, 2005); and a teacher shortage in the mid-1990s which saw significant overseas-trained teachers placed in front of New Zealand children, especially in low-decile (low-socio-economic status (SES)) schools (pp. 6–7).

A radical change or business as usual?

The shape of New Zealand's National Literacy Strategy cannot be considered without recognising the changes wrought in the working lives and classroom practices of the country's teachers as a result of National Party curriculum reforms begun in 1991, described by one educator as 'the most radical restructuring of the education system in 100 years' (Codd 1993, cited in McFarlane 2000: 98). Two of the structural parameters the Achievement Initiative rested on included:

1. the establishing of clear achievement standards for all levels of compulsory schooling, first in the basic subjects of English, mathematics, science and technology, and later in other subjects; and 2. the developing of national assessment procedures at key stages of schooling, by which the learning progress of all students can be monitored in those basic subjects.

(MOE 1991: 1)

Teachers have always grappled with ways of sequencing learning in their classroom. While the authors of *English in the New Zealand Curriculum* (ENZC) mapped overlapping levels of achievement stating 'the objectives are intended to be seen as cumulative and express learning as progressively more complete language behaviours and skills' (MOE 1994: 19), others viewed this curriculum restructuration as based on a flawed model of progression articulated as ladders of achievement objectives at eight levels (Duthie Educational Consultancy 1994; Elley 1996). Teaching was no longer framed to the child; the child was to be framed to a normative ladder of discrete, decontextualised learning outcomes whence content had been drained. While official rhetoric called for a reprofessionalisation of teachers in the decade of the 1990s via what was euphemistically called professional development, the real impact of reform implementation was more akin to deprofessionalisation in the context of an increasingly managerial, audit culture (Locke 2001). Whatever a Literacy Taskforce might recommend, it would be constrained by these models of progression, which would become increasingly reified via the technologies of diagnostic testing regimes (for example, Assessment Tools for Teaching and Learning (asTTle)), systems of exemplars indexed to 'levels' and, more recently, literacy learning progression statements (MOE 2010). Bearing in mind the shift that had already occurred via curriculum upheaval, we return to the engendered crisis.

Even those with a balanced response to New Zealand's international literacy survey performance (such as Wilkinson 1998) viewed the emergence of gaps as a cause for concern and tailored their response to the particular educational needs of boys, Maori, the poor and students from non-English-speaking households. In this respect, the construction of a literacy 'crisis' was different from what happened in England, where the driving metaphor for the National Literacy Strategy was the need for a systemic overhaul involving a radical change in teacher professional and pedagogical knowledge. Reading Stannard and Huxford (2007), one has little sense of a strategy directed to the needs of particular student groupings. Rather the strategy as implemented was a one-size-fits-all model, albeit with room for flexibility or *differentiation*, to use the preferred term (Stannard and Huxford 2007: 93–106).

The measures recommended by New Zealand's Literacy Taskforce's report to the Minister included the following (all page references below are to MOE 1999):

- 'a description of the knowledge, skills, and attitudes that nine-year-olds demonstrate when they are reading and writing for success, together with a description of the features of appropriate texts, be developed and promulgated to teachers and parents' (p. 5);

- 'a statement of best practice be drawn up and promulgated to schools' (p. 9);
- that the requirement of a broad continuum continue, but that monitoring requirements in years 1–4 be focused on literacy and numeracy;
- priority be given to the provision of certain resources (e.g. a video illustrating how to take and analyse running records in English and Maori; developing teaching guidelines for teaching reading and writing in Maori-medium education; material suited for struggling readers; and guidelines for schools in resource selection);
- an investigation into how 'teacher education programmes, particularly in respect to literacy learning, are approved for the purpose of teacher registration' (p. 12);
- the development of a 'comprehensive professional development package to assist teachers to implement best practice in their teaching of reading and writing' (p. 13);
- support for the development of literacy leadership in schools and that 'appropriate materials and opportunities be provided for principals to allow them to update their understanding of literacy learning' (p. 14);
- 'a nationally co-ordinated system of interventions targeted at those most in need be established by reviewing and building on the interventions that already exist, in particular, Reading Recovery and the Resource Teachers of Reading' (p. 16);
- 'assessment be an essential component of teacher education' and the 'development of further externally referenced assessment tools' to help 'assess progress and achievement in literacy in each of the first four years of instruction' and that 'schools be required to use externally referenced assessment tools on an annual basis and that this data be sampled to monitor the system's progress towards the goal' (pp. 18–19).

The Taskforce also recommended that funds be made available to Decile 1 and Decile 2 schools from a Reading, Writing and Mathematics Proposals pool to assist with the set-up costs of programmes clearly aimed at meeting the needs of children 'identified as making limited progress' (p. 19).

As Stannard and Huxford (2007) make abundantly clear, the aim of the NLS in England was a major intervention at the level of classroom instruction, based on the general principle of 'changing teaching behaviours in order to change minds' (pp. 113–14). While the New Zealand Taskforce would have been aware of events in England, they stopped short of such a revolutionary agenda. In contrast to advocates of the English NLS, they generally endorsed the status quo in New Zealand, asserting that 'our literacy strategies are more effective for most students than those in many other similar countries' (p. 7). They also endorsed the professional decision-making capability of teachers at school and classroom level: 'Decisions about teaching strategies, teaching approaches and materials to use are professional decisions that are best made at the local school level in response to the needs of particular groups of children and individuals' (p. 8).

However, it added the rider that given the gaps discussed earlier, more of the same would not do and listed a set of principles of best practice (p. 8) that should underpin effective literacy instruction and thereby help serve the needs of those students clearly needing help. Also, in the light of the current government's imposition of National Standards, it is interesting to note that the Taskforce saw dangers in setting 'minimal competency levels', and preferred the use of such devices as curriculum exemplars to set 'national *expectations* for teachers and parents' (p. 4; our emphasis). The Taskforce in New Zealand (as in England) took note of debates around phonics, deriding the way it had been played out in the media and taking a balanced view of the need for the explicit teaching of word-level skills. Finally, by way of contrast with the situation in England, the Taskforce, while advocating a range of measures, was careful *not* to argue for more time for literacy per se, or even for a *special* time. Rather it emphasised the value of a broad curriculum (including, for example, art and physical education) and the fact that literacy can be actively reinforced via integrated learning.

The writing question

English in the New Zealand Curriculum (ENZC) (MOE 1994) was to transform and alter the teaching of writing in New Zealand primary classrooms. Not only were teachers presented with a document that had a completely different theoretical and pedagogical base for teaching writing, indicating a major shift from a writer-oriented to a text-oriented document (Hyland 2002), but teachers also had to differentiate learning in terms of levels of achievement. The uptake by schools and teachers of a genre-based, functional approach to teaching writing was partly because the government wanted greater control of curriculum knowledge and a written product would enable achievement to be measured more easily (Sawyer 1995; McFarlane 2000). It was also in response to concerns about New Zealand students' ability to write a range of genres, in particular, argumentational texts (Lamb 1987). Teachers themselves were anxious about their own knowledge of genres and associated grammatical features. Professional development was limited, so teachers and schools globally shopped around.

Professional development for many primary schools and teachers meant looking to Australia and buying into First Steps Writing workshops introduced by the Education Department of Western Australia. The *Writing Resource Book* and the *Writing Developmental Continuum* (both Educational Department of Western Australia 1994) became a central teaching resource for many teachers, and genre writing frameworks originating with the Australian Genre School (Cope and Kalantzis 1993) provided scaffolding for teaching genres and text structure. Emphasis on linguistic aspects of genre, the schematic structure of text and associated grammar features dominated language teaching as teachers had to learn a new metalanguage to talk about texts (Macken-Horarik 2002). The resulting writing orientation was more teacher directed and text oriented, and was to influence writing pedagogy in New Zealand for the next two decades.

The non-negotiable, 'levelled' also impacted on teaching practice, as teachers had to find ways of assessing children's achievement against level objectives, when, as Elley (1996) pointed out, 'The inherent progression in language is not captured by these level statements' (p. 14). Despite problems with interpreting the achievement objectives, which are still not addressed, teachers found themselves assessing and comparing students' achievement in writing against levels-based outcomes. As we shall see, the Literacy Taskforce 'supported the Ministry of Education's proposal to develop exemplars for the achievement objectives related to reading and writing in *English in the New Zealand curriculum* so that teachers are clearer about the standards that should be achieved at each level of the curriculum' (MOE 1999: 26).

An emphasis on writing was curiously absent from the *Report of the Taskforce* (MOE 1999) and writing was poorly represented in the literacy research which backgrounds the report. Perhaps fuelled by a media 'beat-up' about reading, the report's focus was on gaps in reading. Skills and understandings related to writing were not recognised and under-researched. As happened in England, there was a kind of tacit assumption that steps to improve reading would have a positive flow-on in writing performance. The various studies mentioned earlier which identified gaps in reading had failed to address student achievement of writing in the early years. For example, the International Association for the Evaluation of Educational Achievement (IEA) Reading Literacy Study (see Elley 1992) reported on reading achievement only.

There were notable omissions from the Taskforce's research base in respect of writing. It failed to acknowledge the writing performance of New Zealand students in the 1984 IEA Study of Written Composition (Lamb 1987) mentioned previously, or the NEMP findings in *Writing Assessment Results, 1998, Report 12* (Flockton and Crooks 1999). Although the *Writing Assessment Results 1998* was published the same year as the Taskforce report, the published findings were not referred to. The NEMP survey randomly sampled, collected and analysed writing data from 2,872 children at year 4 and year 8. Tasks assessed expressive and functional writing, writing conventions and student attitudes. Significant findings noted in *Forum Comment* (Flockton and Crooks 1998) celebrated the 'good news' that 'Students were able to engage in a wide variety of writing tasks in a short time without preliminary motivation and guidance from a class teacher. Many students' attempts at independent writing under these assessment conditions were impressive', and that 'There is evidence of considerable improvement in functional writing and spelling between year 4 and year 8. Typical gains of over 30 percent are amongst the highest seen in NEMP subject reports' (p. 2). Furthermore, in relation to confidence and attitudes to writing, the NEMP report stated that, '72 percent of year 4 students and 60 percent of year 8 students reported a positive feeling about writing. This is a considerable improvement over attitudes reported in local and international surveys in the past. It may reflect the influence in recent years of more liberal approaches to writing' (p. 2), and many students believe that the best ways to become a good writer are to 'use your imagination' and 'try out new ideas' (p. 2).

While the Taskforce was framing its report, then, the NEMP survey was suggesting that students' ability to construct functional texts had improved substantially. NEMP writing concerns were focused on self-editing. Like the reading surveys discussed earlier, however, a concerning gender gap was identified. In addition, 'A very wide range of ability in writing was evident. Differences in performance were especially apparent between low decile schools and the rest, indicating a polarisation of achievement levels in our schools' (Flockton and Crooks 1998: 3).

In summary, the Ministry of Education's desire to close the gap between low and high achievers was based on reading research findings. Although it is widely acknowledged that learning to read and write involves reciprocal understandings and skills (Clay 1991, 2002; Smith and Elley 1997), as Stannard and Huxford (2007) point out, writing needs its own research base. In England and New Zealand, there was a tendency to clump reading and writing research together, because more data are available on reading outcomes and they are easier to measure.

> There is a common assumption that, because competent writing almost always presupposes the ability to read, reading should be the first priority, and that with reasonable encouragement and opportunity for writing, children's experiences will carry across to their writing. This is not necessarily the case, as data on reading and writing attainment over the years has shown.
>
> (p. 53)

The research data, which formed the basis for Taskforce recommendations to the Ministry, failed to identify areas of strength and concerns in students' writing performance. As mentioned earlier, a strong set of pedagogical principles was endorsed by the Taskforce, but the emphasis in the interventions discussed (for example, Reading Recovery) was on reading.

The Taskforce did, however, recognise the need to identify features that would demonstrate successful reading and writing, where writers are self-motivated and able to construct texts with accuracy and fluency. They presented key indicators for 9-year-olds 'writing for success' (listed in Appendix B, MOE 1999: 34–5). In claiming that there were 'no national indicators for children's writing' (MOE 1999: 8), the writers failed to acknowledge the 'criteria for quality writing' or the 'characteristics of the writer' (for emergent, early and fluent writers) as articulated in the Ministry's own handbook, *Dancing with the Pen* (MOE 1992: 121–4). If the Taskforce failed to recognise the composition of written texts as having its own particular concerns, the Literacy Strategy as implemented certainly tried to shift the balance.

Implementing the literacy strategy

The National Literacy Strategies (NLS) that would direct teaching and learning of language literacy in England and New Zealand classrooms were different beasts. In New Zealand the focus was to enhance effective practice, and to refine and improve what was already in place in schools to lift the achievement of all students but especially those languishing in the assessment 'tail'. As Stannard and Huxford (2007) describe it, the NLS in England was a 'strongly interventionist process of informed prescription' (p. 1) driven by a view that major restructuring and professional development was needed.

> In terms of the balance sheet, the biggest deficit was probably teachers' knowledge about language and its relevance to the curriculum at every level: word, sentence and text. The immediate purpose of the Framework for Teaching was to generate a common and practical progression of objectives to support teachers and steer their planning, but its wider purpose was to create an agenda for professional development. What was in the Framework in terms of its content and structure was ahead of the knowledge of many teachers at the time.
>
> (p. 46)

Teaching practices and organisation for the Literacy Hour were sourced from a range of contexts. New Zealand's Reading Recovery programme and classroom practices were to strongly influence the Literacy Hour, owing to its proven research base in respect of mainstream and slower readers (including an emphasis on explicit instruction). Practices introduced to the Literacy Hour included whole-class and instructional grouping, shared reading, guided reading, dialogue, peer conversations, shared writing, teacher modelling and teacher demonstrations, features already part of daily practice in New Zealand schools.

To uplift teacher capability for writing, multiple projects were initiated. In the case of teaching writing the emphasis focused on increased opportunities for professional development; the production of a wider range of resources to enhance teacher pedagogy; and the development of a range of assessment tools to monitor and compare student achievement. These have been introduced earlier in the chapter and are elaborated on in light of their influence on teaching writing.

As Ministry writers themselves described it, the Literacy and Numeracy Strategy was not a single, coherent intervention, but rather something that gave 'direction and alignment for a range of policies, projects, and programmes' (MOE 2002a: 1). It had three overarching themes:

1   developing community capability, particularly by encouraging and supporting family, whanau,[2] and others to help students;
2   lifting professional capability throughout the system so that everyone plays their part in ensuring that the interaction between teachers and students is as effective as possible;

3   raising expectations for students' progress and achievement (MOE 2002a: 1).

Like its English counterpart (with respect, for example, to the three-wave metaphor), it emphasised 'improving first practice' (but later broadened from the first four years of schooling to every level of the education system) and supplementing this with 'specific interventions for students with clearly identified needs beyond the classroom' (MOE 2002a: 1).

Developing community capability

This theme was taken up by the Feed the Mind public information campaign launched in May 1999 and aimed at giving parents, family members and others suggested ways of helping young children develop literacy and maths skills. The campaign was backed up by a range of materials, including pamphlets (with versions translated into Maori and five Pasifika languages) and posters. In general, resources became more inclusive of Pasifika and Maori communities and languages.

Lifting professional capability

The second theme was focused on effective practice – at the classroom level and with interventions targeted at at-risk students beyond the classroom – and on the support structures required for effective practice to occur. The following features were identified by the Literacy Strategy as 'dimensions of effective practice': expectations, instructional strategies, engaging learners with texts, partnerships, knowledge of the learner, knowledge of literacy learning (MOE 2002a: 3). Three of these relate to either professional content knowledge or pedagogical content knowledge in the classroom teacher (Shulman 1986). Initial measures related to this theme included:

- *The production of two resources for teachers* intended, as their titles suggested, to set out what evidence suggests as *Effective Literacy Practice* (MOE 2003a, 2006).
- *Targeted professional development.* In-service professional development was not all-encompassing as it was England. An example of this was the Early Childhood Primary Links via Literacy (ECPL) Project, which engaged in concentrated professional development with early childhood and new entrant teachers in Mangere and Otara (see Phillips *et al.* 2002).[3]
- *A literacy leadership programme.* This was a national professional development initiative which commenced in February 2000 and which aimed in the first instance at principals and school 'literacy leaders', focusing on enhancing Year 1–6 literacy programmes and school-wide policies and practices.
- *Building support from out-of-school professionals,* namely resource teachers: literacy (RT: Lits), who work with clusters of schools working with teachers

on meeting the needs of specific students, and School Support literacy advisers based in teacher education institutions, who focus largely on classroom practice.

* *The Reading, Writing, and Mathematics Proposals pool* (RWMP pool). Established in June 1999, this was a contestable fund aimed at helping schools with set-up costs for programmes targeted at Year 1–8 pupils underperforming in literacy and/or numeracy.
* *Pasifika literacy initiatives.* Begun in 2001, there were two prongs to this: improving English for Speakers of Other Languages (ESOL) teachers' qualifications via fees scholarships, and Pasifika home–school partnerships aimed at enhancing student performance through strengthening school relationships with families.
* *Resource production.* Following Taskforce recommendations, a large variety of print and audio-visual resources were produced for classroom use and teacher development purposes.

Reading Recovery, a literacy intervention programme pioneered in New Zealand by Marie Clay for what Stannard and Huxford (2007) term 'Wave 2' children continued to operate in primary schools.

Two major professional development initiatives were implemented with different outcomes. The first initiative focused on school leadership. 'The desired outcomes for students, however, did not eventuate' (Timperley and Parr 2009: 139). The second initiative, the Literacy Professional Development Project (LPDP), begun in 2004, became a key ingredient of the Ministry's literacy strategy. Schools could apply to join the LPDP which aimed to build teachers' content knowledge and their understandings of pedagogy and practice, 'based on the premise that effective classroom teaching will lead to improved student achievement' (LPDP 2006: 7). The LPDP project was a national school-wide project for years 1–8. 'Schools engage with the project for two years and select either a reading comprehension or writing focus to begin the inquiry into effectiveness of literacy teaching and learning in their school' (Bareta and English 2007: 3). The professional learning model was whole-school focused, based on site, with the intention of building a strong professional learning community. The project team based at Learning Media consisted of a team of researchers and consultants from the University of Auckland, and a regional team which led each cluster of literacy facilitators. The facilitators worked with literacy leaders, principals and teachers of participating schools, 'supporting them to make an inquiry and evidence-based approach to increasing the effectiveness of the literacy practices in their school' (English *et al.* 2008: 3).

New Zealand teachers have been well served in terms of literacy resources compared with their English counterparts. (Stannard and Huxford lament 'the emphasis on individualised teaching also encouraged a growth in the use of exercises, worksheets, comprehension programmes' (2007: 14).) Teachers already had access to *Ready to Read*, graded readers (for years 1 to 3), *Junior Journals* (for years 2 to 3), *School Journals* (for years 4 to 8), *School Journal Story Library* (high-interest material for years 6 to 10) and *Choices* (years 9 to 10) reading texts. The Literacy Strategy continued with the free publication of reading material, complementing this measure with the highly successful teacher support notes which provided guidance for teaching the *Ready to Read* graded readers and the school journals. Audio CDs were also developed and provided further listening opportunities and reading aloud material to support readers. High-interest multimedia CD-ROMs were designed to help raise the performance of reluctant readers in years 7 to 10. These interactive texts placed an emphasis on content which would engage Maori and Pasifika boys.

In terms of teacher handbooks the *Effective Literacy Practice in Years 1 to 4* (MOE 2003a) and later *Effective Literacy Practice in Years 5 to 8* (MOE 2006) provide guidance for the teaching of reading and writing (though heavily oriented to print). Further publications on *Guided Reading: Years 1 to 4* (MOE 2002b) and *Guided Reading: Years 5 to 8* (MOE 2005) with supporting video and DVDs were used for teacher development. Parallel books have yet to be written to support the teaching of writing. More recently, texts have been published for teachers providing guidance and support for oral language programmes. The *Learning through Talk: Oral Language in Years 1–3* and *Learning through Talk: Oral Language in Years 4–8* were published in 2009 (MOE 2009a and b). The most recent publication for teachers is *The Literacy Learning Progressions: Meeting the Reading and Writing Demands of the Curriculum* (LLP) (MOE 2010). 'It describes and illustrates the literacy-related knowledge, skills and attitudes that students need to draw on in order to meet the reading and writing demands of the New Zealand Curriculum from year 1 to year 10' (MOE 2010: 3). Where as the *Literacy Learning Progressions* identify skills and knowledge children are expected to achieve at the end of each of their years at school, the *Effective Literacy Practice* handbooks provide information for teaching and assessing writing and reading in primary schools.

Monitoring student progress and achievement

The third theme of 'raising expectations for students' progress and achievement' was in part played out in the rolling out of a number of measures aimed at helping schools 'gather, analyse, and use good-quality assessment information' (MOE 2002a: 1, 12), in part because of an emphasis on assessment for learning through formative assessment (Black & Wiliam 1998). National testing was introduced into British schools in 2002 as part of the Literacy Strategy. In New Zealand the Literacy Strategy worked alongside a National Assessment strategy that was less focused on testing than on helping schools gather, analyse and interpret quality assessment data ultimately to identify students' learning needs, and track and compare individual student progress and cohorts of children against national norms, so as to identify those students performing at the 'tail-end'.

Several new assessment tools were developed for literacy/language learning:

- National Exemplars – examples (in English and Maori) of student work referenced to curriculum levels showing expected qualities and characteristics for particular learning objectives (commenced in 2003);[4]
- Assessment Tools for Teaching and Learning (asTTle) which assess reading and writing skills at curriculum levels 2–6 (begun in 2003);[5]
- Assessment Resource Banks (ARBs), to assess reading, writing and visual language at levels 2–5;[6]
- School Entry Assessment (SEA), which assesses emergent literacy knowledge (introduced in 2000);
- Supplementary Tests of Achievement in Reading (STAR) for children's reading levels 2–9.

The National Educational Monitoring Project (NEMP),[7] begun in 1995, continues to provide national curriculum literacy data on the performance of year 4 and 8 students. Progressive Achievement Tests (PATs) in reading comprehension and reading vocabulary years 4–10 were updated and revised in early 2008. These assessment tools have all become part of the classroom teacher's tool kit for gathering evidence, developing programmes and monitoring student progress. Their relationship to the current determination to impose National Standards is currently being worked out. To restate a point made earlier, what can be seen in a number of these measures is a reification of the Achievement Initiatives determination to introduce levels-based thinking into the New Zealand educational system. In a nutshell, normativity is driving performativity.

For writing, two key assessment tools have been introduced: the New Zealand Curriculum Writing Exemplars and asTTle writing. Ministry of Education writing exemplars provide teachers with level-based exemplars relating to the so-called expressive and poetic writing function achievement objectives of the former English curriculum (MOE 1994). Each exemplar provides a sample of authentic student work, annotated and linked to a matrix of progress indicators, which define the deep and surface features of texts, and 'Illustrate key features of learning, achievement, and quality of different stages of student development' (MOE 2003b: 3). These exemplars are used widely especially in junior schools as they begin at level one and include subset exemplars at this emergent level. Teachers use them widely as models of writing when teaching, for moderating school-wide writing exemplars, and for assessing individual progress against the curriculum framework levels.

The Assessment Tools for Teaching and Learning (asTTle) were developed for the Ministry of Education by the University of Auckland to test reading, writing and mathematics skills and are available in both English and Te Reo Māori from curriculum levels 2 to 5 (years 5 to 10). The asTTle tools 'are designed to have a dual purpose: they are designed to provide teachers with information about their students, specifically to assist their teaching for increased learning outcomes in the areas of reading, writing and numeracy. They are also designed to allow teachers to compare their students with others using the norms for the assessment tasks selected' (Glasswell *et al.* 2001: 1–2). AsTTle provides standardised data for New Zealand teachers analysing and reporting on student performance. The reports generated from the tests allow schools and teachers to see trends, patterns and needs across individual or selected cohorts, or to make comparisons with similar cohorts and New Zealand norms. Schools and teachers can select reading or writing aspects that they want to assess or track cohorts in the school.

AsTTle tools are being used by a number of New Zealand researchers (such as the LPDP team) as well as by schools to show changes in student literacy achievement within the school. There is also evidence of pressure for schools to use it as a measure in the new world of national standards. However, asTTle writing tools have had a mixed reception amongst teachers, teacher educators and educational researchers. Teachers voice concerns about appropriate writing contexts for some tasks, the time required for the pen and paper tests (approximately 40 minutes) and the variance in teacher marking. Glasswell and colleagues (2001) acknowledge the influence of Martin (1989) and others in the decision to adopt the Australian 'Genre School's' view of genre as linked to purpose rather than text form. However, the authors of this chapter would see the adoption of six 'genre' categories for asTTle – to explain; to argue or persuade; to instruct or lay out a procedure; to classify, organise, describe and report information; to inform and entertain through imaginative narrative; and to inform and entertain through recount – as posing issues of construct validity. As we see it, the assessment tool presents a somewhat narrow view of writing and fails to acknowledge the way in which writing in the real world (editorials, book reviews, travel writing and so on) is predominantly multifunctional.

A change for the better?

How did the various NLS strategies work in the New Zealand context? We refer to a small number of instances without making any grand claims one way or another. On the basis of their own reporting, the LPDP worked with cohorts of schools successfully and made a difference to student achievement. Of the first cohort of 97 schools (2004–5), 45 of these schools selected to focus on student writing with asTTle: writing as the monitoring tool of choice. A representative sample of 10 per cent of the data was analysed. The project was deemed successful in that 'The whole cohort had a mean gain of 2.5 curriculum sub-levels over the two years (compared with the national mean gain of 1 curriculum sub-level over two years), and the lowest 20% of the students at Time 1 gained 4 curriculum sub-levels' (LPDP 2006: 5). In terms of sub-group shifts, 'the lowest 20% of each year group of Maori students has a greater achievement shift than each year group as a whole' (LPDP 2006: 5). However, the project reported a persisting gender gap.

The third cohort (2006–7) involved 127 schools, with 62 choosing a writing focus, and 65 a reading comprehension focus. 'The analysis of the impact of the projects learning and changed practices on the literacy outcomes of students . . .

was once again positive, with rates of progress for the majority of students being greater than those seen without project intervention and in accelerated progress for those sub-groups of students traditionally over represented in the lower bands of achievement' (English *et al.* 2008: 5). The Observation Survey (Clay 2002) used to assess 5 and 6-year-olds' reading and writing progress found 'There was a noticeable shift in stanine mean and decrease in the proportion of students in stanine 1–3 for all tasks and for all sub-groups' (English *et al.* 2008: 5–6). For years 4–8, asTTle reading and writing tools were used to assess student achievement. Positive findings indicated that in all year groups, both boys and girls and Pasifika students were achieving at cohort expectation or better when compared to the national picture associated with the asTTle tool. The project also reported that, 'The mean score for students in the lowest 20% for all year groups is now closer to each group's mean and is close to or better than the national picture' (English *et al.* 2008: 6).

The most recent NEMP Writing Assessment Results (Crooks *et al.* 2007) presents another perspective of how New Zealand students and sub-groups of students at years 4 and 8 are performing as writers. For expressive writing, students were given opportunities to write inventively. The characteristics sought included the 'ability to write coherently, to communicate personal feeling, to communicate stories or ideas clearly and vividly, and to follow conventions associated with particular forms of writing' (p. 3). 'The trend analyses showed a substantial improvement since 2002 for year 4 students, and a modest improvement for year 8 students' (p. 3). For functional writing, students had opportunities to act as reporters, fill in forms, write instructions and create advertisements. Characteristics sought included presenting information clearly and accurately. 'Trend analyses showed a small improvement between 2002 and 2006 for year 4 students and a slight improvement for year 8 students' (p. 3).

In respect of NEMP data on sub-groups, 'There have been reduced disparities from 2002 to 2006 in overall scores between Pakeha and Māori students, and between Pakeha and Pasifika students . . . and differences in achievement between Pakeha and Māori were smaller at year 8 than year 4, suggesting a trend towards improvement for Māori students as they advance from year 4 to year 8' (NEMP 2008, Writing 2006: Good News ¶3, 5). The report also indicated that Pasifika students were more enthusiastic about writing and talking about their writing with others than were Pakeha and Maori students. The report, like the PDLP findings, however, indicated that, 'Despite the overall reduction in disparity between Pakeha and Pasifika students, Pasifika students are still achieving at substantially lower levels at both year 4 and year 8' (NEMP 2008, Writing 2006: Concerns ¶3). However, the gender gap persists: 'This is a serious concern, with the gap larger than in all other areas assessed in NEMP' (NEMP 2008, Writing 2006: Concerns ¶2).

Conclusion

In 2006, along with 37 other countries, New Zealand participated in a Progress in International Reading Literacy Study (PIRLS). As reported by Tunmer and colleagues (2008), the results were little different from the 2001 study, which would have been too soon to have measured an impact on literacy achievement from the New Zealand Literacy Strategy. The long tail was still evident with the difference between 5th and 95th percentiles exceeded by only nine other countries. In this 2008 article, Tunmer and colleagues position themselves as prophets who had predicted this apparent lack of progress (2004; see also Chapman *et al.* 2007). For them, New Zealand's NLS was doomed to fail because it imposed a 'literature-based, constructivist approach to teaching literacy' (p. 108), as a 'one size fits all' to all children. For these writers, the major NLS strategies were misguided, in particular the *Effective Literacy Practice* handbooks and the use of Reading Recovery. (For a vigorous rebuttal of the latter claim, see McDowall 2008.) For these critics, a remedy for the current situation is the discriminating use of systematic phonics instruction for those students who constitute New Zealand's long tail, especially those from poor SES backgrounds and with Maori and Pasifika ethnicities.

There is another way to read the 2006 PIRLS results of course. Given the rapidly changing ethnic face of New Zealand's school-based population and the accelerating income gap between rich and poor, a result of 'little different' might be viewed as an achievement. In 2010, you might say, not a lot has changed. The gaps remain; the phonics debate refuses to debate; and the air of crisis continues to hang in the air. Against the wishes of most teachers and teacher educators, the current coalition government, dominated by pragmatic, right-wing politicians, has imposed its own National Literacy and Numeracy Strategy in the form of National Standards, the impact of which is already being felt in a narrowing primary-school curriculum, anxieties about league tables and the spectre of various measurement instruments being used to drill students to master the guise of this or that 'literacy' competence.

Notes

1 Findings in respect of the New Zealand 1990–91 sample have not been challenged in the academic literature in this country, though questions *have* been raised about the meaningfulness or reliability of *rankings* in such surveys as IEA and PISA (Progress in International Reading-Literacy Study) (see Elley 2004, who argues that 'New Zealand reading standards have remained remarkably stable over the past 30 years, *despite* enormous increases in the numbers of immigrants and ESOL children in schools' (p. 32)).

2 Maori word for 'family' in the sense of 'extended family'.

3 Suburbs in South Auckand with large numbers of Maori and Pasifika pupils.

4 These can be accessed at http://www.tki.org.nz/r/assessment/exemplars/eng/index_e.php.

5 See http://www.tki.org.nz/r/asTTle/.

6 These can be accessed at http://arb.nzcer.org.nz/.

7 See http://nemp.otago.ac.nz/.

References

Anon. (2008, September 28). New Zealand's income gap doubles. *The Press*. (Retrieved March 25, 2010) from http://www.stuff.co.nz/national/649243.

Bareta, L., and English, C. (2007). Evidence-based inquiry: A collective responsibility. Paper presented at the August Literacy Symposium: Lifting the Achievement of the Underachieving Reader and Writer in the New Zealand Mainstream Classroom. Wellington: Learning Media.

Black, P., and Wiliam, D. (1998). Assessment and classroom learning. *Assessment in Education: Principles, policy and practice*, 5(1), 7–74.

Chapman, J., Greaney, K., and Tunmer, W. (2007). How well is Reading Recovery really working in New Zealand? *New Zealand Journal of Educational Studies*, 42 (1&2), 59–71.

Clay, M. (1991). *Becoming literate: The construction of inner control*. Auckland: Heinemann Education.

Clay, M. (2002). *An observation survey of early literacy achievement* (2nd edn). Auckland: Heinemann.

Cope, B., and Kalantzis, M. (eds). (1993). *The powers of literacy: A genre approach to teaching writing*. Pittsburgh, PA: University of Pittsburgh Press.

Cotterell, G., von Randow, M., and Wheldon, M. (2008). *An examination of the links between parental educational qualifications, family structure and family wellbeing, 1981–2006*. Wellington: Ministry of Education. (Retrieved March 25, 2010) from http://www.educationcounts.govt.nz/publications/assessment/32057/5.

Crooks, T., and Flockton, L. (2005). *National Education Monitoring Project: Reading and speaking assessment results 2004*. Dunedin: Educational Assessment Research Unit.

Crooks, T., Flockton, L., and White, J. (2007). *National Education Monitoring Project: Writing assessment results 2006*. Dunedin: Educational Assessment Research Unit.

Douglas, S. (2002). The Literacy Strategy for New Zealand: A focus on learning. *Reading Forum New Zealand*, 1, 22–4.

Duthie Educational Consultancy (1994). *Responses to the Draft National Curriculum Statement English in the New Zealand Curriculum*. Wellington: Duthie Educational Consultancy.

Educational Department of Western Australia (1994). *Writing developmental continuum*. Melbourne: Longman Australia.

Educational Department of Western Australia (1994). *Writing resource book*. Melbourne: Longman Australia.

Elley, W. (1992). *How in the world do students read?* Hamburg: Grindeldruck GMBH.

Elley, W. (1996). Curriculum reform: Forwards or backwards. *DELTA*, 48(1), 11–18.

Elley, W. (2004). New Zealand literacy standards in a global context: The uses and abuses of international literacy surveys. *English Teaching: Practice and Critique*, 3(1), 32–45.

English, C., Bareta, L., and Winthrop, M. (2008). Evidence of improved student outcomes: From the schools that participated in the Literacy Professional Development Project February 2006–November 2007: LPDP Report. Wellington: Learning Media. (Retrieved June 9, 2010) from http://literacyonline.tki.org.nz/content/download/15644/92614/file/LPDP+Cohort+2+%282006–07%29+findings.pdf.

Flockton, L., and Crooks, T. (1997). *Reading and speaking assessment results 1996: National Education Monitoring Report 6*. Wellington: Ministry of Education.

Flockton, L., and Crooks, T. (1998). *Forum comment*. (Retrieved April 2, 2010) from http://nemp.otago.ac.nz/forum_comment/1998_reports.htm.

Flockton, L., and Crooks, T. (1999). *Writing assessment results, 1998*. (National Education Monitoring Report No. 12). Dunedin: Educational Assessment Research Unit, University of Otago.

Glasswell, K., Parr, J., and Aikman, M. (2001). Development of the asTTle writing assessment rubrics for scoring extended writing tasks: Technical report 6. Auckland: Project asTTle, University of Auckland.

Hyland, K. (2002). *Teaching and researching writing*. Harlow: Longman.

Lamb, H. (1987). *Writing performance in New Zealand schools: A report on the IEA Study of Written Composition in New Zealand*. Wellington: Department of Education.

Limbrick, L. (2000). New Zealand's response to the literacy issues of the 1990s. *Reading Forum New Zealand, 2*, 5–12.

Literacy Professional Development Project (LPDP). (2006). LPDP Cohort 1 (2004–05) findings: Report. (Retrieved June 9, 2010) from http://literacyonline.tki.org.nz/content/download/15643/92611/file/LPDP+Cohort+1+%282004–05%29+findings.pdf.

Locke, T. (2001). Curriculum, assessment and the erosion of professionalism. *New Zealand Journal of Educational Studies, 36*(1), 5–23.

Locke, T., Vulliamy, G., Webb, R., and Hill, M. (2005). Being a 'professional' primary school teacher at the beginning of the 21st century: A comparative analysis of primary teacher professionalism in New Zealand and England. *Journal of Education Policy, 20*(5), 555–80.

McDowall, S. (2008). Commentary: How well is Reading Recovery really working in New Zealand: Reply to Chapman, Greaney and Tunmer. *New Zealand Journal of Educational Studies, 43*(2), 121–6.

McFarlane, J. (2000). Implementing the new English syllabus. In J. Soler and J. Smith (eds), *Literacy in New Zealand: Practices, politics and policy since 1900* (pp. 98–115). Auckland: Pearson Education.

Macken-Horarik, M. (2002). 'Something to shoot for': A systemic functional approach to teaching genre in secondary school science. In A.M. Johns (Ed.), *Genre in the classroom: Multiple perspectives* (pp. 17–42). London: Lawrence Erlbaum.

Martin, J. (1989). *Factual writing: Exploring and challenging social reality*. Oxford: Oxford University Press.

Ministry of Education (MOE) (n.d.). *Processes of reading comprehension: A summary of the results from the Progress in International Reading Literacy Study (PIRLS) 2001*. Wellington: Ministry of Education.

Ministry of Education (1991). *Education Gazette*, 70 (7).

Ministry of Education (1992). *Dancing with the pen*. Wellington: Learning Media.

Ministry of Education (1994). *English in the New Zealand curriculum*. Wellington: Learning Media.

Ministry of Education (1999, March). Report of the Literacy Taskforce: Advice to the Government on achieving its goal that: 'By 2005, every child turning nine will be able to read, write and do maths for success'. Wellington: Ministry of Education.

Ministry of Education (2002a, July). *Curriculum update: He Korero Marautanga, 50*. Wellington: Learning Media.

Ministry of Education (2002b). *Guided reading: Years 1 to 4*. Wellington: Learning Media.

Ministry of Education (2003a). *Effective literacy practice in Years 1–4*. Wellington: Learning Media.

Ministry of Education (2003b). *The New Zealand curriculum exemplars: English*. Wellington: Learning Media.

Ministry of Education (2005). *Guided Reading: Years 5 to 8*. Wellington: Learning Media.

Ministry of Education (2006). *Effective literacy practice in Years 5–8.* Wellington: Learning Media.

Ministry of Education (2009a). *Learning through talk: Oral language in Years 1–3.* Wellington: Learning Media.

Ministry of Education (2009b). *Learning through talk: Oral language in Years 4–8.* Wellington: Learning Media.

Ministry of Education (2010). *The literacy learning progressions: Meeting the reading and writing demands of the curriculum.* Wellington: Learning Media.

Ministry of Social Development (2009). *Ethnic composition of the population. In 2009: The social report.* Wellington: Ministry of Social Development. (Retrieved March 25, 2010) from http://www.socialreport.msd.govt.nz/people/ethnic-composition-population.html.

NEMP (October, 2008). *Forum comment.* (Retrieved June 8, 2010) from http://nemp.otago.ac.nz/forum_comment/2006_reports.htm.

Phillips, G., McNaughton, S., and MacDonald, S. (2002). *Picking up the pace: A summary.* Manukau: Strengthening Education in Mangere and Otara (SEMO)/Ministry of Education.

Sawyer, W. (Ed.). (1995). *Teaching writing: Is genre the answer?* Springwood, NSW: Australian Education Network.

Shulman, L. (1986). Those who understand: Knowledge growth in teaching. *Educational Researcher, 15*(2), 4–14.

Smith, J., and Elley, W. (1997). *How children learn to write.* North Shore City, NZ: Addison Wesley Longman.

Stannard, J., and Huxford, L. (2007) *The literacy game: The story of the National Literacy Strategy.* London/New York: Routledge.

Statistics New Zealand (2008). *National Ethnic Population Projections: 2006 (base)–2026.* Wellington: Statistics New Zealand. (Retrieved March 25, 2010) from http://www.stats.govt.nz/~/media/Statistics/Browse%20for%20stats/NationalEthnicPopulation Projections/HOTP06–26/nationalethnicpopulationprojections2006basehotp.ashx.

Timperley, S., and Parr, J. (2009). Chain of influence from policy to practice in the New Zealand literacy strategy. *Research Papers in Education, 24*(2), 135–54.

Tunmer, W., Chapman, J., and Prochnow, J. (2004). Why the reading achievement gap in New Zealand won't go away: Evidence from PIRLS 2001 International Study of Reading Achievement. *New Zealand Journal of Educational Studies, 39*(1), 127–46.

Tunmer, W., Nicholson, T., Greaney, K., Prochnow, J., Chapman, J., and Warrow, A. (2008). PIRLS before swine: A critique of New Zealand's National Literacy Strategy. *New Zealand Journal of Educational Studies, 43*(2), 105–20.

Wagemaker, H. (1992). Preliminary findings of the IEA literacy study: New Zealand achievement in the national and international context. *Educational Psychology, 12*(3 & 4), 195–214.

Wilkinson, I. (1998). Dealing with diversity: Achievement gaps in reading literacy among New Zealand students. *Reading Research Quarterly, 33*(2), 144–67.

Chapter 6

NLS1 and NLS2

Implications of a social literacies perspective for policies and practices of literacy education

Brian Street

Introduction: The Literacy Game and NLS1

My concern with literacy is with the uses and meanings of reading and writing in everyday life. Like many colleagues who take a 'social practice' approach to literacy (see below), I see the school domain of literacy as one amongst many, with its own features, styles, genres, requirements. What is the relationship of this 'schooled literacy' (cf. Street and Street, 1991) to the everyday literacy practices that we all engage in remains a question for research. The 'New Literacy Studies' (NLS1) approach (cf. Street, 1984; Gee, 1990), which I describe below, argues that what this relationship is cannot be assumed, rather we need to find out exactly how it works in given contexts. Indeed we might expect, from what research in this field already tells us, that it will vary from one context to another and one time to another. So I approach the debates about the National Literacy Strategy (I refer to this as NLS2 since it began and the acronym was coined about a decade after NLS1) with this question in mind – what is the relationship between the kinds of reading and writing that have been developed by NLS2 strategists, teachers, examiners and policy makers and the actual uses of reading and writing that the pupils they are interested in actually engage with in their daily lives?

Reading *The Literacy Game* (Stannard and Huxford, 2007) I am surprised to find that the authors and the majority of people they cite are not actually interested in this question. They are concerned with strategies, management, conflicts over policy, teaching methods, assessment and evaluation, measurement – but I find myself asking, of what? Although the term Literacy appears twice in the title of the book, it seems not to be about Literacy so much as about Strategy. The main concern of policy makers, educators and the authors is how to raise the attainment levels of pupils especially those at Key Stage 2 in UK schools, with various targets being set over the decade in which NLS2 has been active, such as for example that 80 per cent and later 85 per cent of pupils at KS4 should attain level 4. But what is the relationship of such attainment to 'literacy' and to the variety of literacy practices in which those attaining it will engage outside of school?

There are some hints in the book. For instance, where the figures for attainment appear to be stalling and not rising as the proponents of NLS2 hoped, various explanations are offered that derive from broader 'social' factors. Whilst the government in the mid-2000 period seemed keen to advocate a 'phonics' approach to learning literacy, thereby explaining some disappointing test results in terms of teaching methods, the authors argue that 'there are other variables impacting on education and development of young children which may prove more recalcitrant' (p. 167).

> Not least amongst these is the growing socio-cultural complexity of modern-day Britain which, over the lifetime of the Strategy, has seen significant increases in the proportion of children from other cultures and language backgrounds with very different experiences of family, community and schooling.
>
> (Stannard and Huxley, 2007, p. 167)

At first NLS1 researchers might be forgiven for thinking this argument means that the educators and policy makers concerned with literacy are beginning to take on board the social practice view that 'children from other cultures and language backgrounds' have 'very different experiences of family, community and schooling'. However, closer analysis reveals that this apparently multiple literacies perspective is in fact simply a deficit view – those children, especially from abroad, are bringing the attainment targets down. There is only one Literacy that matters and this is the one embedded in the attainment targets and curriculum of the NLS2.

Another hint in the wider direction that is then also withdrawn concerns the fraught debate about the different attainments of KS2 children regarding reading and writing. At first NLS2 concentrated on reading skills and indeed the figures for these were seen to rise for a while. But then it was noticed that the figures for writing were not nearly so 'successful', so that when the 'English' results, comprising both reading and writing, were composited, the improvements were less dramatic. Explanations were needed and again at first there seemed to be a 'literacy practices' dimension to these. For instance, a distinction was drawn between comprehension and production in language skills, with reading at the comprehension end and speaking and writing at the production end. In order to improve writing, the Strategy proposed more guidance for teachers on production, on 'sentence and text level principles for text composition':

> While schools are evidently improving children's comprehension abilities, there are clear messages here about the fundamental importance of language production and how we promote this effectively in the classroom.
>
> (Stannard and Huxley, 2007, p. 172)

Again, however, an apparent move in the direction of recognising the variation in language and literacy practices on which NLS1 focuses is withdrawn as the underlying assumption returns directly to the autonomous model. The authors add that the message about production refers to '*especially the more articulated and formal styles associated with context-free communication, including writing*' (p. 172; my italics). It is astonishing for NLS1 researchers and practitioners to find this autonomous view of writing still espoused after more than two decades of research and practice drawing attention to the fundamental principle that literacy practices, both reading and writing, are always embedded in social contexts from which they take their meanings. Writing, far from being 'context-free', is always a product of a particular context, of the specific participants and the institutional and cultural pressures under which they produce text (Barton *et al.*, 2000; Heath, 1982; Street, 1982, 2003, 2006) – in the present case the context of school and early twenty-first-century institutional and political pressures regarding what counts as written text. If senior proponents of the UK Literacy Strategy still believe that writing is context-free and insert this belief into the curriculum and teaching and assessment of literacy, then it may not be surprising to find that the attainment figures for children are 'disappointing'. One pedagogic effect of such a belief may be that the opportunity is missed to build upon children's own rich engagement with writing, which could be used as a basis for development of those specific genres required in the academy. Most good learning theory these days certainly assumes that it is better to build on the learner's prior knowledge and it is certain that children do have prior knowledge of writing, but perhaps less often 'the more articulated and formal styles' associated with schooled literacy. So maybe a good way to achieve the latter might be to work with the former. A literacy practices perspective, grounded in NLS1, then has implications for pedagogy as well as for research, as a number of authors have recently demonstrated (cf. Pahl and Rowsell, 2005, 2006; Street *et al.*, 2006).

In this chapter I will briefly recall some of the moves evident in NLS2 and some of the responses to them, then bring the story up to date with recent proposals from the Rose Reports and the Cambridge Review. I will then relocate these debates in the context of NLS1.

NLS1

Whilst the concern with cognition and with 'problems' of acquisition continue to dominate the Literacy Game in England, a recent shift in perspective, recognised in at least some international fields (cf. Unesco, 2006; Letter Programme, cf. Street *et al.*, 2006) has emphasised understanding of literacy practices in their social and cultural contexts. This approach has been particularly influenced by those who have advocated an 'ethnographic' perspective, in contrast with the experimental and often individualistic character of cognitive studies of literacy, and the textual, etic perspective of linguistic-based studies of text. These social developments have sometimes been referred to as 'New Literacy Studies' (Gee, 1990; Barton *et al.*, 2000; Collins, 1995; Heath, 1982, 1983; Street, 1993). Much of the work in this tradition focuses on the everyday meanings and uses of literacy in specific cultural contexts and links directly to how we understand the work of literacy programmes, which themselves then become subject to ethnographic enquiry (Robinson-Pant, 2005).

In trying to characterise these new approaches to understanding and defining literacy, I have referred to a distinction between an 'autonomous' model and an 'ideological' model of literacy (Street, 1984). The 'autonomous' model of literacy works from the assumption that literacy in itself – autonomously – will have effects on other social and cognitive practices, much as in the early 'cognitive consequences' literature cited above. The model, I argue, disguises the cultural and ideological assumptions that underpin it and that can then be presented as though they are neutral and universal. Research in the social practice approach challenges this view and suggests that in practice dominant approaches based on the autonomous model are simply imposing Western (or urban, etc.) conceptions of literacy on to other cultures (Street, 2001). The alternative, ideological model of literacy offers a more culturally sensitive view of literacy practices as they vary from one context to another. This model starts from different premises than the autonomous model: it posits instead that literacy is a social practice, not simply a technical and neutral skill; that it is always embedded in socially constructed epistemological principles. The ways in which people address reading and writing are themselves rooted in conceptions of knowledge, identity and being. The 'autonomous' model is, then, itself deeply ideological; indeed it is characteristically so in the sense that a significant meaning of ideology is that it attempts to disguise its partial and loaded character, precisely by presenting itself as 'neutral' and 'universal'. The ideological model, on the other hand, makes explicit its own loading and in particular its recognition that literacy is always contested, both its meanings and its practices – hence that particular versions of it are always 'ideological', they are always rooted in a particular world view and a desire for that view of literacy to dominate and to marginalise others (Gee, 1990). The argument about social literacies suggests that engaging with literacy is always a social act even from the outset. The ways in which teachers or facilitators and their students interact is already a social practice that affects the nature of the literacy being learned and the ideas about literacy held by the participants, especially the new learners and their position in relations of power. It is not valid to suggest that 'literacy' can be 'given' neutrally and then its 'social' effects only experienced or 'added on' afterwards.

For these reasons, as well as because of the failure of many traditional literacy programmes (Abadzi, 2003; Street, 2005), academics, researchers and practitioners working in literacy in different parts of the world are beginning to come to the conclusion that the autonomous model of literacy on which much of the practice and programmes have been based was not an appropriate intellectual tool, either for understanding the diversity of reading and writing around the world or for designing the practical programmes this required which may be better suited to an ideological model (Aikman, 1999; Heath, 1983; Doronilla, 1996; Hornberger, 1997, 2002; Kalman, 1999; King, 1994; Robinson-Pant, 1997). The question this approach raises for policy makers and programme designers is, then, not simply that of the 'impact' of literacy – to be measured in terms of a neutral developmental index providing 'rates' and 'levels', as in the UK case – but rather of how local people 'take hold' of the new communicative practices being introduced to them, as Kulick and Stroud's (1993) ethnographic description of missionaries bringing literacy to New Guinea villagers makes clear. Literacy, in this sense, is, then, already part of a power relationship and how people 'take hold' of it is contingent on social and cultural practices and not just on pedagogic and cognitive factors. This raises questions that need to be addressed in any literacy programme: What is the power relation between the participants? What are the resources? Where are people going if they take on one literacy rather than another literacy? How do recipients challenge the dominant conceptions of literacy?

This approach has implications for both research and practice. Researchers, instead of privileging the particular literacy practices familiar in their own culture, now suspend judgement as to what constitutes literacy among the people they are working with until they are able to understand what it means to the people themselves, and which social contexts reading and writing derive their meaning from. Many people labelled 'illiterate' within the autonomous model of literacy may, from a more culturally sensitive viewpoint, be seen to make significant use of literacy practices for specific purposes and in specific contexts. For instance, studies suggest that even non-literate persons find themselves engaged in literacy activities so the boundary between literate/non-literate is less obvious than individual 'measures' of literacy suggest (Doronilla, 1996). Academics have, however, often failed to make explicit the implications of such theory for practical work. In the present conditions of world change such ivory tower distancing is no longer legitimate. But likewise, policy makers and practitioners have not always taken on board such 'academic' findings, or have adopted one position (most often that identified with the autonomous model) and not taken account of the many others outlined here. These findings, then, raise important issues both for research into literacy in general and more locally for policy of the kind we can see in the England National Literacy Strategy (NLS2) to which I now turn.

NLS2

How, then, does the development of literacy policy in England look in the light of these debates? I will briefly remind us of the development of the National Literacy Strategy (NLS2) and indicate some responses to it, before moving on to look at current debates in this context. As others in this volume have indicated, NLS2 is a national primary programme that emerged from the Literacy Task Group set up by the Labour opposition in 1996. The National Literacy Project 1996–7 led to a National Literacy Strategy in 1998 when Labour took power. Riley (2001) describes how the reports were based on larger claims for literacy in modern society: 'personal growth, quality of life, self image, ability to function . . . ways of thinking and understanding the world' – claims that I would see as based on the autonomous model of literacy. Comparisons were provided of statistics for literacy internationally and it appeared that in England a greater than average proportion of children were achieving poorly – what was referred to as the 'long tail'. It was in the context of these larger claims and comparisons that the aims of the programme were set, namely to 'improve standards of literacy . . . through a national network, support, dissemination and evaluation and the setting of targets'. For instance, a central target was for 80 per cent of 11-year-olds to attain level 4 in KS2 tests by 2002 (whereas the figure had been 57 per cent in 1996). This was to be achieved through a Framework for Teaching with objectives set for word level, sentence level and text level and a Literacy Hour was designed whereby teachers would work through different levels of the aims (DfES, 2002, 2003). 'How' this was to be achieved, as Riley (2001) explains, was through professional development with training days for teachers and the support of a Literacy Training Pack. It is evident that the programme was based on what I term an 'autonomous' model of literacy, that assumed a de-contextualised universal 'skill' that all should attain, that could be measured and that would then ensure participation in wider social activities. Without analysing it in quite this way, there was already evidence emerging during the early 2000s that such a model was as inadequate for meeting the social ends of children in England as research has shown in more international contexts (see above under NLS1).

For instance, Moss *et al.* (2003), in an Economic and Social Research Council (ESRC) Report, argued that the English curriculum was highly standardised, with mechanisms for monitoring what and how, and that this led to 'centralised control with little room for local autonomy'. Whilst some targets had been met, there was in fact considerable variation between schools and pupils, lack of scope for individual development 'for their own purposes' as well as 'little room for local autonomy', which was having a distorting effect on teaching and weakening 'teacher morale'. There was a need 'to revise and allow greater local autonomy'. Much of this might have been couched in terms of NLS1 and linked to international developments in the field that recognised the importance of individual variation with regard to the uses of reading and writing in context; local factors, social practices and cultural variation all figure in the acquisition and use of literacy. But in the English context such views were mostly marginalised and even the moderate proposals put forward by the researchers on this ESRC Project were not able to enter the 'Game' as defined by the dominant strategists and policy makers. However, the national debate did continue at a highly political and public level and I will just signal here two major developments that are still being contested as I write, which indicate that beneath the apparent certainties of the Literacy Game were indeed fundamental issues of theory and practice that the NLS1 position highlights. The Rose Report of 2006 and the subsequent Rose Review of the Curriculum (2009) received considerable national publicity, and at the same time a key research report, the Cambridge Primary Review (Alexander, 2009), challenged many of the premises of both NLS2 and of Rose in ways that highlight many of the themes raised in the present volume.

Evidence based on a brief study in Clackmannanshire that showed 'gains' in student literacy following an intervention that added two letters a week to student knowledge, in all positions in words, led the Rose Report (2006) to recommend that synthetic phonics be adopted as a systematic approach in all schools. A key theme was that such an approach would be 'discrete' from the broader, social and literary comprehension of written language that many teachers and researchers advocated. Rather, the report sought to differentiate word recognition and language comprehension in teaching plans. This approach was adopted by the government in England and made compulsory for all schools. A critique by Wyse and Goswami (2008), leading experts in language and literacy, unlike the members of the Rose team, strongly undermines the claims made in the report and in subsequent government propaganda and highlighted the tensions between deep research on the one hand and superficial levels of political policy on the other. Wyse and Goswami put forward theoretical perspectives that challenged the idea of language learning being reduced to phonic skills and threw doubt on the cross-language comparisons cited in the Rose Report. Conclusions by linguistic experts are that 'a range of different teaching approaches' can be effective rather than the Rose Report view of 'discrete phonics' which 'is not supported by empirical research evidence' (Wyse and Goswami, 2008, p. 706). Instead 'systematic tuition in phonics that is contextualised is more effective'. So national policy in the UK is not, it appears, justified by research. As they and other researchers state, reading is not simple and if 'In written language as in spoken language the ultimate aim is communication and comprehension then a rigorous synthesis of methods is necessary not one discrete method'.

In 2009 an alternative report was published, the Cambridge Primary Review (CPR) (Alexander, 2009), aiming to establish a sound basis for the teaching of primary education. Based on six years of work – three years planning and consultation, and three years research, involving 28 specially commissioned surveys of research – the report has now been followed by a lengthy period of dissemination and discussion. Like Wyse and Goswami and other experts in the field, CPR found the government position in general and the Rose Report in particular inadequate for handling the complexities of primary education in general and literacy and language learning in particular. CPR was the first comprehensive review of English primary education since the Plowden Inquiry in 1967. In particular it noted that changes in society since that time require a new view that is more multicultural. It cited the need for economic equality, noting that many minority children and families are still at the margins, whilst globalisation entails us all linking to a wider and broader world than that envisaged by the Plowden report – and, we may add, by Rose. The aim of the report was to 'identify the purposes of Primary Education' in this new context; the curriculum and learning environment it should provide; the conditions necessary for consistent quality; and to draw upon evidence from international research. It made 75 recommendations of which a few were:

- Reduce underachievement, narrow the gap.
- New curriculum based on clear aims (not vice versa) guaranteeing breadth, depth and balance.

- Language, literacy and oracy primary (not just 'phonics') but integrated with rest of the curriculum; teaching which is 'dialogic' (cf. Bakhtin) 'where classrooms are full of debate and discussion that is collective, reciprocal, supportive, cumulative, critical and purposeful'.
- Combine national framework with locally devised community curriculum (links with community groups, employment, local associations, local authorities, etc., e.g. North Yorkshire 'Talk for Learning', dialogue with regard to issues and problems, e.g. the Second World War, build shelters together and talk about issues, etc.; Essex 'pupil–clients' – pupils asked to improve design of their school, with help of architects; work in teams to produce drawings, words and pictures, displays; aim to inspire creativity, develop sensitivity to design, e.g. learning spaces, outdoor and social spaces, toilets, etc. and actually affect government's building programme).
- Listen to children not what the media say about them, e.g. 'crisis', '3Rs', rather children as agents, 'Children who feel empowered are more likely to be better and happier learners'.
- Bridges between home and school (not necessarily 'open door') and traffic flow both ways.
- 'Cognition' not in fixed stages but complex processes of learning from experience, effective interaction, interpreting the world – teachers to exploit these developments and potentials via talk, diversity of experiences, creative activities, linguistic and social interactions.
- Current formal curriculum too early: start a year later, i.e. age 6, and allow foundation stage to ensure 'children glide rather than trip over the threshold into mainstream primary education' to enable first language and study skills; then single primary stage 6–11.
- Locate ICT not as separate domain or 'core skill' (as in Rose) but integrated in language component – spoken, reading, writing, literature, non-print media (multimodality?).
- 'Standards' – move away from limited view that has led to 'long tail of underachievement' and instead provide 'a more comprehensive framework which relates to the entirety of what a school does and how it performs' – 'measuring what we value, not valuing what we measure'. New model for school inspection with 'greater focus on classroom practice, pupil learning and the curriculum as a whole' (rather than limited proxies).

Public and government responses have not been very positive and the change of government in 2010, from a conservative Labour government to a new Coalition of Conservative and LibDems, has left open what exactly will be the official response and what direction primary education and literacy teaching will take. But the first moves seem to indicate a resistance to such research-based 'liberal' thinking and a return to earlier versions of the narrow 'standards' debate. The Labour government in fact left Rose undertaking a further review of primary education and, interestingly enough for the arguments here, it appears that Rose suggested some changes to the original narrow curriculum and pedagogy that he put forward in 2006.

The Rose Review (2009) instead proposed a new Primary Curriculum starting in 2011 that advocated extending the play-based approach to learning from the Early Years Foundation Stage (EYFS) into Key Stage 1 and a primary curriculum based on six areas of learning. News has emerged that the Coalition government has abandoned this approach. Schools minister Nick Gibb said:

> A move away from teaching traditional subjects like history and geography could have led to an unacceptable erosion of standards in our primary schools.
>
> Instead, teachers need a curriculum which helps them ensure that every child has a firm grasp of the basics and a good grounding in general knowledge, free from unnecessary prescription and bureaucracy.
>
> It is vital that we return our curriculum to its intended purpose – a minimum national entitlement organised around subject disciplines.
>
> (DfE, 2010)

Ministers have said that they intend to change the national curriculum to focus on the basics and give teachers more flexibility. They will shortly announce their next steps.

Conclusion

Where, then, does all of this leave us as we attempt to respond to NLS2? Andrew Goodwyn, in his overview of the current position and the justification indeed for the present volume, suggested that 'the signs are that the era of the NLS is over and the Strategies are being revised'. Although this is true, it does not appear at present that the revisions at government level are moving far in the direction that research suggests is needed. Indeed, the claims cited above from government ministers that the curriculum should return to 'basics' and the need to maintain 'standards' indicate more of the same that we have seen in the past decade. On the other hand, the complexity of the arguments put forward by the Cambridge Review and the fact that they represent the largest review of the field for fifty years suggests that research might be hard to ignore. How, then, might research such as this move on to influence policy – or are the two fields inevitably irreconcilable, as Hammersley suggests?

> It no longer seems possible, if it ever was, simultaneously to pursue the goals of contributing to disciplinary knowledge and serving educational policy making and practice, while at the same time framing research within some all-embracing political philosophy.
>
> (Hammersley, 1994, p. 148)

Similarly, a leading colleague in the USA, herself deeply involved in trying to link research and policy, indicates some of the tensions between researchers and policy makers that in England we have characterised the 'Literacy Game'.

Kris Gutiérrez, the current President of the American Educational Association (AERA), has written a Presidential address to members in anticipation of a forthcoming meeting under the heading 'Inciting the Social Imagination: Education Research for the Public Good' in which she states:

> Like Twain (writing about the Mississippi River) we in education research have worked really hard to recognise the ever-changing shape and force of the river, to move away from one-dimensional representations of social phenomena that are inaccurate and can lead to reductive policies and practice. However, in the move toward complexity, we sometimes find ourselves in tension with the world of political reality.
>
> (Gutiérrez, 2010, p. 487)

I find this note an insightful place to conclude this discussion of the 'Literacy Game' in England and look forward to a time when we do indeed come 'to recognise the ever-changing shape and force of the river', in this case the multiple flows and tides evident in the uses and meanings of literacy in our everyday social lives.

References

Abadzi, H. (2003) *Improving Adult Literacy Outcomes*, Washington: World Bank.

Aikman, S. (1999) *Intercultural Education and Literacy: An ethnographic study of indigenous knowledge and learning in the Peruvian Amazon*, Amsterdam: Benjamins.

Alexander, R.J. (ed.) (2009) *Children, their World, their Education: Final report and recommendations of the Cambridge Primary Review*, London: Routledge.

Barton, D., Hamilton, M. and Ivanic, R. (2000) *Situated Literacies: Reading and writing in context*, London: Routledge.

Collins, J. (1995) 'Literacy and Literacies', *Annual Review of Anthropology*, 24, 75–93.

DfE (2010) 'Government Announces Changes to Qualifications and the Curriculum', Press Notice, 25 August.

DfES (2002) *The Literacy and Numeracy KS3 National Strategies: Guidance*, London: DfES.

DfES (2003) *Skills for Life: The national strategy for improving adult literacy and numeracy skills*, London: DfES.

Doronilla, M.L. (1996) *Landscapes of Literacy: An ethnographic study of functional literacy in marginal Philippine communities*, Hamburg: UIE.

Gee, James P. (1990) 'Orality and Literacy: from The Savage Mind to Ways with Words', in *Social Linguistics and Literacy: Ideology in Discourses*, London: Falmer Press.

Gutiérrez, K. (2010) 'From the Desk of the President' of AERA, *Educational Researcher*, 39(6), 487.

Hammersley, M. (1994) 'Ethnography, Policy Making and Practice in Education', in B. Troyna and D. Halpin (eds) *Researching Education Policy: Ethical and methodological issues*, London: Falmer, pp. 139–53.

Heath, S.B. (1982) 'What No Bedtime Story Means: Narrative Skills at Home and School', *Language and Society*, 11, 49–76.

Heath, S.B. (1983) *Ways with Words*, Cambridge: Cambridge University Press.

Hornberger, N. (1997) 'Indigenous Literacies in the Americas', Introduction to ed. *Indigenous Literacies in the Americas*, Berlin: Mouton de Gruyter, pp. 3–16.

Hornberger, N (ed.) 2002 'The Continua of Biliteracy: A framework for educational policy, research and practice in multiple settings', Afterword by B. Street, Bristol: Multilingual Matters.

Kalman, J. (1999) *Writing on the Plaza: Mediated literacy practices among scribes and clients in Mexico City*, Cresskill, NJ: Hampton Press.

King, L. (1994) *Roots of Identity: Language and literacy in Mexico*, Stanford, CA: Stanford University Press.

Kulick, D. and Stroud, C. (1993) 'Conceptions and Uses of Literacy in a Papua New Guinean Village', in B. Street (ed.) *Cross-Cultural Approaches to Literacy*, Cambridge: Cambridge University Press.

Moss, G. *et al.* (2003) 'Building a New Literacy Practice through the Adoption of the National Literacy Strategy', ESRC Report, Swindon: ESRC.

Pahl, K. and Rowsell, J. (2005) *Literacy and Education: The New Literacy Studies in the classroom*, London: Sage.

Pahl, K. and Rowsell, J. (eds) (2006) *Travel Notes from the New Literacy Studies: Case studies in practice*, Clevedon: Multilingual Matters.

Riley, J. (2001) 'The National Literacy Strategy: Success with literacy for all?' *Curriculum Journal*, 12(1), 29–58.

Robinson-Pant, A. (1997) *'Why Eat Green Cucumbers at the Time of Dying?': The Link between women's literacy and development*, Hamburg: Unesco.

Robinson-Pant, A. (2005) *Cross-cultural Perspectives on Educational Research*, Buckingham: Open University Press.

Rose, J. (2006) *Independent Report of the Teaching of Early Reading*, London: DfES.

Rose, J. (2009) *Independent Review of the Primary Curriculum*, Nottingham: DCSF.

Stannard, J. and Huxford, L. (2007) *The Literacy Game: The story of the National Literacy Strategy*, London: Routledge.

Street, B. (1984) *Literacy in Theory and Practice*, Cambridge: Cambridge University Press.

Street, B. (ed.) (1993) *Cross-cultural Approaches to Literacy*, Cambridge: Cambridge University Press.

Street, B. (ed.) (2001) *Literacy and Development: Ethnographic perspectives*, London: Routledge.

Street, B. (2003) 'What's New in New Literacy Studies?' *Current Issues in Comparative Education*, 5(2): http://www.tc.columbia.edu/cice/.

Street, B. (ed.) (2005) *Literacies across Educational Contexts: Mediating learning and teaching*, Philadelphia, PA: Caslon Publishing.

Street, B. (2006) 'New Literacies for New Times', 'Invited Address' *55th Yearbook of the National Reading Conference*, ed. J. Hoffman and D. Schallert, Oak Creek, WI: NRC, pp. 21–42.

Street, B. and Street, J. (1991) 'The Schooling of Literacy', in D. Barton and R. Ivanic (eds) *Literacy in the Community*, London: Sage, pp. 143–66.

Street, B., Rogers, A. and Baker, D. (2006) 'Adult Teachers as Researchers: Ethnographic approaches to numeracy and literacy as social practices in South Asia', *Convergence*, 39(1), 31–44.

Unesco (2006) *Education for All: Global Monitoring Report*, Paris: Unesco.

Wyse, D. and Goswami, U. (2008) 'Synthetic Phonics and the Teaching of Reading', *British Educational Research Journal*, 31(6), 691–710.

Chapter 7

The impact of the Framework for English

Teachers' struggle against 'informed prescription'

Andrew Goodwyn

Lessons to be learned: why English teachers did not learn to love Literacy

> The National Literacy Strategy, initiated in England in 1997, was the most ambitious educational reform programme in the world. While it achieved significant success, there are lessons to be learned at every level from government through local administration to school leaders and teachers.
>
> (Stannard and Huxford, 2007, back cover)

This chapter explores a remarkable paradox, which is that English teachers in England do not see themselves as teachers of Literacy (with a capital L). The claim above is undoubtedly accurate. It is also interesting as it leaves out educational researchers in its list; this is also accurate on one level as their research evidence was, indeed, left out of the rationale for the National Literacy Strategy (NLS), this will be further considered below.

One, and perhaps the most important, of the lessons to be learned from the NLS is that 'informed prescription', i.e. telling teachers what to do and how to do it on the assumption that they are currently not 'doing it right', is both utterly patronising and utterly ineffective.

In reviewing the NLS we have *The Literacy Game* (2007), the book by Stannard and Huxford that both tells some of the story of the Strategy's inception and implementation and might be categorized as an 'apologia'. It certainly captures the political frenzy that catapulted a half-thought-through initiative with an incomplete pilot into a gigantic enterprise. Given its remit, that is to review the NLS, it has nothing to say about the secondary follow on, the Framework for English (FWE). There is no equivalent apologia for the FWE, nor have its authors been explicitly identified. The closest text is perhaps the review of research published in 2002 (Harrison) three years after the secondary strategy had begun.

How can this paradox be explained, that English teachers have become anti-Literacy, especially when comparable teachers in the USA and Australia, for example, are very comfortable with the term and have simply added it to their job title? This chapter will begin with a brief historical contextualization (more detailed accounts are available elsewhere; see for example Goodwyn, 2010), and it will then describe and analyse the Framework essentially as a manifesto style text. It will review the evidence offered for the approach of the Strategy towards the subject of English. It will then consider what the impact has been on the profession of English teachers and how it has affected their sense of professional identity, especially their foregrounding of literature. Finally it will consider what the FWE's relationship was to the NLS and whether students are in some sense more, or perhaps differently, literate than in the past.

All individual accounts are partial for a number of reasons, and I acknowledge that my account has many limitations but it is never intended to be merely partisan. It is written entirely in the spirit of what we can learn from the period of the Literacy Strategies. What I would argue in support of this account is the knowledge and experience I bring to it at every level from the personal, and anecdotal, to systematic evidence gathered through research. I taught English in secondary schools between 1978 and 1988, the last four years as a head of department. I experienced at first hand a period of considerable autonomy and radical change to English with the introduction of the GCSE and features such as 100 per cent course work. I then moved into teacher education and ran an English PGCE course for 20 years and continue to run an MA in English and Language in Education that began in 1990. In that time I have worked with hundreds of prospective English teachers and equal numbers of serving teachers. I have visited English departments in secondary schools year in year out through the period of the National Curriculum and the subsequent strategies. All the major strategies discussed below have affected me professionally as well as personally. It was my professional duty to ensure that my student teachers were fully informed about every government initiative and could cope with its demands in school. However much I disagreed with any particular dictat, I endeavoured to give my students an understanding of it and also the capacity to be critical of it whilst being able to undertake it in the way that their host department would require. I have been inspected by Ofsted on numerous occasions and asked to justify the content and approach of the English PGCE. I have been a consultant a number of times for the Ministry of Education (under its many changing names), have worked for other agencies (e.g. the Qualifications and Curriculum Authority (QCA), the British Educational Communications and Technology Agency (BECTA), the Training and Development Agency (TDA), etc.). I worked for Ofsted for three years as an evaluator of the New Opportunities Fund IT training, focusing specifically on English departments and emergent best practice in using ICT in English.

Since 1988, I have worked with many teachers on their research and many teachers have participated in my research. My research has taken many forms and certainly includes the full range from highly qualitative to chiefly quantitative. One of its main concerns has been to investigate what the school subject of English is like in practice and what English teachers both believe about their subject and 'do' when teaching it. Between 1988 and 2010 I have undertaken several national-scale projects to attempt to capture the views of the profession, several of these more recent projects will be discussed below. Throughout that period I have also been an active member of the National Association for the Teaching of English (NATE).

All this national activity must be put in the context of the international. I have also undertaken research in the USA, Australia and New Zealand. I have visited schools in these countries and other English-speaking nations. I have been to many international conferences and met with many hundreds of teachers and researchers from these countries. I am a founding member of the International Association for the Improvement of Mother Tongue Education that brings together mother tongue educators from all over the world to examine common issues and the latest research. So although I have worked intensively in the national context of English as school subject it has never been a parochial understanding.

To some readers I hope this will establish a degree of credential, to others it might confirm me as an insider with a deeply partisan view. I argue that I have developed (and continue to develop) a deep and lived knowledge of the school subject of English and its teachers and that is a very valuable strength in attempting to sum up the effects of the NLS and FWE over the last 13 years. I acknowledge a real empathy towards those teachers and a sympathy as regards the prescription they have endured during that time. However, the enterprise of research is to find out what is significant, not what one wishes to find. Throughout this period my research has been as objective and rigorous as I (and many collaborators) could make it. So this chapter is, unquestionably and appropriately, a critique of the Strategies but chiefly as a wasted opportunity and as something to learn from for the future.

A brief history lesson about English

The school subject of English has a complex and torturous history even in its relatively short life on the curriculum compared to Maths and Science. Its gradual displacement of Classics took perhaps a hundred years from the 1860s to the 1960s when what has been called a 'progressive' model of English began to appear. For the purposes of this chapter that shift is important because in the 1970s the dominance of Literature, especially English Literature, was challenged by a new emphasis on language, the Bullock Report (DES, 1975) representing a high point in that challenge. However, all the way through the history of the subject, the contested notion of grammar was a constant. It might be argued that both the NLS and the FWE are part of the grammar movement, that is to say a focus on linguistic themes rather than on the broader conceptualization of English which includes literature.

What has rarely been contested, certainly not since the Newbolt Report of 1921, is both the centrality of subject English to schooling and its pre-eminence. This latter point explains why in 1988 the first subject to be defined within the National Curriculum was English. What makes this even more striking is that there had just been another major review of English, the Kingman Report (1988), which had investigated teachers' Knowledge About Language and concluded that there needed to be a whole new approach backed up by a national in-service programme (sounds like an early version of the FWE?). This report was to a large extent overtaken by the juggernaut of the National Curriculum. However some of the report's recommendations were implemented and the Language in the National Curriculum project 1989–92 was undertaken. However, other recommendations, including a national project about language in education and also more emphasis on language in initial teacher training, were never implemented. The most striking outcome of all, however, was the banning of the materials produced by the project in 1992; they were simply not to the liking of the government. No reason was ever offered except that the materials were not approved as suitable for the use of classroom teachers. The actual reason was that the project, led by the most eminent Professor of Linguistics at that time, Ronald Carter, adopted essentially a 'Language in Use', sociolinguistic approach which did not emphasize grammatical rules.

 Ironically the National Curriculum for English in its first version, designed by Cox and his Committee, was well received by English teachers (see Goodwyn, 1992), that version lasted about three years (1989–92). The National Curriculum was not only revised but the assessment system that was introduced, particularly the Key Stage tests or SATs, was deeply unpopular. In fact English teachers boycotted the SATs for several years, refusing to mark them. The government got round this by making the SATS marked externally and by making it the head teachers' legal duty to ensure the tests took place. This system was finally in place in 1996.

In that very year the idea of the NLS was conceived in what turned out to be the last year in office of the Conservative government. As *The Literacy Game* (2007) demonstrates, the concept was seized upon by New Labour and the strategy came into being with extraordinary rapidity in 1997. There are key points to consider in relation to secondary schools and also in reflecting on the nature of this 'reform'.

The first is that the situation was treated as a crisis, the implication being that, in less than a decade, i.e. between 1988 and 1996, the National Curriculum had, at worst, lowered literacy standards, at best, failed to raise them. There was some suggestion that in the formation of the primary curriculum on a subject-defined model, its teachers had begun to neglect literacy (English 2003; English *et al.*, 2002). Interestingly the National Numeracy Strategy was created as both an afterthought and on a relatively small scale. It is worth noting that more recent research and analysis identifies a much deeper and authentic problem in the teaching of Mathematics in England compared to a number of other countries. This point is important because there was no genuine evidence of a crisis in literacy standards (see Wyse, 2003) although there has been much debate about this (Beard, 2003, 2000a, 2000b). The typically right-wing obsession with reading standards and that they must be falling, is a convenient myth that New Labour grasped with relish. The 'Tories' had identified the crisis and in proving New Labour's credentials as a centre right party, they would deal with the crisis.

The second key point is that this generated atmosphere of crisis allowed the NLS to be presented to the public in terms of a crusade, with literacy as the Holy Grail. Much of the discourse in both the NLS documents and the subsequent Framework for English is imbued with an evangelical fervour. A striking feature of research about the implementation of the FWE is the way its proponents, whether political or educational, for example its army of consultants, spoke and acted as if on a holy mission. The NLS/FWE was genuinely then more of an act of faith than an act of reason. Its absurdities and excesses are much more easily understood on this basis than any other. Not least because evangelical faith is predicated on an absolute sense of being right and that unbelievers must be saved from their ignorance. This is not rhetoric; the entire training model for the NLS and the subsequent FWE were designed as if teachers were 'doing things wrong' and had to be put right for their own good. The infamous clock of the 'Literacy Hour' is a spectacular symbol (see Andersen *et al.*, 2000) of how primary teachers were patronized. The reaction to the training for secondary teachers will be discussed below.

One other crucial aspect of a crusade is that the end can justify the means, in order to secure a Holy Grail. There are three inseparable and powerful elements in such a crusade. The first is that in the public's mind a Holy Grail is a powerful, mystical symbol not really subject to much close analysis. The second element is that it is somehow a good thing that is incontestable, there must surely be no one who could question that its pursuit is worthwhile? In fact, the act of questioning its pursuit must surely be a sign of not lack of faith, but anti-faith. Finally, given all these certainties, the pursuit must begin immediately, the army recruited and equipped, the enemy, where identified, must be dealt with remorselessly. Again this is not fanciful rhetoric as any reading of *The Literacy Game* will attest.

The Holy Grail of Literacy is never truly or clearly defined. Indeed the emergence of the term 'Literacy' in the period approximately between 1950 and 1990 has an interesting history given that 'illiteracy' was a much more commonly used term in the nineteenth and twentieth centuries (see Street, 1984). Although both the NLS and the FWE are characterized by an extraordinary proliferation of manuals, guides, exemplars and directives, mostly in textual form, there is no singular definition of literacy. An analysis of the many documents reveals an implied definition which was perhaps derived from the traditional notion of 'becoming lettered', i.e. able to read and write using a pen. Ironically, this inability to produce a simple definition is correct. The term literacy is problematic and the research community have increasingly accepted this Holy Grail cannot be reduced to an actual simple 'object'. However, the public (and political) perception remains that literacy is a simple thing, the so-called experts are demonized in their failure to produce a neat simple definition. This point is especially important in understanding why English teachers have rejected the L in NLS, which will be elaborated below.

On this basis Barber's (1995) model of 'informed prescription', i.e. the end justifies the NLS means, actually becomes ill-informed and ill-defined prescription. Of course the Grail, as everyone surely knows, must be found. The infidels, of course, not only create obstacles by questioning the means, some of them even question whether the Grail exists in any simple form.

In the period 1996 to 2000, secondary schools were, in a sense, spectators of the crusade. They were busy with the revised, more prescriptive and detailed National Curriculum and the dominating force of the fully established Key Stage Three (KS3) tests, and they were coping with the frequent attention of Ofsted and the glare of league tables. In English departments the KS3 test was especially dominant, affecting the whole of the Key Stage. Many departments questioned the validity of the KS2 test in English and spent much of Year 7 retesting pupils, then training them for the SATs in Years 8 and 9. However, towards the end of that period, they were beginning to consider what to do with the new-style pupils who would be entering secondary schools from the year 2000 onwards. They knew there was going to be a new National Curriculum but it was not clear whether there was going to be a NLS-style initiative for secondary education. This was partly because the crusaders had been fixated on primary education, as *The Literacy Game* demonstrates, the Grail should have been found by the end of Year 6. It is hard to determine the facts but it seems very probable that no real thinking had been done about the secondary curriculum until the NLS was well underway. What seems to have happened is that the political imperative ensured that the crusade continued, especially because the short-term improvement in results at KS2 were already neither substantial enough nor sustainable. By 2000 the NLS evaluation team were already explicitly telling the crusaders (see Earl *et al.*, 2003) that the Holy Grail was not secured and that the foot soldiers (the primary teachers) were already wilting on the long march.

Essentially the period 1997–2000 in secondary schools was marked by two characteristics (Goodwyn, 2003a, 2003b; Goodwyn and Findlay, 2003a, 2003b). At whole school level there was an emphasis on whole school literacy, reminiscent of the post-Bullock Report era when many secondary schools developed Language across the curriculum policies, driven by working parties of enthusiastic teachers (see Goodwyn and Findlay, 2002). This emphasis was partly in pragmatic preparation for the NLS pupils and partly in response to a genuine renewal of interest in literacy. Secondary schools were intrigued by the frenetic activity of the Literacy Hour in all their feeder schools and made more effort to consider how to enable smooth transition between Years 6 and 7. One of the arguments for the NLS, as it had been for the National Curriculum, was that it would help to overcome the negative impact of moving to secondary school.

The research into the activities of English departments (Goodwyn and Findlay, 2002) revealed a genuine excitement about a new challenge for all teachers. Many English teachers visited nearby primary schools and were extremely impressed by the teaching of literacy, including the literal 'Literacy Hour', and were certainly somewhat in awe of these pupils who seemed confident using technical vocabulary about language. They were also beginning to think about the dominant pedagogy of word, sentence and text level and what its implications might be for Year 7 and beyond. At this stage there was no Framework to either challenge or limit their thinking.

2000–3

The initial period of the FWE was marked by a dramatic change of attitude in English departments. The reaction to the training for the implementation of the FWE was dramatic. The research undertaken in the first two years of the Framework (Goodwyn, 2003a, 2003b; Goodwyn and Findlay, 2003a, 2003b) found that teachers loathed the patronizing style of the training sessions and their dogmatic adherence to the materials produced. The teachers were at first shocked and then confused by being told that lessons had beginnings, middles and ends and that 'pace' was important. This all seemed so blindingly obvious that they felt they must be missing something. They also felt that this sudden plethora of supporting materials, some for training uses, videos for example, some for the classroom, were of good quality and worth using, but overall not especially innovative.

2003–9

This period was essentially one of quiet compliance. The training continued but was toned down and became less prescriptive. Equally English teachers attended training with low expectations after the first three years. It became clear that dutiful attendance was necessary but need not lead to any real change to practice. The plethora of initiatives also continued, supported by materials, and English departments had shelves groaning with training manuals and DVDs. They demonstrated a real willingness to make use of these materials but found that one initiative could not be absorbed before another one came along.

This period ends with a dramatic and significant finale, the abolishing of the KS3 tests. In many ways everything about this debacle is representative of the absurdity of the NLS/FWE monolith. These tests were boycotted by English teachers for several years (1992–5) before the government enforced them on head teachers (as already mentioned) and they were never supported by the teachers themselves. Nevertheless, English teachers found themselves in a Catch 22 situation. Although individual children gained no benefit from reaching a particular level, the school would be judged in a league table by the collective success or failure of the SATs results. So without believing in the benefit of preparing students for these tests, English teachers found themselves curiously dedicated to just that preparation. Once the legal change enforced this dedication, then Year 9 became dominated by test preparation and over the subsequent years the whole of KS3 was affected, especially as the FWE put such emphasis on focusing on levels and targeting students' progress in an atomistic way.

The tests were not just unpopular with English teachers, their Maths and Science colleagues were equally disaffected. The teaching unions vociferously spoke against them including those representing the head teachers. As soon as Wales was able to govern its own schools it abolished the tests. But the government stubbornly resisted all calls for change until 2009. In 2008 there had been a huge media furore about the administration and marking of the tests. Hundreds of schools challenged the outcome of the marking, their tests were then remarked and, very often, much higher levels awarded. Many schools did not receive their results for weeks after the deadline. The government then changed the organization which managed the SATs with a promise of major improvements. The effect was the exact opposite and everything that had become problematic with the SATs was doubly worse. The result was a quick and politically expedient decision to scrap them.

However, one ironic effect of this unplanned action was to create a sudden vacuum. English teachers, deeply enculturated into teaching towards the tests, had no time to adjust and many schools continue to test their students, SATs-style, long after the SATs themselves have gone. It is clear that it will be several years before the dominance of the test is truly diminished.

The experience of the Strategy for English

The outline above demonstrates that English teachers went from a period of positive anticipation about the 'impact' of the NLS (Allen, 2002), to a state of initial shock and anger about the actual nature of the Framework for English and its training regime, to a final period of compliance but relative indifference with an exception in relation to the status of literature(see below for detail).

Some of that 'experience' was governed by the evangelical rhetoric of the Literacy crusade. Much of that rhetoric was enacted in training sessions and other real-time events; its traces are everywhere in the training manuals and DVDs produced throughout the period. The essence of the Framework can best be captured through an example or two from the main document itself. It must be stressed that there is much other rhetoric, often problematic, in official documentation, and this certainly includes the National Curriculum for English in its various guises since 1989.

For example, this statement acted as a preamble to the National Curriculum for English from 2000–8 (see the QCA website):

The importance of English

English is a vital way of communicating in school, in public life and internationally. Literature in English is rich and influential, reflecting the experience of people from many countries and times. In studying English pupils develop skills in speaking, listening, reading and writing. It enables them to express themselves creatively and imaginatively and to communicate with others effectively. Pupils learn to become enthusiastic and critical readers of stories, poetry and drama as well as non-fiction and media texts. The study of English helps pupils understand how language works by looking at its patterns, structures and origins. Using this knowledge, pupils can choose and adapt what they say and write in different situations.

(National Curriculum for English, 2001)

In considering the status of literature, if we examine the two key sentences about Literature in English then the first articulates that such literature is 'influential'. Such a claim is hard to substantiate but if one took as one piece of evidence the number of students studying it around the world then the claim would seem reasonable. Equally, if one measured influence by sales of texts, the same would apply. However the pervasiveness of this literature is also part of the imperialistic past (and present) and 'influence' might usefully be interrogated as a very negative force.

Is such literature 'rich'? It seems that 'rich' is used in the sense of *full of abundance* or *of great worth*, etc. but it unavoidably carries connotations of wealth and power. Perhaps this ambiguity is of value in itself? The comment that it is 'reflecting the experience of people from many countries and times' is both true and misleading, we really ought to add 'some' before people. However this interpellation shades towards the pedantic. My own experience as a reader is unquestionably that I have gained enormously from such reading and I do believe that I have been provided with innumerable insights into the experience of others over both time and space.

The second sentence which contains the words 'Pupils learn to become enthusiastic and critical readers of stories, poetry and drama' is simply untrue, and in the previous (and current) assessment regime, increasingly untrue. The research discussed below provides strong evidence to support this point. However, was it ever true? I think probably to a much lesser extent than English teachers would wish. It is not only the National Curriculum for English that has made grossly inflated claims for the enduring benefits of studying literature in school; and I do not mean here the extraordinary evangelisms of Leavis and his host of followers (see Eagleton, 1975). The justifications for studying English Literature (which is almost always the actual topic) bear no close examination because the habits of adult consumers of texts clearly demonstrate that 'Literature' (with that capital L) is not to their 'taste'. I am clear that some pupils can 'become enthusiastic and critical' and I am also extremely clear that insisting (which is what we do) that pupils encounter literature in school is a perfectly reasonable requirement. Any adult should be able to select a literary form of reading when they wish to and there is nothing 'natural' about it. It is learnt and most definitely can be taught. I am arguing very strongly for a mode of literary reading that includes words such as 'engagement', 'immersion' and 'reflection' in relation to complete texts and this would include texts, such as plays and novels, that cannot be held easily in the mind in their entirety.

A significant part of the problem with the rhetoric (and reality) of the Framework was neatly encapsulated in this paragraph from the DCSF (Department for Children, Families and Schools), placed on their Standards website, acting as a preface to the Framework for English (2001 onwards) and aims to help 'fulfill the requirement for the teaching of literature':

> There is clearly a balance to be achieved between providing classroom time to support the reading of longer texts and the imperative to secure progression. Having clear objectives lends pace and focus to the study of longer texts: there is less need to teach all possible angles on the text and more reason to focus on those aspects that cluster around the objectives. The aim is to provide enjoyable encounters, which serve the objectives well but do not demand a disproportionate amount of time. Teachers already use a repertoire of techniques (such as the use of priority passages, support tapes, abridgement, televised extracts, and recapitulation) to move quickly through longer texts without denying attention to the details and quality of the text.
>
> (DES 2001, p. 15)

'The imperative to secure progression' is a phrase redolent with all the negative connotations of the last decade (Frater, 2000; Hunt, 2001; Goodwyn, 2010). Its utter banal simplicity smacks of endless unreachable targets, measured against standards and benchmarks. How ironic that certain forms of more 'liberal' pedagogy have always been somewhat patronizingly called 'progressive'. More to the point, this paragraph reveals the fundamental problem with an obsession with apparently focused objectives and the nature of learning, especially of something as usefully ambiguous, interpretable and personal as 'literature'. At a practical level it might be summed up as follows 'why read the whole thing when an extract will do?'

The research evidence below, again, bears out a deep unease amongst English teachers (of all ages and stages) with the dominance of teaching through extracts (see Goodwyn, 2008a). Of course, the final sentence about teachers and their repertoire is, at least in my view, absolutely right and proper. Good English teachers learn just such skills of selection in order to introduce learners to all kinds of valid textual experiences, if anything I think they should have opportunities to make such selections autonomously far more often. But the issue for teachers was that they felt under such pressure that the rather messy and slow process of engaging with a longer text was conceptualized as either a luxury that cannot be afforded or as a desirable experience that must wait for the survivors of 5–16 who select studying at A level. I would argue that becoming a 'literary' reader must involve the experience of a longish literary text and reflection on that experience by the reader. I would also argue that this experience needs to be refined through positive repetition coupled with maturation. Put simply, learners need this experience several times a year for several years.

The two 'manifestos' above are both problematic in their own ways as has been demonstrated. However the former is certainly more aligned with what practitioners both preach and practice when teaching literature and the latter was far more an attempt to dislodge that practice in order to respond to the 'imperative to secure progression'.

The confirmation of Literature not Literacy: the view of English teachers at the end of the NLS/FWE period

This section focuses on what has become, in retrospect, a final phase of the Strategy model and analyses the findings of three interrelated research projects, undertaken over that period, 2006–9. The first study was a survey of student teachers of English as they completed their PGCE courses in 2007. The second was a national survey of serving teachers in the period 2006–7. The final study (see below) was a small, qualitative study of student teachers undertaken in 2007–8.

In this section I report on the key findings of two national surveys of English teachers, in a relatively short chapter there is space only for a selected proportion of the findings. Study 1 focused on student teachers of English in their final weeks of their training year; there were 182 respondents from 10 universities. Study 2 investigated practising teachers – there were 254 individual respondents from 180 schools. In both cases these numbers are well below the statistical level that would allow for a claim of being truly representative, and this is acknowledged. However these surveys follow on from many years of work investigating English teachers views about the Literacy Strategy and the Framework for English and the findings have a clear pattern of continuity (Goodwyn, 2003a, 2003b, 2004a, 2004b, 2008a). Initially the two surveys will be combined to maximize the sample and also because a number of the questions were the same, then they will be treated distinctly for more fine-grained analysis and because some questions were specific to the sample. Key Stages 3 and 4 are treated as one unit in these findings. The questions used are included in an appendix and the findings here are a selection from the data with the emphasis being on those questions that most directly relate to the 'condition' of literature teaching.

As a preamble it is worth noting that the reasons given for becoming an English teacher were remarkably consistent and can be summarized as follows:

- love of/enthusiasm for/passion for the subject
- working with young people
- love of literature/reading
- being good at the subject.

These four are in order of importance and it is interesting to note that the first and third points are very similar but that 'love of reading' is given a distinct status. Respondents do not put, for example, 'love of language' or 'love of writing'. This survey, like others (Goodwyn, 2008b), shows that the 'next generation' of teachers wanted to become English teachers at least partly because of a love for literature; they share that passion with several previous generations.

The three factors below are also significant:

- teaching is creative/full of variety/not an office job
- the influence of an inspirational English teacher
- good career/money/holidays.

When asked to rate the personal importance of Literature to them then, 75 per cent said 'Very', 20 per cent just 'Important' and 5 per cent 'Fairly', suggesting that from the teachers' perspective Literature remains central to their teaching and their professional identity.

As regards its importance within the current curriculum then the results diminished its importance somewhat. Its current place was rarely seen as 'Very Important', only 20 per cent, the next two categories were 'Important' 45 per cent and 'Fairly Important' 30 per cent and these figures are almost repeated for the prediction of the next few years. These figures suggest a solid place for literature although many comments were far more pessimistic, especially from experienced teachers who predicted the predominance of 'Functional English' and a much more Linguistic than literary orientation within the curriculum.

Estimates of curriculum coverage and numbers of Schemes of Work (SOW) devoted to Literature again support a strong role for literature. All respondents were positive about having SOWs devoted to literature with about 5 per cent stating that all their SOWs were such. However about 20 per cent stated that three-quarters were literature, and the great majority, 60 per cent, estimated about half. It is worth noting here that the respondents who returned the survey may well be those teachers for whom literature IS very important. This may have influenced both their choice of school and how they interpret a SOW.

This point is partly balanced by the fact that the student teachers had no choice over school and were also administered the questionnaires in class. Overall it is clear that teachers *perceive* that a great deal of work in English is centred on Literature in some way or another. As regards estimates of time, over three-quarters stated that they spent at least half their time on literature teaching.

An interesting difference is evident in the enjoyment of teaching. Of the student teachers, the great majority very much enjoyed teaching literature, with none saying they did not enjoy it. The experienced teachers were a good deal less enthusiastic. About half still put 'very much' but almost half put 'to some extent' and comments tended to be about the negative pressure of assessment, the need to cover too much ground (especially poetry at KS4) and a general sense that their teaching was not really interactive or creative and certainly not 'inspiring' in they way they felt it should be.

Respondents were invited to reflect on the impact of the Framework for English on literature teaching, the student teachers were encouraged to draw on their con- versations with more experienced teachers as well as their own views: 100 per cent said there had been a strong impact. Of the approximately 50 per cent who chose to respond by adding comments, 90 per cent commented in the negative, all stating, in one way or another, that literature teaching had become much more instrumental, dominated by narrow objectives and focused on textual extracts. Half of these commentators expressed extreme frustration at the lack of opportunity to study a whole text in any detail or depth. Many experienced teachers also commented on literature teaching becoming 'scripted' and on the emphasis being constantly on the assessment objectives and 'a right answer'.

Respondents were also asked to reflect on pupil response to literature and were asked:

> When students are being assessed on their response to literature, what kind of response is given most importance (regardless of whether you agree with this emphasis)? Please put these in order, 1 to 4, with 1 being the most dominant.
>
> *Analytical*   *Personal*   *Formal*   *Creative*

They were also asked to comment on their view of this order.

There were some differences between Key Stages 3 and 4 but fundamentally, and taken together, 80 per cent put the emphasis on 'analytical' and 'formal', with 'personal' and 'creative' as either 3 or 4. Of the half who chose to comment, the great majority expressed this emphasis as the key negative impact of the last few years stressing that they felt pupils were missing out on the real point of literary study. Equally they emphasized how disengaging the effect was on all pupils, even the most able, but disastrously so for the less capable.

As regards Shakespeare all teachers wanted to include him in both KS3 and 4. About 60 per cent stated that if there had to be SATs tests then including Shakespeare was reasonable but 95 per cent stated that the SATs were distorting and ruining KS3. What the teachers wanted was freedom to choose which Shakespeare to teach and when and to be able to differentiate teaching for different groups. The great majority, three-quarters, felt that the real qualities of Shakespeare such as dramatic power and poetry of the language were being obscured by the testing apparatus. Since the survey the formal testing situation has been changed and the Shakespeare test has gone for now. However it is most unlikely that the curriculum itself as taught or the way English teachers teach Shakespeare will rapidly or radically change as huge amounts of energy have been invested in the apparatus of the testing model; further research will be needed.

About 60 per cent of teachers felt that the then GCSE requirements did encourage students to go on to A level but their comments were clear that this could only happen with the right teaching and that, in themselves, the requirements could be discouraging. More than a third were definitely of the view that the requirements were discouraging because there were too many texts covered superficially, especially poetry, and too much teaching was driven by assessment objectives rather than personal response.

One of the most striking findings related to the teachers' views about how things might be improved in the future. These views were expressed as comments and were analysed for key words and phrases. In KS3 over 80 per cent wished to see the end of the Framework for English which was characterized as prescriptive, limiting, not student-centred and assessment obsessed. All these teachers wanted much more autonomy and flexibility. At KS4 almost three-quarters of teachers also wanted much more flexibility and autonomy. They also wanted much more personal engagement with texts and with students choosing some of their own texts.

The third, small-scale study of fifteen student teachers consisted of semi-structured interviews in which each student was asked to reflect on their own literary experiences and to consider how these experiences might inform their own teaching. These were volunteers and therefore a random self-selection but suggesting an interest in discussing literature and its teaching. The interviews were conducted about halfway through their one-year programme and after they had experience of two schools and therefore two English departments. They were asked to articulate their rationale for asking school students to engage with literature and to propose what makes a text 'literary'. They were also asked to consider the notion of the kind of reader that they have become through both literary experience and literary study. A short section of the interview asked them to consider the status of literature in secondary schools; as well as being relevant to the current study, these questions link to an ongoing project by the researcher investigating attitudes to literature in schools more generally.

The findings support the idea that reading literature has benefited the participants, that it was a key reason for them becoming teachers and that they believe the right kinds of teaching can have similar benefits for children. They also demonstrate that participants do believe that 'literary reading' is part of the spectrum of reading but with particular properties and characteristics that do justify its special status in society and in education.

As a group they feel literature retains status but most feel this is now highly compromised by the assessment regime and the Strategies, i.e. teachers and students simply 'have to do it'. In other words literature's importance per se is obscured. The group also expressed concerns about how much time was spent on extracts and how little on complete texts. They recognized the challenge of teaching longer texts but felt that much more was lost by such an emphasis on extracts. One student, Emma (pseudonym), commented:

> Overall I suppose it's very much exam texts, it's focused on exam texts and the only freedom is in Year 7 and Year 8 and possibly, I mean, the school I was in last term they were doing texts in the first term of Year 9 so that they could actually do something other than SATs work and then putting all the SATs work into this term um but at that level you can't do a Dickens or something like that. I mean we did do a bit of Dickens through extracts but it wasn't very satisfying because you want to say you know *Great*

Expectations is a fabulous book but actually they are too young or haven't, maybe not too young some of them but haven't got the skills to really appreciate that. Um ... but I think because I just love to lose myself in a book I find it frustrating sometimes that it's very exam orientated you know and sometimes you get the impression from the teachers that 'we've *got to do* this book'. It's not that 'we are *going to read* this book' it's 'we are *going to do* this book' and all the connotations that that has and all the pupils equally is 'we are *doing* Shakespeare'. 'We are *doing* our exam text'. 'We've got to get through it and write a piece of coursework on it'. Or 'learn it for the exam and then we will never touch it again'.

Most of the group felt that some teachers knew how to escape the assessment regime particularly by using 'dramatic approaches', 'creative responses' and 'keeping it interactive'. But they also felt they were witnessing a great deal of stultifying teaching.

One of the most striking findings relates to the 'hypothetical' questions asked about retaining literature. In response to the idea that the government might require English to leave out Literature at KS3, the universal response was of 'horror'. The suggestion was characterized as 'shocking, 'horrifying', 'devastating', etc. and the rationale given was that literature was the most engaging and interesting element in the curriculum and that it allowed for interesting ways of teaching the 'other stuff', like grammar. Over half said emphatically that they would not wish to be an English teacher in these circumstances. There is a strong relationship here to their original decision to become a teacher.

However, the hypothesis about KS4, i.e. should it be taught only to those who choose it, produced more diverse responses. Four of the group were clear that the age of 14 was just too young to decide and the benefits of literature were far too important to be optional. Four saw the rationale for offering choice to 'young adults' but felt that some literature should be retained in compulsory English. Four felt that the advantages in having only enthusiastic students were very significant, and that it was a workable idea.

Despite these intriguing differences, this group of beginning English teachers had much in common: one very strong commonality was that they all considered that their own interest and experience of literature was a very strong motivator in choosing to teach English. The following points are also characteristic of the whole group who:

- have also been strongly influenced by 'inspirational' teachers of literature;
- consider that literature retains status in schools but it principally has importance because of the assessment regime rather than per se;
- feel that there is too much reliance on extracts and not enough on whole texts (challenging though whole texts can be);
- feel that much teaching is 'stultifying' and 'impersonal';
- would be horrified if literature was removed from KS3;

- have mixed feelings about making it an option in KS4 but most would retain it;
- want to be inspirational, passionate teachers of literature;
- are certain that literature offers much to all students;
- are certain that they have gained enormously from literary reading;
- feel that literary reading is characterized by a powerful, emotional state of mind;
- believe that this experience is possible for school students but that, under current circumstances, certain students are more likely to benefit from it than others.

What these findings make clear is that beginning English teachers have joined the profession because of a strong attachment to literature and to helping students have a meaningful literary experience. After just a few months, they had experienced the stultifying effects of the FWE and its narrowing of the curriculum and the especially negative effect of the testing regime; at this point the Key Stage test was firmly in place with no sign of it being changed, never mind abolished.

Conclusions

It is very evident that English teachers have never developed a positive relationship with 'The Strategies'. There was a period, before the FWE was itself in place, when secondary schools and English teachers in particular were strongly interested in the potential benefits of the Literacy Strategy for students moving up to the secondary phase. This positive anticipation turned to first disbelief and then hostility when the full impact of the FWE was felt and especially the deeply patronizing training and endless succession of initiatives and accompanying folders and DVDs. In a sense they 'came to terms' with the FWE by coping with it and complying with what had to be done but without enthusiasm or conviction.

Despite the powerful pressure of the Framework and its mighty evangelical band of consultants preaching the imperative to secure progression, literature teaching in secondary schools still has a strong 'presence' but its apparent material dominance masks a much deeper issue. It is still highly valued by English teachers both personally and professionally but its true status was diminished. This was principally because very narrow assessment objectives and high-stakes testing were making literature, and especially extracts from literature, merely a vehicle for mechanistic outcomes. The more creative and personal responses to literature that teachers especially value have been drastically diminished. For example, the kind of depth that teachers feel can be gained from a thorough engagement with a longer and more complex text are almost impossible to manage given 'the imperative to secure progression'. It is perhaps too trite to mention 'personalized learning' here but an engagement with literature is clearly one of the most authentically personal experiences that a young person can gain. The available empirical studies of literary reading (see Miall, 2006) are very clear that the personal is central to meaning-making at all levels of engagement with a literary text.

If English teachers are granted any influence, post the NLS/FWE era, if some of their autonomy is restored, then the curriculum will change, the assessment regime will be radically revised and literature will regain some of its significance in schools in the way that teachers see it as significant. However, perhaps with some irony, the rather taken-for-granted notion of reading a literary text will also need revisiting. The inflated claims made for reading Great English Literature (see Eagleton, 1975; Mathieson 1975), trumpeted so often since the nineteenth century, have long since been discredited. Indeed those claims were marked with an evangelical fervour very comparable to the rhetoric of the NLS/FWE. The emergent claims of the twenty-first century are less grandiose and based far more on the experiences of actual readers. Equally, they do resonate with those previous claims in suggesting that 'literary reading' is an experience with quite remarkable qualities and benefits for those who genuinely engage with it. Even though it can be argued that Rosenblatt started this reader response view of literary reading back in 1938, it is still an emergent field.

How much research has actually explored how young readers begin to experience the phenomenon of literary reading and, of equal importance, why so many do not ever have that experience? Whatever the excesses of the FWE, they in themselves would not explain why some readers fail to experience literary reading. English teachers know a very great deal about how to engage young people, especially when teaching literature, and with some of the current restrictions perhaps removed, then good practice may be liberated. The findings of the two large-scale surveys are clear that English teachers are seeking to offer their students an authentic engagement in literature where assessment promotes and enables a personal response. The changes to the National Curriculum for English and to the assessment frameworks may signal a new set of opportunities for English teachers and their students. However the introduction of tests in Functional English may act as a counterpoint, it is too soon to evaluate their impact.

Overall, the term 'literacy', as promoted by the NLS and FWE, has not become accepted by secondary English teachers. In the period 1997–2000, they were sympathetic to notions of 'whole school literacy' and to working with all other subject teachers on this enterprise. However once the ill-informed prescription of the FWE was forced upon them, their attention turned to surviving its demands and its attempts to narrow the curriculum and promote a functionalist model of English. The evidence is clear that they found the whole Strategy antipathetical to their professional identity and their value for the personal and the literary in English. English teachers very evidently want their students to be highly literate, but to them being literate is an affective, not simply cognitive, capability. The NLS and FWE bandwagons missed a great opportunity to work with English teachers in order to secure true literacy for far more students.

The most significant lesson from the NLS and FWE period is that 'informed prescription' is not an effective way to produce educational change or to 'raise standards'. Such an approach positions teachers as the problem and it is deeply patronizing. This is partly because it diminishes teaching to a technical function, that much-mentioned phrase to 'deliver the curriculum'. Delivering is what lorry drivers do and, with no offence to them, they really do not have to concern themselves too much with the contents of the lorry. Equally, and this was especially true of the training models employed, it confuses teachers by telling them what they already know as if they need to change their practice. Many quotations in my surveys over the period would comment on the fact lessons almost always have beginnings, middles and ends, why do trainers assume we do not know that? Ultimately the obsession with objectives, tests and formulaic and scripted approaches to teaching led to what I have described above as a form of indifferent compliance. However, in the last period of the FWE, English teachers were becoming deeply anxious about the loss of meaningful content in their teaching and about the increasing disengagement of their students. It is a tribute to them as professionals that they 'soldiered on' during this period and endeavoured, whenever they could, to provide their students with rich and meaningful learning, not derived from the model of Literacy advocated in the Strategy, but from the positive traditions and best practice which are at the heart of the subject English.

References

Allen, N. (2002) Too Much, Too Young? An analysis of the Key Stage 3 National Literacy Strategy in practice, *English in Education*, 36, 5–15.

Anderson, H., Digings, M. and Urquhart, I. (2000) Hourwatch: Monitoring the inception of the National Literacy Strategy, *Reading*, 34(3).

Barber, M. (1995) *The Learning Game*, London: Routledge.

Beard, R. (2000a) Research and the National Literacy Strategy, *Oxford Review of Education*, 26(3&4), 421–36.

Beard, R. (2000b) Long Overdue? Another look at the National Literacy Strategy, *Journal of Research in Reading*, 23, 245–55.

Beard, R. (2003) Not the Whole Story of the National Literacy Strategy: A response to Dominic Wyse, *British Educational Research Journal*, 29, 917–28.

Departmental Committee of the Board of Education (1921)*The Teaching of English in England: Being the report of the departmental committee appointed by the President of the Board of Education to inquire into the position of English in the educational system of England* (The Newbolt Report), London: HMSO.

DES (1975) *A Language for Life* (The Bullock Report), London: HMSO.

DES (1988) *The National Curriculum for English 5–16*, London: DES.

DES (1988) *Report of the Committee of Inquiry into the Teaching of English Language* (The Kingman Report), London: HMSO.

DES (2001) *The Framework for Teaching English, Years 7, 8 and 9*, London: HMSO.

DfEE (1999) *Key Stage Three Strategy National Strategy: Framework for Teaching English*, London: DfEE.

Eagleton, T. (1975) *Literary Theory: An introduction*, Oxford: Blackwell.

Earl, L., Watson, N., Levin, B., Leithwood, K., Fullan, M. and Torrance, N. (2003) *Watching and Learning 3: Final Report of the external evaluation of England's National Literacy and Numeracy Strategies*, London: Department for Education and Employment.

English, E. (2003) All change! The National Literacy Strategy and its influence on the teaching of reading, *Studies in Training and Learning*, 4, 18–23.

English, E., Hargreaves, L. and Hislam, J. (2002) Pedagogical dilemmas in the National Literacy Strategy: Primary teachers' perceptions, reflections and classroom behaviour, *Cambridge Journal of Education*, 32, 9–26.

Frater, G. (2000) Observed in Practice. English in the National Literacy Strategy: some reflections, *Reading*, 34(3).

Goodwyn, A. (1992) *English Teaching and Media Education*, Buckingham: Open University Press.

Goodwyn, A. (2001) Second Tier Professionals: English teachers in England, *L1–Educational Studies in Language and Literature*, 1(2), 149–61.

Goodwyn, A. (2003a) Literacy or English: The struggle for the professional identity of English teachers in England, in *English Teachers at Work: Narratives, counter-narratives and arguments*, Australian Association for the Teaching of English/Interface, Kent Town: Wakefield Press.

Goodwyn, A. (2003b) Breaking Up is Hard to Do: English teachers and that LOVE of reading, *English Teaching, Practice and Critique*, 1(1), 66–78.

Goodwyn, A. (2004a) What's in a Frame? The English Framework – Three years on, *English, Drama, Media*, 2, 39–43.

Goodwyn, A. (2004b) Literacy versus English: A professional identity crisis, in Goodwyn, A. and Stables, A. (eds) *Learning to Read Critically in Language and Literacy Education*, London: Sage, pp. 192–205.

Goodwyn, A. (2008a) Student Teachers and Literary Reading, paper presented at the British Educational Research Association (BERA), University of Warwick, September.

Goodwyn, A (2008b) The Status of Literature in Secondary Schools in England, paper presented at the BERA conference, University of Warwick, September.

Goodwyn, A. (2010) *The Expert Teacher of English*, London: Routledge.

Goodwyn, A. and Findlay, K. (2002) Secondary Schools and the National Literacy Strategy, in Goodwyn, A. (ed.) *Improving Literacy at KS2 and KS3*, London: Paul Chapman, pp. 45–64.

Goodwyn, A. and Findlay, K. (2003a) Shaping Literacy in the Secondary School: Policy, practice and agency in the age of the National Literacy Strategy, *British Journal of Educational Studies*, 51(1).

Goodwyn, A. and Findlay, K. (2003b) Literature, Literacy and the Discourses of English Teaching: A case study, *L1–Educational Studies in Language and Literature*, 3(2).

Harrison, C. (2002) *Key Stage 3 National Strategy: Key Stage 3 English: Roots and research*, London: HMSO.

Hunt, G. (2001) Democracy or a Command Curriculum: Teaching literacy in England, *Improving Schools*, 4, 51–8.

Mathieson, M. (1975) *The Preachers of Culture*, London: Allen and Unwin.

Miall, D.S. (2006) *Literary Reading: Empirical and Theoretical Studies*, New York: Peter Lang.

Stannard, J. and Huxford, L. (2007) *The Literacy Game: The story of the National Literacy Strategy*, London: Routledge.

Street, B. (1984) *Literacy in Theory and Practice*, Cambridge: Cambridge University Press.

Wyse, D. (2003) The National Literacy Strategy: A critical review of empirical evidence, *British Educational Research Journal*, 29, 903–16.

Chapter 8

The great literacy debate as makeover television

Notes on genre proliferation

Adam Lefstein

Education policy in the public sphere, on prime time

Deliberative democracy, in contrast to procedural or formal democracy, is based upon the idea that the people should form and exercise their will through reasoned, informed debate in the public sphere (Calhoun, 1992; Habermas, 1984, 1989). While the notion of citizens freely exchanging ideas and reaching consensus through deliberation is appealing in principle, it is rather problematic in its practical enactment in conditions current in Western democracies. First, issues on the public agenda are complex, require specialised knowledge and access to reliable information and evidence. Second, public discourse is rarely conducted in face-to-face encounters; rather, it is mediated by print and broadcast journalism, which play a critical role in shaping the public agenda, informing debate and giving voice to participants (Page, 1996).

How the media perform this role – whether in the service of deliberative democracy or its suppression – depends upon a number of factors, including who has access to and control over the media (Garnham, 1992), and – more subtly – how technology, economics and culture interact to privilege certain messages and/or communicators.[1]

Television, in particular, has been criticised as a threat to the quality of public discourse. Postman (1986), for example, argues that television is good at entertainment, at telling stories, but bad at logic and analysis. Richards and King (2000) note the medium's tendency to gravitate to, highlight and polarise conflict. Ekstrom (2002) emphasises the centrality of the visual mode: television 'represents reality, creates powerful engagement, identification, fascination, thoughts and values through pictures' (p. 264). For Scheuer (1999), the main problem with television is that it is intolerant of complexity:

> Television . . . thrives on action, immediacy, specificity, and certainty. It filters out 1) more abstract and conceptual structures or relationships, including systems (which are relationships that interact over time to produce particular results or to maintain a particular balance); 2) causality, particularly remote causal histories and destinies, evolutionary change, and uncertain or

incomplete processes of change; 3) context, which is likewise relational and causative; and 4) ambiguity, i.e. uncertainty of meaning, and ambivalence, or uncertainty of value.

(Scheuer, 1999, pp. 121–2)

Though these criticisms apply to much of what we see on television, there are important differences between, for example, situation comedies, sports coverage, a C-SPAN live feed from Congress, reality television, commercial advertisements, a breakfast television show, music videos and the evening news. And, indeed, the particular conventions of each genre can be seen as constraints on what can be legitimately and intelligibly communicated through them. In other words, how events are shown and spoken about on the news is part of what makes audiences recognise these events *as news*, and thus what lends them their authority and credibility. This approach to genre will be further elaborated in its application to analysis of the inter-mixing of current affairs reporting and makeover genres in the *Newsnight* synthetic phonics series.

Literacy policy: from Bullock to Rose

Literacy is caught up in the public imagination with a host of anxieties about social order, national identity, economic competitiveness, moral character and the ability to think (Street and Lefstein, 2007). For that reason, the 'Great Debate' (Chall, 1965) in academic and professional circles about code-based (phonic) vs. meaning-based (whole language) approaches to early reading instruction is frequently transformed in the public sphere into ideologically and politically motivated 'Reading Wars' (Snyder, 2008). Disputes (or skirmishes) about how to teach reading periodically flare up, and in response English governments periodically appoint independent committees to review the evidence and make recommendations. To get a sense of the extent to which English policy has shifted in the past thirty years, consider the work of two such commissions: the 1975 Committee of Inquiry into the teaching of reading and other uses of English, chaired by Sir Alan Bullock (the *Bullock Report*) (DES, 1975), and the 2006 Independent Review of the Teaching of Early Reading conducted by Sir Jim Rose (the *Rose Review*) (Rose, 2006). The discussion of methods for teaching reading in the *Bullock Report* opened with the following caveat:

Controversy about the teaching of reading has a long history, and throughout it there has been the assumption, or at least the hope, that a panacea can be found that will make everything right. This was reflected in much of the correspondence we received. There was an expectation that we would identify the one method in whose adoption lay the complete solution. Let us, therefore, express our conclusion at the outset in plain terms: there is no one method, medium, approach, device, or philosophy that holds the key to the process of learning to read.

(DES, 1975, para 6.1)

Thirty-one years later, the *Rose Review* arrived at the opposite conclusion:

> Despite uncertainties in research findings, the practice seen by the review shows that the systematic approach, which is generally understood as 'synthetic' phonics, offers the vast majority of young children the best and most direct route to becoming skilled readers and writers.
>
> (Rose, 2006, p. 4)

The government immediately endorsed the *Rose Review* recommendations, and shortly thereafter schools were instructed to use a 'high-quality, systematic phonics programme' that, among other criteria, is 'underpinned by a synthetic approach to blending phonemes in order all through a word to read it, and segmenting words into their constituent phonemes to spell them' and is 'delivered in discrete daily sessions at a brisk pace that is well matched to children's developing abilities' (DfES, 2006, p. 8).

What happened to bring about such a radical policy shift? How did English education get from *Bullock* to *Rose*? Comprehensive treatment of this question is beyond the scope of this chapter, but I will briefly touch on some central events and processes, focusing on the public debate on the eve of the *Rose Review*. Changing government policies in the past two decades reflects a gradual and steady swing toward phonics teaching, both in terms of relative emphasis in the curriculum and the degree of specification with regard to curriculum delivery. Key developments – and corresponding peaks in press activity – are represented visually on the chart in Figure 8.1 of fluctuations in the volume of newspaper coverage regarding *phonics* and *literacy* in UK national newspapers between 1988 and 2010. The BBC *Newsnight* reports took place between May and July 2005, during the period of most intense press activity.

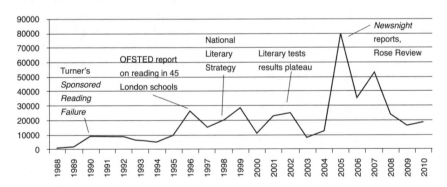

Figure 8.1 Number of words per year in articles mentioning phonics and literacy, UK national press.

The 1970s and 1980s were characterised by a large degree of teacher autonomy over both curriculum and teaching method, and the available evidence suggests that teachers employed both phonic-based readers and real books in teaching children to read (HMI, 1991). Teacher freedom – or, as its detractors characterised it, lack of accountability – was criticised in a series of speeches, reports and policy proposals leading up to the Educational Reform Act of 1988, which established, among other measures, a National Curriculum.[2] The new Curriculum included phonics as the third of three areas of reading knowledge: the relevant Attainment Target for 5–7-year-olds was to 'use picture and context cues, words recognised on sight and phonic cues in reading'.

Controversy erupted one year later with the publication and related media coverage of Martin Turner's (1990) *Sponsored Reading Failure: An Object Lesson*, which appeared to demonstrate that reading standards had dramatically declined in the Inner London Educational Authority. Turner claimed that

> a curriculum trend . . . is heavily implicated in the debacle: during the 1980s there has been a 'progressive' but, in view of the research into reading, capricious movement in the teaching of reading which has confused and disconcerted infant teachers. This is a hydra-headed beast named:
>
> • real books
> • storybook method
> • emergent reading
> • wholistic approach.

Heated debate ensued regarding this 'crisis', including whether or not standards were indeed falling, how reading was being taught in schools, and what should be the role of phonics in the curriculum.[3] In its wake, national testing to monitor achievement was introduced, and the National Curriculum was revised to place a greater emphasis on the importance of phonic knowledge. The relevant section of the revised scheme (1995) included:

> Pupils should be taught the alphabet, and be made aware of the sounds of spoken language in order to develop phonological awareness. They should also be taught to use various approaches to word identification and recognition, and to use their understanding of grammatical structure and the meaning of the text as a whole to make sense of print.

Note that phonics is given a much more prominent position in this version, though other cues are still included alongside it.[4]

The dispute was rekindled in the wake of an Ofsted report about poor pupil literacy levels in three London boroughs, which was again attributed to a lack of direct, systematic phonics teaching among other factors (Ofsted, 1996; see also Mortimore and Goldstein, 1996, for a contemporaneous critique of this report). The next year, the New Labour party rose to power with the promise that their top three priorities would be 'education, education, education'. New Labour

introduced in 1998 an ambitious National Literacy Strategy (NLS), a comprehensive reform programme that included detailed teaching objectives, a dedicated
daily 'literacy hour', elaborate curricular materials, professional development and
intervention programmes to support pupils that fall behind. The model of reading
that underpinned the NLS *Framework for teaching* (DfEE, 1998) was known as
the 'searchlights' model.[5] This model consists of a range of strategies – phonic,
contextual, grammatical and word recognition – that 'can be depicted as a series
of searchlights, each of which sheds light on the text' (p. 3). The anonymous
NLS author(s) apparently considered the phonics searchlight to be the least widely
used in classrooms at that time:

> Most teachers know about all these [strategies for reading], but have
> often been over-cautious about the teaching of phonics – sounds and
> spelling. It is vital that pupils are taught to use these word level strategies
> effectively. Research evidence shows that pupils do not learn to distinguish
> between the different sounds of words simply by being exposed to books.
> They need to be taught to do this ... At Key Stage 1, there should be a
> strong and systematic emphasis on the teaching of phonics and other word
> level skills.

In its second year the NLS supplemented these exhortations and the Literacy
Hour structure with the *Progression in Phonics* programme in order to assist
teachers in meeting the Strategy's word-level objectives.

The NLS *Framework* was criticised from multiple angles (see Street *et al.*, 2007,
for an overview). Some argued that the NLS tendency to chop everything up –
time, into 15–20 minute slots for activity; language, into word, sentence and text
levels; and texts, into excerpts for demonstrating specific features or practising
discrete skills – took the enjoyment out of reading and the creativity out of writing
(e.g. Ashley *et al.*, 2005). Critics from the phonics camp objected to the
searchlights model, which they argued confounded word recognition and text
comprehension processes, and perpetuated the problematic strategy of reading
by guessing on the basis of contextual cues (e.g. Stuart, 2003).

Initial, post-NLS rises in test scores were encouraging, but progress appeared
to have stalled after the Strategy's third year (see Earl *et al.*, 2003, for an evaluation
of the NLS, and Adey, 2003, and Tymms, 2004, for sceptical interpretations).
Motivated by an 'unacceptably high' rate of failure, the House of Commons Select
Committee on Education and Skills conducted a series of hearings between
November 2004 and February 2005 on competing methods for teaching reading.
The Committee was impressed by claims advanced for the effectiveness of synthetic
phonics teaching, especially a recent, highly publicised experiment conducted in
Clackmannanshire, Scotland (Johnston and Watson, 2005).[6] In the Committee's
conclusions, published in March 2005, it recommended an immediate review of
the place of synthetic phonics in the NLS and further study to compare the NLS

mixed approach with a 'phonics fast, first and only' model. Synthetic phonics was also championed by the opposition Conservative party, who used the issue – together with the NLS failure to achieve its pupil attainment targets – as a means of attacking the government.[7]

These political developments were accompanied by growing media interest in the issue. In the most comprehensive and in-depth coverage, *Newsnight*, the BBC's flagship television news programme, investigated the implementation of a synthetic phonics intervention in an East London school with 'some of the worst national curriculum results in the country'. The producers gave Ruth Miskin, charismatic developer of the *Read Write Inc.*[8] commercial synthetic phonics programme, 16 weeks to 'turn the school around'. A film crew visited the school periodically to document Miskin introducing her programme to the staff at the school and coaching them in its implementation. *Newsnight* broadcast three in-depth reports on the 'experiment', on 26 May, 20 June and 20 July 2005.[9] These reports were accompanied by panel discussions in the studio with prominent educational researchers and politicians as guests.[10]

I have chosen to focus on the *Newsnight* reports for a number of reasons. First, *Newsnight* enjoys an international reputation as a television news programme of the highest standards. In 2005 it won Media Tenor's 'Global TV award' based on objectivity, diversity, range of issues and balance. *Newsnight*'s self-description directly defies the negative characterisations of television discussed above:

> Television news has a lot to be said for it, but *Newsnight* has always lived on the edge of that world. In news, nuances tend to be ironed out, blemishes covered up, stories packaged. On *Newsnight* we aim to keep the rough edges, explain the awkward details.
>
> (Barron, 2005)

The show's aims include 'to give you the best daily analysis of news and current affairs on television', 'to help make sense of it all' and 'to break original stories, analyse developments in depth and put it all in perspective'. Moreover, since it is run by the BBC, it is not subject to the same commercial pressures as corporate media outlets. In short, if any television news programme can be expected to break the *Sound-bite Society* mould, it should be *Newsnight*.

Second, I conducted ethnographic research on the implementation of both *Read Write Inc.* and the NLS (in other schools), thereby giving me a good vantage point from which to comment on the way these programmes have been represented.[11]

Third, the news reports played a prominent role in a public debate that ultimately led to a policy shift. Then Secretary of State for Education Ruth Kelly appointed Sir Jim Rose to chair an Independent Review of the Teaching of Early Reading shortly after the first report was aired. As I noted above, the *Rose Review* recommended adoption of synthetic phonics, and the government almost immediately accepted this recommendation.[12] The searchlights model has since been replaced by the 'simple model' of reading, which separates word recognition and language comprehension (Primary National Strategy, 2006); *Letters and Sounds*, a new phonics programme has been produced; and a set of criteria for selecting commercial programmes have been published (partially quoted above).

Newsnight's synthetic phonics reports

The first episode introduces the pupils, teachers and school, and a challenge: Can Ruth Miskin get every child in this failing school to read within 16 weeks? The second instalment reports that the school has made encouraging progress, but that it is battling discipline and attendance problems. The third and final report proclaims the experiment an unmitigated success, details the progress attained and discusses the possibility of replicating the achievements in all English schools.

Episode 1: introducing the problem and solution

Speaking from the *Newsnight* studio, presenter Kirsty Wark introduces the first report thus:

> One in five children in England and Wales leave primary school unable to read or write properly. Following some startling research from primary schools in Clackmannanshire which found that teaching reading through synthetic phonics resulted in children achieving a reading age three and a half years ahead of their actual age, the Select Committee on Education has strongly recommended an immediate review of the way we teach children to read. We've learned that the Government is planning to look again at its National Literacy Strategy. And in the wake of that, *Newsnight* has gained exclusive access to a struggling Primary school in London, where the Headteacher has brought in a phonics expert to try to emulate Clackmannanshire's success. We'll be following their progress over the next few weeks. Here's Jackie Long's first report.

The programme then cuts from the studio to a school playground in which children play energetically; in the background an equally energetic song is played, with the words 'are you ready?' and staccato syllables somewhat similar to the phonic drills viewers will later encounter. Then follows a quick progression of images (music still playing in the background): children dancing, Miskin reciting phonemes, the camera panning out from the Canary Wharf financial district (visible from the school), children playing, children learning, Miskin pointing at a chart, a child performing a cartwheel, teachers reciting phonemes, children skipping in the playground. Jackie Long says in a voiceover: 'Britannia Village primary school is in the grip of a revolution: a radical plan to teach the children to read.' The school, which is located 'in a deprived area of East London', has 'some of the worst National Curriculum results in the country . . . in the league tables, out of around 13,500 primary schools, it sits in the bottom 200'.

To demonstrate just how poorly Britannia Village pupils read, Long provides three sources of evidence. First, we are introduced to two pupils, Marie-Paul Lukun and Eddie Jackson-Cash, who are 9 and 8 years old respectively, but whose reading levels are well below the norms for their ages. The camera focuses on Marie-Paul's face as she struggles to sound out the word 'drank'. Eddie has an easier time of it, but Long characterises the book he is reading (*My Dog Ned*) as intended for children 4–5 years his junior. Eddie seems oblivious to his underachievement, appearing pleased that he knew all the words.

Second, *Newsnight* arranges a photogenic 'test' of children's word recognition: the words 'Thank', 'Rubbed', 'Bright' and 'Mine' are written on a pane of glass. One by one, children run across the room, stop in front of the pane, try to read the words and then run off. By positioning the camera in back of the glass, the programme captures their expressions of bewilderment. Their exuberant running to and from the test provides a striking contrast to their dumbfounded responses of 'dunno' to most of the words.

Third, Long quotes statistics about the scope of the problem at the school:

> Three quarters of 6–7-year-olds are failing to reach even the national average for reading. A third of 7–8-year-olds have only just begun to read at all. And by year 4, that's 8–9-year-olds, there's been no improvement. 70% are two or more years behind where they should be.

What are the ramifications of this literacy problem? Head teacher Linda-May Bingham explains that poor reading abilities prevent pupils from accessing the rest of the curriculum. Later we meet Geraldine Jackson-Cash, Eddie's mother, who attributes Eddie's behavioural problems to his poor reading skills, and expresses fear that her 8-year-old son may 'go down that road' into crime. Six months ago she phoned the local education authority to 'beg for help':

> If something isn't done quickly with, you know, his school environment, with the school itself – if somebody doesn't step in, and start pulling the school the right way, then my son is going to end up being one of these children that you don't notice until you hear on the TV that he's just killed someone.

This startling prediction resonates with a widespread view of literacy as the key factor in a 'great divide' separating civilised and primitive societies (see Street, 1984, for critical review). Literacy is thus linked not only to cognitive and economic consequences, but to the moral and social order.

Jackson-Cash appeals for external help, for someone to 'step in'; this outside intervention is precisely what *Newsnight* documents. Head teacher Bingham turns to Ruth Miskin, developer of *Read Write Inc.*, to help the school tackle its literacy problem. *Newsnight* glosses Miskin's synthetic phonics method as follows (in Long's recapitulation at the beginning of the second episode):

First you teach the children the individual letter sounds. [Seven pupils hold up letter cards and pronounce the phonemes: 'p', 'rrr', 'oh', 'g', 'rrr', 'eh', 'sss'.] Then they learn to blend the sounds together. [The pupils say in unison, 'proh', 'gress'.] So instead of guessing, children are able to sound out the words they don't know. [Pupils: 'progress!']

The viewer receives only momentary glimpses of this method in action: a number of scenes from the teacher training sessions, in which Miskin demonstrates and the teachers practise pronouncing, 'rrr', 'mmm', 'zzz'; a teacher pointing to a chart of graphemes and prompting the pupils to say the appropriate phoneme; pupils reciting sounds and making hand motions; a teacher and her pupils repeating, 'mmm, mountain, mmm, mountain'. Outside of the context of a coherent lesson, these fragments are all rather baffling.

By isolating phonics from the rest of the reading process, and by isolating teaching method from other aspects of schooling, the reports mystify literacy education and its improvement. Consider the reports' omissions. First, the show ignores a host of problems with the 'teach the individual letter sounds . . . and blend the sounds together' approach: reading is more than merely sounding out words (it is principally about meaning), pronunciations vary with accent, and English orthography is not transparent – i.e. one letter refers to more than one sound, and many spellings are irregular. Although these issues are central to the phonics-whole language debate, and are thoughtfully addressed by Miskin in her training sessions, they are conspicuously absent from the *Newsnight* reports.

Moreover, the *Read Write Inc.* programme tackles school improvement with a comprehensive approach that includes much more than the transmission of a phonetic decoding strategy. *Read Write Inc.* features the following innovations to teaching, learning and school organisation:

- Five principles of good teaching manner: participation, positive teaching, pace, purpose and passion
- Cooperative learning: children are paired up with partners, and take turns teaching one another
- Classroom management rituals and techniques
- Homogeneous grouping by ability (rather than age)
- Regular diagnostic assessment and regrouping of pupils
- Use of teaching assistants as teachers of small groups
- 'Ten minute tutoring' for pupils falling behind
- Appointment of dedicated programme manager to oversee assignment of pupils to groups and teacher implementation of the programme
- Ongoing monitoring of and support for teachers.

Each of these elements are emphasised by Miskin in her training sessions and in interviews with me as being critical to the programme's success, but were either omitted or barely mentioned in the *Newsnight* reports.[13] The complexity of teaching reading and changing schools is reduced to 'learning their sounds'.[14]

Episode 2: complications and adversity

A key theme of this episode is progress. Seven pupils pronounce the word, phoneme by phoneme, at the beginning and end of the report, and it is also repeatedly invoked throughout to describe what is happening in the school. The episode starts with a recapitulation of the problem and solution as described in the first report, including many shots of energetic teachers conducting phonics lessons. In her gloss of these shots, Long reports, 'it's hard work, but the early signs are encouraging'. Head teacher Bingham explains the achievements in each of the various pupil groups, summarising, 'everywhere we are seeing progress'.

However, immediately afterwards the report cuts to a scene of two adults wrestling with an out-of-control child. 'But not everything is going quite so well,' Long explains. 'Staff have been forced to restrain a pupil.' The pupil, whose face is blurred to conceal her identity, screams, 'Let go of me.' The two adults drag her, feet trailing lifelessly, out of frame. The music turns ominous as Long explains that while this is now a rare occurrence, it used to happen on a daily basis at the school, which was engaged in an 'all-consuming battle to maintain order'. The topic of pupil discipline is then explored in the rest of the episode: in an interview with two veteran teachers, in an update on Eddie's positive progress (including vis-à-vis his behaviour), in a scene of a teacher disciplining a disruptive child, and in a discussion of attendance problems. Finally, Long interviews June Turner, 'a behaviour specialist who has worked in education for 23 years', whom *Read Write Inc.* has made 'optimistic about the children's future in a way she never thought possible'.

At the end of the episode viewers meet again with Miskin, who is 'very confident that . . . we're going to see fantastic progress at the end of this term'. Long summarises the report thus:

> Success is what this school badly needs. The staff have worked hard to combat the problems which have held the school back in the past. It is moving forward, but can synthetic phonics take the children far enough, fast enough to ever really catch up?

Note the shift in agency. The *staff* have worked hard in the past, but responsibility for present and future progress lies with *synthetic phonics*. (I return to this issue below.)

Episode 3: success!

In his introduction to the third and final report, *Newsnight* presenter Eddie Mair summarises its message thus:

> Full marks for a learning method that helped the unteachable read. [Cut to children decoding words: 'said', 'chip', 'quick', 'want'.] Three months ago these words were beyond these children. Should everyone get the chance to try synthetic phonics?

The episode is structured around a series of before and after shots. We see Marie-Paul Lukun struggling before the *Read Write Inc.* intervention, but reading the same text with ease 16 weeks later. Pupils who responded to the sprint–stop–decode–sprint test with shrugs of 'dunno' before, now confidently and successfully read all the words. Jackie Long says about this test: 'not hugely scientific perhaps, but an illustration of the progress now surging through the school.' The illustration is further grounded by a battery of impressive statistics: from April to July Year 1 pupils' reading levels improved by an average of one year, Year 2 pupils by an average of four terms, and Years 3 and 4 by five terms or more.

These improvements are shown to be having a positive effect on pupil confidence, participation in and access to other curricular areas. The experience has also had a significant impact on teaching assistant Jane Harris, who has decided that 'through the successes that I've seen I'm actually going to go on to do a teaching degree. So, yes, it has meant a lot to me'. Finally, Geraldine Jackson-Cash, who feared her son Eddie would 'fall into a life of crime and violence' before, now proudly hugs him and says, 'I can only see things now going from better to better.'

'Britannia Village Primary has clearly been won over by synthetic phonics', concludes Long. 'Will the reading review panel be as convinced?' She directs this question to head teacher Bingham, who responds, 'Look at my figures'. And given the experiment's dramatic achievements, how could anyone disagree? The report raises only one objection, which is worthy of being quoted in full.

> JACKIE LONG [interviewing three teachers in a classroom]:   One of the criticisms is that it's very prescriptive. It tells you very literally what to do at every stage. Is that a problem for you as teachers? Has that been annoying?
>
> STEPHANIE THOMAS: Yes.
>
> GEORGINA HARRIS: Has it for you?
>
> STEPHANIE THOMAS: Yeah, yeah. Completely. Yeah, it's – the first week it was nice to have that, you know, level of guidance, and I found it reassuring, but you know after that when you're doing the same thing every day I get bored, the children get bored, I think it loses its effect to an extent so you know I've been happy to bring in some (foreign) ideas to make it the sessions more pacey.
>
> [cut to] JACKIE LONG [monologue in playground]:   While most of the teachers in the school say it's a price worth paying, outside some of the teaching unions remain unconvinced. They're worried the ongoing reading review will recommend more structured phonics programmes, which they say will undermine the skill of individual teachers. Ruth Miskin is unimpressed.
>
> [cut to] RUTH MISKIN: First of all, when your children are learning their sounds, we are there for them, aren't we? Not to amuse the teachers.

But if that sounds awful, but I mean, the children have just got to know those sounds. And if they haven't got those sounds they're going absolutely nowhere. So my sympathy is more with the children there.

The reports have juxtaposed three different arguments, which initially appear to be responding to one another, but on closer inspection actually fail to connect. First, teacher Stephanie Thomas is asked whether the prescriptive nature of *Read Write Inc.* was a problem and/or annoying. Her response speaks to three issues: the advantage of detailed prescription (reassuring at first), the disadvantage of repetitive structure (teacher boredom, which leads to pupil boredom) and a solution (introducing other ideas to liven up the lessons).

Next, Long represents teaching unions who are unconvinced that the disadvantages of prescriptiveness are a price worth paying. According to Long, they are concerned that more structured phonics programmes 'will undermine the skill of individual teachers'. A plausible argument can be made for such a relationship between government prescription and teacher skill (e.g. Apple, 1981), but it involves a complex line of reasoning, and makes little sense as presented here without elaboration. Moreover, Long misleadingly speaks about the skill of *individual* teachers, rather than the authority and status of the teaching *profession* as a whole.

Newsnight then cuts to Miskin, who is 'unimpressed' with this argument. But Miskin does not respond to the deskilling problem, but to some version – we do not hear the exact question – of Thomas's concerns regarding teacher boredom. But whereas Thomas tied her own boredom to pupil engagement and learning, and was proactive in suggesting a solution, Miskin sets up a stark choice: we must choose between serving the children or 'amusing' the teachers.

I have paused to examine this sequence in detail for two reasons. First, it calls to mind Postman's argument that television is ill-suited to logical argumentation. While this example does not necessarily support such a sweeping claim, it does illustrate how easily and seamlessly arguments can become mangled in the medium. Second, it is noteworthy how the teachers are positioned in this segment. They are not interviewed as experts in their field – addressing, for example, the relative strengths of the scheme in relation to other methods they have used; rather, the teachers are questioned about their personal feelings (i.e. 'Has that been annoying?'). Thomas's answer serves to redirect the question to professional concerns, but the subsequent treatment of her comments presents her as frivolous and self-centred – seeking amusement at the expense of her pupils' welfare. This representation is especially significant inasmuch as Thomas's comments are a rare occasion in which one of the teachers appears to be exercising agency.

The reports' producer, Carol Rubra, graciously responded to and discussed with me an earlier draft of this chapter; her perspective is instructive. She rejected criticisms regarding the reports' omissions by noting that 'a report for *Newsnight* can rarely compete in 10–15 minutes with the space available in a piece of academic research'. It would certainly be a frivolous and futile exercise to judge television journalism according to the criteria of an academic journal article (or vice versa, see Hammersley, 2003). The critical issue is not how exhaustive the reports have been in their description of Miskin's programme, but how the television medium constrains the scope and complexity of news exposition. Likewise, in responding to my analysis of the way the third report juxtaposed Thomas, the unions and Miskin's responses to the prescriptiveness issue, Rubra discussed the 'conventions of current affairs reporting' and the need to distil a large amount of information into a coherent narrative. To my mind, the key point here is that a more complex and nuanced exposition would have yielded a less engaging story.

Rubra's most vigorous disagreement relates to my interpretation of how *Newsnight* positioned the teachers. Indeed, she seemed genuinely distressed by the possibility that the reports may have presented the teachers as anything but 'professional agents in control of a very difficult situation'. I do not doubt her intentions, yet those intentions are severely constrained by the reports' genre, to which I now turn.

News as reality makeover television

All texts resonate with the voices of other texts that have preceded them. By evoking, imitating, building upon and/or arguing with these inter-textual models and resources, authors and readers make meaning. Key to this process are *genres*, the relatively stable communicative patterns that emerge in recurrent activity in different social spheres (Bakhtin, 1986). We fashion our utterances on the basis of generic resources, and likewise genres shape our interlocutors' expectations and interpretations. Particularly significant for the current case is the way in which linguistic and textual features 'knit together with specific points of view, specific approaches, forms of thinking, nuances and accents characteristic of [a] given genre' (Bakhtin, 1981, p. 289). Choice of genre has implications for what can and cannot readily be said (or understood) within the genre; the associations, or 'indexical tinge' (Briggs and Bauman, 1992, p. 141), that accompany the genre; and the relative authority speakers of the genre tend to command (see Hanks, 1996, p. 244, on 'officialisation').

Newsnight's synthetic phonics reports employ resources from a number of different genres. First and foremost, they are cast as documentary news, broadcast as part of the prestigious *Newsnight* programme, a framing that lends the reports considerable gravity and credibility. However, the series also resonates with other forms. The beginning of the third episode recalls the classic television commercial in which the situations before and after use of the advertised product are compared (cf. Postman, 1982, on 'The Parable of the Ring Around the Collar'). The introductory and transitional sequences employ techniques common in music video clips. The reports' narrative structure resemble that of a heroic fairy tale: a damsel in distress (the school), is rescued by a brave heroine (Miskin) wielding a magic weapon (synthetic phonics). Most significantly, the reports draw upon the emerging genre of social makeover television.

Makeover television shows are a relatively recent invention – starting in 1996 with *Changing Rooms* in the UK – but have come to dominate prime-time television in the UK, USA and elsewhere (Moseley, 2000; Dover and Hill, 2007). Most makeover programmes include the following components: a likable, ordinary subject who unfortunately suffers from some lack, e.g. of style, expertise, beauty or charm; an expert or experts to 'makeover' the subject, transforming her or his person or home, thereby making it stylish, beautiful and/or charming; a description of the makeover process, including further discoveries about the abominable state of the subject's taste/house/lifestyle/situation; a startling revelation, in which the subject meets her/his new face/home for the first time; and reflection on the makeover's success, on how much better life has or will become in its wake.

An important element of these programmes, which grants them much of their entertainment value, is the relationship between the subject and expert(s). The former appear hopelessly ignorant, tasteless and incompetent next to the glamorous designer-experts (Philips, 2005). The latter vary: some are gracious and caring (e.g. *Extreme Makeover: Home Edition*), others playful and sarcastic (e.g. *Queer Eye for the Straight Guy*), and still others firm and brutally honest (e.g. *What Not to Wear*). Invariably, the expert knows what is best for the subject, and the subject – though sometimes initially resistant – ultimately entrusts his/her fate to the expert's wise judgement, relinquishing all agency in the face of the latter's seeming omnipotence. Unlike traditional gardening or home improvement shows, in which the camera focused on the craftsperson's hands as s/he demonstrated techniques, in makeover programmes the subjects' and experts' emotions are the primary object of interest, and the close-up of the subject's face during the revelation is the climactic moment (Moseley, 2000). Finally, it is important to note the overlapping functions of makeover television programmes as entertainment, information and advertising (Lowrey *et al.*, 2005). The audience is provided not only with the spectacle of another's transformation, but with details of the products used and, often, information about how to acquire them. The designer's expertise and good taste are thus commodified; by purchasing the strategically placed products, the audience can imitate the makeover in their own lives and thereby participate in the subject's good fortune.

The makeover genre promotes a set of ideological assumptions about success, happiness, transformation and expertise. First, many of the programmes are premised upon (and also promote) the idea that personal appearance and propriety are fundamental ingredients of success and happiness, that commodities have the power to effect personal transformation (Miller, 2008), and that knowledge of e.g. what not to wear, how to decorate one's house, successfully manage one's children, etc. are the possession of experts, whose knowledge can be readily accessed (e.g. through viewing the programme). Second, and this is particularly significant in the case of the synthetic phonics reports, most problems can be readily solved through adoption of relatively simple solutions; our problems are not rooted in their complexity, competing interests and/or inherent trade-offs, but rather in our own ignorance and unawareness.

While the original makeover programmes focused on personal lifestyle topics (e.g. style, home, body), more recently makeover shows have begun to target social issues such as parenting (e.g. *Supernanny*) and public health (*Jamie's School Dinners*). The latter programme is particularly salient for the *Newsnight* reports, given its focus on schools and facilitating large-scale social change. Celebrity chef Jamie Oliver created his *School Dinners* series in order to reveal the appalling state of nutrition in British schools and, by making over one borough, to demonstrate what could be done in all English schools. Following on from the show Oliver initiated a 'Feed me better' campaign and successfully petitioned the government to increase spending on school meals. The success of the campaign has turned its star into the icon of an emerging 'social makeover' genre. Hence, for example, a group of children's book authors entitled a recent collection of essays decrying the ills of the National Literacy Strategy, *Waiting for a Jamie Oliver* (Ashley et al., 2005).

The *Newsnight* synthetic phonics reports draw upon makeover in many respects, weaving elements of the genre together with features of more traditional television news reporting. The synthetic phonics reports are produced in the visual and verbal language of a news report. They look and feel like news, due to their use of familiar visual techniques, e.g. the reporter walking toward and talking to the camera in a crowded playground, the long shot of the school while describing the social conditions in which it operates, interviews with key participants, alternating between the studio and from the field (see Montgomery, 2007). Likewise, Kirsty Wark and Jackie Long speak like television journalists: they address the camera, enunciate clearly, use formal, standard language, focus on facts and adopt, at least explicitly, an objective position vis-à-vis controversial issues they cover.

However, the content and to an extent structure of the reports adhere to the makeover model, specifically in their presentation of the school's deficiencies, a made-for-television intervention by a confident and omnipotent external expert, transformation of the school and teachers, and revelation and celebration of the makeover's success. This framing of the synthetics phonics question as a makeover has a number of consequences for the shape – and moral – of the story.

First, with Miskin in the role of makeover expert, the teachers are 'naturally' positioned in the role of the trusting subjects. Although not a tear-jerker like e.g. *Extreme Makeover: Home Edition*, the synthetic phonics reports do expose viewers to the hopes and fears of the show's subjects. Indeed, Long focuses more on the teachers' emotional lives than their approaches to teaching reading. Thus, in an interview at the beginning of the first programme, *Newsnight* uncovers teacher Georgina Harris's fragility and despair. First, Harris expresses confidence that the school is poised to improve with the new programme:

Long asks, 'But if it doesn't work?'

'Then maybe I should train to be something else,' Harris responds, laughs nervously and looks away. She shrugs her shoulders and looks back at the camera, serious: 'I don't know. We don't know where you go from that. And – but we don't think it will fail.'

And, of course, it does not fail, and in the third episode the audience is given the opportunity to bask in the warmth of the teachers' pride, the pupils' pleasure and parent Geraldine Jackson-Cash's new-found optimism.

A second consequence of casting the synthetic phonics story as a makeover is that, as noted above, both problems and solutions are narrowed and simplified. The processes of reading and its acquisition are reduced to 'learning their sounds'. The complicated practice of teaching – including e.g. managing behaviour, diagnosing children's difficulties, differentiating instruction, developing relation-ships, and negotiating multiple curricular aims and related concerns – is reduced to teaching phonemes. And the very thorny problem of how to change classroom practice at scale (see e.g. Cohen and Ball, 2006; Lefstein, 2008b) is reduced to 'adopting synthetic phonics'. I expect that the pupils, teachers, Miskin and the *Newsnight* team encountered and wrestled with the wide range of problems posed by these issues during their collaboration on the programme. However, the complexities and uncertainties were squeezed out in the *entextualisation* process – the process of turning what happened at the school into a coherent text in the hybrid makeover-news genre.[15]

In concluding this chapter I would like to reflect upon the relationship between makeover and literacy policy, on and off television. Above I described the proliferation of the makeover genre – in topics (from fashion and interior design to parenting), scope (from the makeover of an individual person, home or family to institutions such as school dinners) and setting (from entertainment to news programmes). Within education, it has also been recently adopted by Teachers TV, as the structure for their *From Good to Outstanding* programme. The narrator summarises the plot of this series in the introduction to each episode:

> Outstanding. The ultimate accolade for teachers. We challenged reception teacher Rachel Atkins to go from good to outstanding. A top inspector observes one lesson. Two experts will fine-tune her practice and improve her presentation. She also gets comments and advice from teachers across the country who've seen her lesson on the web. Rachel then has three weeks to put all the advice into action before the inspector comes back for the final verdict.
>
> (Episode published 7 December 2009, available at
> http://www.teachers.tv/videos/rachel-atkins)

'Good' and 'outstanding' are of course categories used in Ofsted inspection judgements, and the makeover format seems to sit very comfortably with that of the inspection. Indeed, in many ways the ritual of school inspection has much in common with the makeover, with its emphasis on external judgement and expertise, processes of diagnosis and transformation, and expectation that inadequate practice be made over according to very short timetables.

One possible interpretation of these phenomena, implied at times above, is that the *Newsnight* and Teachers TV producers have extended makeover beyond its legitimate domain in entertainment, and have erred in using the genre as a way of representing teaching practice and its improvement. However, in some respects, the use of makeover to represent educational problem-solving was *all too appropriate* – in light of the extent to which makeover logic and values have become integral to thinking and discourse about English education policy. In an analysis of policies regarding school leadership, for example, Helen Gunter and Pat Thomson (2009) argue that television makeover programmes are 'illuminating metaphors for how leadership development is being constructed and imposed in English education' (p. 471). Likewise, policies such as the National Strategies reflect makeover assumptions about the locus of expertise, confidence in 'what works', ease of change, the 'transferability' of 'best practice' and the limited role of teacher agency.

Indeed, this convergence of education policy and makeover may explain why audiences did not object to mixing of news reporting and makeover genres in the synthetic phonics reports. Here is a thought experiment: imagine how audiences might have received a *Newsnight* report that similarly mixed news and makeover in investigating other pressing current affairs, such as for example the war in Afghanistan (making over the most beleaguered company in Helmand province), or the global financial crisis (8 weeks to turn around Northern Rock)?

Notes

1   Some observers have cast this issue in terms of media accuracy and ideological bias; indeed, in recent years there has been a proliferation of accusations from right and left concerning the alleged slants of the right-wing corporate media or the dominant clique of liberal journalists (e.g. Alterman, 2003; Bozell, 2005). Such critiques of media bias problematically assume that an objective representation of reality is possible and, more importantly, ignore factors which have been found to be far more influential in actual news production, e.g. professional norms, cultural traditions and narrative conventions (Schudson, 2002, 2003). This chapter concentrates on how these latter considerations combine with technological affordances and constraints to shape television journalism.
2   On these and related developments (not focused on literacy) see Beck (2008), Mahony and Hextall (2000) and McCulloch (2001).
3   See Soler and Openshaw (2006) for a detailed account of this and other literacy 'crises'.
4   See Cox (1995) and Raban-Bisby *et al.* (1995) for discussions of the early 1990s debates over the English curriculum, in which phonics was one of many controversial issues.
5   See Stannard and Huxford (2007) for details of NLS background, design and implementation, including an explanation of the searchlights metaphor (they take exception to its widespread characterisation as a 'model').
6   See Ellis (2007) for a detailed discussion of what happened in Clackmannanshire, and for a fascinating Scottish perspective on how this study was received in England.

7   See Rosen (2006) for an amusing take on the absurdity of contemporary politics, in which synthetic phonics was the first of only three policy proposals (all concerned with education) appearing in Conservative party leader David Cameron's party conference address on 4 October 2005.

8   'Inc.' stands for 'inclusive'. See the programme's website at http://www.ruthmiskinliteracy.com/, and discussion below.

9   Two additional programmes (on 7 June and 1 December) discussed the synthetic phonics intervention in the context of other reports. The reports can currently be viewed online at the BBC website, which also includes a brief textual summary of the series: http://news.bbc.co.uk/1/hi/programmes/newsnight/4584491.stm, and http://news.bbc.co.uk/1/hi/programmes/newsnight/4700537.stm.

10 In this chapter I focus exclusively on the reports. See Lefstein (2008a) for analysis of the studio debates.

11 My study of *Read Write Inc.* included participant observation in lessons and staff activities, interviews with teachers, and audio-recording of lessons in one school for 10 weeks in Spring 2003; participant observation in two training sessions; and a number of interviews with its director, Ruth Miskin. See Lefstein (2008b, 2009) for relevant studies of NLS enactment.

12 See Wyse and Styles (2007) for critical discussions of the *Rose Review* and especially the evidence base for the claims that synthetic phonics is more effective than other approaches. See Brooks (2007) for a response to Wyse and Styles, and also the latter's rejoinder in that same journal issue.

13 Once Long alludes to 'partner work' being an important part of the scheme, occasionally mentions streaming, and notes the use of teaching assistants as controversial policy, but does not elaborate on these facets, nor discuss their importance to the programme. In the third episode, Long wonders whether any other programme using streaming and smaller classes would have succeeded just as well, thereby acknowledging the importance of these elements to the success of *Read Write Inc.*, but at the same time suggesting that it is possible to isolate *the one key ingredient* in successful literacy teaching (i.e. streaming and smaller classes instead of synthetic phonics).

14 The programme producer disagrees with my analysis here. I discuss her perspective at the end of this section. It is also worth noting that Miskin's approach to the teaching of reading does not fit neatly into the stereotypical reading wars categories: while *Read Write Inc.* is a structured phonics programme, the means of teaching and learning it employs – especially the emphasis on cooperative learning – are more typical of progressivist, whole language pedagogy.

15 On entextualisation see Silverstein and Urban (1996). For a fascinating ethnographic study of the entextualisation of one (print) news item, see Van Hout and Macgilchrist (2010).

References

Adey, P. (2003). Are the Strategies *Lowering* Achievement? *Times Educational Supplement*, 11 April, p. 21.

Alterman, E. (2003) *What Liberal Media? The truth about bias and the news*, New York: Basic Books.

Apple, M.W. (1981) Curricular Form and the Logic of Technical Control, *Economic and Industrial Democracy*, 2(3), 293–319.

Ashley, B., Blake, Q., Fine, A., Gavin, J., Morpurgo, M., Powling, C., *et al.* (2005) *Waiting for a Jamie Oliver: Beyond a bog-standard literacy*, Reading: National Centre for Language and Literacy.

Bakhtin, M.M. (1981) *The Dialogic Imagination*, Austin: University of Texas Press.

Bakhtin, M.M. (1986) *Speech Genres and Other Late Essays*, Austin: University of Texas Press.

Barron, P. (2005) The Newsnight Mission (BBC). Available online at: http://news.bbc. co.uk/1/hi/programmes/newsnight/newsnight25/4198849.stm.

Beck, J. (2008) Governmental Professionalism: Re-professionalising or de-professionalising teachers in England? *British Journal of Educational Studies*, 56(2), 119–43.

Bozell, L.B. (2005) *Weapons of Mass Distortion: The coming meltdown of the liberal media*, New York: Three Rivers Press.

Briggs, C.L. and Bauman, R. (1992) Genre, Intertextuality, and Social Power, *Journal of Linguistic Anthropology*, 2(2), 131–72.

Brooks, G. (2007) Rationality and Phonics: A comment on Wyse and Styles (2007), *Literacy*, 41(3), 170–3.

Calhoun, C.J. (1992) *Habermas and the Public Sphere*, Cambridge, MA: MIT Press.

Chall, J.S. (1965) *Learning to Read: The great debate; an inquiry into the science, art, and ideology of old and new methods of teaching children to read*, New York: City College of the City University of New York.

Cohen, D.K. and Ball, D.L. (2006) Educational Innovation and the Problem of Scale. In B.L. Schneider and S.K. McDonald (eds) *Scale Up in Education: Volume 1: Ideas in Principle*, Lanham, MD: Rowman and Littlefield.

Cox, C.B. (1995) *Cox on the Battle for the English Curriculum*, London: Hodder and Stoughton.

DES (Department of Education and Science) and Bullock, A. (1975) *A Language for Life: Report of the committee of inquiry appointed by the Secretary of State for Education and Science under the chairmanship of Sir Alan Bullock*, London: HMSO.

DfEE (Department of Education and Employment) (1998) *The National Literacy Strategy: Framework for teaching*, London: DfEE.

DfES (Department of Education and Skills) (2006) *The Primary Framework for Literacy and Mathematics: Core position papers underpinning the renewal of guidance for teaching literacy and mathematics*, London: DfES.

Dover, C. and Hill, A. (2007) Mapping Genres: Broadcaster and audience perceptions of makeover television. In D. Heller (ed.) *Makeover Television: Realities remodelled* (pp. 23–38), London: I.B. Taurus.

Earl, L.M. and Ontario Institute for Studies in Education (2003) *Watching and Learning 3: Final Report of the external evaluation of England's National Literacy and Numeracy Strategies*, Nottingham: DfES.

Ekstrom, M. (2002) Epistemologies of TV Journalism, *Journalism*, 3(3), 259–82.

Ellis, S. (2007) Policy and Research: Lessons from the Clackmannanshire Synthetic Phonics Initiative, *Journal of Early Childhood Literacy*, 7(3), 281–97.

Garnham, N. (1992) The Media and the Public Sphere. In C.J. Calhoun (ed.) *Habermas and the Public Sphere*, Cambridge, MA: MIT Press.

Gunter, H. and Thomson, P. (2009) The Makeover: A new logic in leadership development in England, *Educational Review*, 61(4), 469–83.

Habermas, J. (1984) *The Theory of Communicative Action*, Cambridge: Polity.

Habermas, J. (1989) *The Structural Transformation of the Public Sphere: An inquiry into a category of bourgeois society*, Cambridge: Polity.

Hammersley, M. (2003) Media Representation of Research: The case of a review of ethnic minority education, *British Educational Research Journal*, 29(3), 327–43.

Hanks, W.F. (1996) *Language and Communicative Practices*, Boulder, CO: Westview Press.

Her Majesty's Inspectorate (HMI) (1991) *The Teaching and Learning of Reading in Primary Schools 1990*, Stanmore: DES.

House of Commons Select Committee on Education and Skills (2005) *Teaching Children to Read: Eighth Report of Session 2004–5*, London: The Stationery Office.

Johnston, R.S. and Watson, J.E. (2005) *A Seven Year Study of the Effects of Synthetic Phonics Teaching on Reading and Spelling Attainment*, Edinburgh: Scottish Executive, Education Dept.

Lefstein, A. (2008a) Literacy Makeover: Educational research and the public interest on prime time, *Teachers College Record*, 110(5), 1115–46.

Lefstein, A. (2008b) Changing Classroom Practice through the English National Literacy Strategy: A micro-interactional perspective, *American Educational Research Journal*, 45(3), 701–37.

Lefstein, A. (2009) Rhetorical Grammar and the Grammar of Schooling: Teaching 'powerful verbs' in the English National Literacy Strategy, *Linguistics and Education*, 20(4), 378–400.

Lowrey, T.M., Shrum, L.J. and McCarty, J.A. (2005) The Future of Television Advertising. In A.J. Kimmel (ed.) *Marketing Communication: New approaches, technologies, and styles*, London: Oxford University Press.

McCulloch, G. (2001) The Reinvention of Teacher Professionalism. In R. Phillips and J. Furlong (eds) *Education, Reform, and the State: Twenty-five years of politics, policy, and practice* (pp. 103–17), London: Routledge/Falmer.

Mahony, P. and Hextall, I. (2000) *Reconstructing Teaching: Standards, performance, and accountability*, London: Routledge/Falmer.

Miller, T. (2008) The New World Makeover, *Continuum: Journal of Media and Cultural Studies*, 22(4), 585–90.

Montgomery, M. (2007) *The Discourse of Broadcast News: A linguistic approach*, London: Routledge.

Mortimore, P. and Goldstein, H. (1996) *The Teaching of Reading in 45 Inner London Primary Schools: A critical examination of Ofsted research*, London: Institute of Education.

Moseley, R. (2000) Makeover Takeover on British Television, *Screen*, 41(3), 299–314.

Office for Standards in Education (Ofsted) (1996) *The Teaching of Reading in 45 Inner London Primary Schools*, London: Ofsted.

Page, B.I. (1996) *Who Deliberates? Mass media in modern democracy*, Chicago, IL: University of Chicago Press.

Philips, D. (2005) Transformation Scenes: The television interior makeover, *International Journal of Cultural Studies*, 8(2), 213–29.

Postman, N. (1982) *The Disappearance of Childhood*, New York: Delacorte Press.

Postman, N. (1986) *Amusing Ourselves to Death: Public discourse in the age of show business*, London: Heinemann.

Primary National Strategy (2006) *The New Conceptual Framework for Teaching Reading: The 'simple view of reading' – overview for literacy leaders and managers in schools and Early Years settings*. Retrieved from http://www.standards.dcsf.gov.uk/primaryframework/downloads/PDF/Paper_on_searchlights_model.pdf.

Raban-Bisby, B., Brooks, G., Wolfendale, S. and United Kingdom Reading Association (eds) (1995) *Developing Language and Literacy in the English National Curriculum*, Stoke-on-Trent: Trentham and United Kingdom Reading Association.

Richards, T. and King, B. (2000) An Alternative to the Fighting Frame in News Reporting, *Canadian Journal of Communication* [Online], 25(4). Available: http://www.cjc-online.ca/viewarticle.php?id=599.

Rose, J. (2006) *Independent Review of the Teaching of Early Reading: Final report* (No. 1844786846), London: DES.

Rosen, M. (2006) *What's Politics Got to Do with It?* Annual Education Lecture, King's College London. http://kcl.ac.uk/content/1/c6/01/75/88/lecture-rosen.pdf

Scheuer, J. (1999) *The Sound Bite Society: Television and the American mind*, New York, Four Walls Eight Windows.

Schudson, M. (2002) The News Media as Political Institutions, *Annual Review of Political Science*, 5, 249–69.

Schudson, M. (2003) *The Sociology of News*, New York: Norton.

Silverstein, M. and Urban, G. (1996) *Natural Histories of Discourse*, Chicago, IL: University of Chicago Press.

Snyder, I. (2008) *The Literacy Wars: Why teaching children to read and write is a battleground in Australia*, Sydney: Allen and Unwin.

Soler, J. and Openshaw, R. (2006) *Literacy Crises and Reading Policies: Children still can't read!* London: Routledge.

Stannard, J. and Huxford, L. (2007) *The Literacy Game: The story of the National Literacy Strategy*, London: Routledge.

Street, B.V. (1984) *Literacy in Theory and Practice*, Cambridge: Cambridge University Press.

Street, B.V. and Lefstein, A. (2007) *Literacy: An advanced resource book*, New York: Routledge.

Street, B.V., Lefstein, A. and Pahl, K. (2007) The National Literacy Strategy in England: Contradictions of control and creativity. In J. Larson (ed.) *Literacy as Snake Oil: Beyond the quick fix*, 2nd edn, New York: Peter Lang.

Stuart, M. (2003) Fine Tuning the National Literacy Strategy to Ensure Continuing Progress in Improving Standards of Reading in the UK: Some suggestions for change, Institute of Education, University of London.

Turner, M. (1990) *Sponsored Reading Failure: An object lesson*, Warlingham, Surrey: Independent Primary and Secondary Education Trust Education Unit (reprinted in Stierer, B. and Maybin, J. (1993) *Language, Literacy and Learning in Educational Practice*, Clevedon: Multilingual Matters.

Tymms, P. (2004) Are Standards Rising in English Primary Schools? *British Educational Research Journal*, 30(4), 477–94.

Van Hout, T. and Macgilchrist, F. (2010) Framing the News: An ethnographic view of business newswriting, *Text and Talk*, 30(2), 147–69.

Wyse, D. and Styles, M. (2007) Synthetic Phonics and the Teaching of Reading: The debate surrounding England's Rose Report, *Literacy*, 41(1), 35–42.

Chapter 9

The public, the personal, and the teaching of English, language and literacy

Dominic Wyse

The learning and teaching of English, language and literacy is a high priority for education in most of the world's nations. The role of language and literacy as fundamental to learning in all other areas; the argument that nations' economic futures are closely aligned with literacy skills; and the continued interest in the evidence base for policy and practice continue to stimulate debate. Within this international context the case of England is noteworthy. In 1997 England began implementation of National Literacy and Numeracy strategies which at the time represented internationally the largest scale reforms of teaching and learning in a nation state (Earl *et al.*, 2003). Yet in 2009 the demise of the strategies was quietly announced in a government White Paper:

> As we move to our new model of how improvement support is delivered to schools, we will not renew the current, central contract for the National Strategies when it comes to an end in 2011. We will delegate the funding for the Primary and Secondary National Strategies to schools, and expect them, with their SIPs [School Improvement Partners], to use it to continue their investment in improving their literacy, numeracy and other core business.
> (Department for Children Schools and Families, 2009, p. 59)

The national literacy and numeracy strategies were central to the New Labour project which placed education at the heart of the government's ambitions, epitomised, in a very early speech by Prime Minister Tony Blair, in his mantra 'education, education, education'. In view of Britain's role on the world stage and the considerable interest expressed in the approach to literacy in England there is much to be learned from the implementation of the strategies.

When reflecting on the implications of this phase of English, language and literacy teaching policy in England there are a variety of theoretical and empirical resources that can be drawn upon in order to better understand the processes and outcomes. Policy theory, in particular the understanding of England's policy in the context of global influences, provides one such resource that informs this chapter. This orientation is particularly relevant to consideration of the public aspects of policy. But, as I argue, policy is also driven by the personal agendas of those involved. The intellectual space where private beliefs encounter public obligations is a stimulus for debate and sometimes acrimony. Pedagogy, and particularly claims about the most effective teaching methods, has been a key area for these debates.

The chapter begins with an outline of key theoretical ideas that were used to orient my analysis of the processes and outcomes of the National Literacy Strategy (NLS). This is followed by consideration of evidence of its success from empirical studies and conceptual analyses. Pedagogy is highlighted as a particularly important feature of the debates, but one unacceptably narrowed by political processes. The chapter concludes with recommendations for future developments in policy and practice.

Ball (2008) has suggested that globalisation is a key idea in relation to policy development. In particular, it forms a spatial frame within which policy discourses and policy formulation are set. For example, education has been implicated in the discourse and processes of globalisation through the idea of the *knowledge economy*. But Ball notes that the idea of globalisation has to be treated with care because the term can be used too casually to 'explain' almost anything. Wyse and Opfer (2010) argue, in their examination of the context for the national curriculum and national literacy strategy in England, that one feature of politicians' understanding of globalisation is their *perception* of risk, and that this perception is implicated in a decline in trust of professionals and subsequent increased regulation of their work.

Globally, reform of education systems has increasingly focused on teachers as a major factor in enhancing learning and educational quality (Tatto, 2007). However, Tatto's thesis is that in many cases top-down political operationalisation of this focus has resulted in control of education being taken away from teachers and teacher educators. This change in the locus of control, Tatto argues, is often at the expense of teacher-owned deep levels of knowledge and critical thinking, the kind of knowledge that may be more likely to result in increases in learning and teaching quality. The debate about political control can also be seen in terms of basic tensions between commitment to the pursuit of a particular form of efficiency and commitment to social justice (Ball, 1997, p. 257).

In view of increasing political appeals to globalisation, for example international league tables of educational attainment, Tikly's (2004, p. 194) cautions are important. The hegemonic role of economics in the development of educational programmes, with associated targets and quantifiable indicators, often ignores processes at the heart of education, namely those of the curriculum and pedagogy. Tikly describes such global economics-driven policy as a *new imperialism* that can be challenged by grass-roots social movements, representing 'globalisation from below' (2004, p. 193), linked to specific forms of critical pedagogy.

Paradoxically, in view of the top-down approach adopted between 1997 and 2009 in England, Coffield *et al.* (2007) noted a new model of public service reform was being proposed that included the idea of 'users shaping the service from below (PMSU 2006, p. 8)'. However this model still did not appear to acknowledge that professionals may be at least as informed and effective as governments at taking decisions about curriculum and teaching methods. Rather than a positive and decisive move based on principle, the model looked more like a politically expedient response to growing tensions resulting from top-down control. Coffield *et al.* (2007, p. 66) complained that the evidence base for the model of public service reform was weak and that the different elements were likely to be in conflict with each other because, 'A simple model [had] been arrived at by the expedient of understating all the difficulties and complexities inherent in each of its four main elements'.

The main themes of this brief theoretical overview have influenced my analyses of the NLS in England. England is a useful case to examine because aspects of its curriculum reform processes have been adopted in other countries, and because the reform effort was located by politicians explicitly in a global context.

The NLS and the rise of the regulatory state

The beginnings of an increase in the regulatory state and its links with political perceptions of globalisation can be clearly seen in the context that was set for the national strategies in England. In 1996 a Literacy Task Force was established by the Secretary of State for Education and Employment. It was charged with developing a strategy for substantially raising standards of literacy in primary schools in England over a five- to ten-year period. The expectation was that the strategy would be implemented if the New Labour government was elected in 1997, which they duly were. The Literacy Task Force report, *A Reading Revolution: How we can teach every child to read well*, unfavourably compared England's performance with other countries: 'International comparisons of children's achievements in reading suggest Britain is not performing well, with a slightly below average position in international literacy "league tables" . . . Most studies show also a long "tail" of underachievement in Britain . . . most [people] are agreed that the educational system bears the main responsibility' (Literacy Task Force, 1997, p. 10). The sources for the 'international comparisons' (op. cit.) were revealed in a retrospective analysis of research and other related evidence, commissioned by the Department for Education and Skills (Beard and Department for Education and Employment (DfEE), 1999), as the International Association for the Evaluation of Educational Achievement (Elley, 1992) and a report by Brooks *et al.* (1996). Brooks *et al.* (1996) did indeed identify a 'long tail' of underachievement in the reading results for England and Wales (a phrase which was used repeatedly as part of the justification for the government's interventions), which they described as the performance of lower ability pupils tailing off drastically which tended to lower the average score in international comparisons. However a point that was not emphasised as part of the Task Force report was that the nature of the data that Brooks *et al.* examined meant that it was 'impossible to deduce any trend over time' (p. 18). The Task Force report went on to comment on national assessment data suggesting that the range of performance among schools with similar intakes was 'profoundly disturbing' (Literacy Task Force, 1997, p. 11). Although it is always the case that performance among schools with similar intakes differs, no evidence was presented that the NLS was the best way to address the perception of profound disturbance. In fact the Task Force report admitted that 'detailed data have not so far been made available nationally on the results in the reading component of English alone' (p. 11). The lack of rigorous attention to evidence was a contributor to policy makers' perception of risk influenced by global factors.

In 1997, the government's 'answer' to the risk posed by international and national comparisons of literacy test results was to implement the NLS as part of its 'crusade for higher standards' (Literacy Task Force, 1997, p. 15) that was a feature of the government's approach to education. At the very heart of the strategy, and arguably the government's educational mission more generally, was the teaching of reading: 'The core of our strategy necessarily relates to improving the teaching of reading in primary schools' (op. cit., p. 16). The single most influential feature of the strategy was the setting of a national target: 'By 2002 80% of 11-year-olds should reach the standard expected for their age in English (ie. Level 4) in the Key Stage 2 National Curriculum tests' (DfEE, 1997, p. 5), by which progress could be measured and control could be maintained. The testing and target-setting system is the most enduring, and powerful, regulatory feature of education in England since 1988; a feature that was intensified from 1997 onwards.

Problems with pedagogy

The pedagogy of the NLS, described in the *Framework for Teaching* (DfEE, 1998), had been developed between 1996 and 1998 as part of the National Literacy Project (NLP) that preceded the NLS. The NLP was a professional development initiative lead by John Stannard, one of Her Majesty's Inspectorate (HMI). It involved local education authorities (LEAs) and schools in England that had identified weaknesses in their teaching of literacy. The NLP established for the first time a detailed scheme of work with term-by-term objectives to be used by schools nationally. The objectives were delivered through the use of a daily literacy hour with strict timings for the different parts of the hour.

The NLP was originally conceived as a five-year project; after that time, an evaluation was to be carried out. In the event, the approach of the NLP was adopted as part of the National Literacy Strategy from 1997 onwards. This decision was taken before the results of any independent evaluation had been reported and long before the planned five-year extent of the National Literacy Project. The only independent evaluation of the project found some gains in standardised reading test scores but as there was no control group these could not necessarily be attributed to the teaching methods of the NLP (Sainsbury *et al.*, 1998).

A problem with the original development of the NLS *Framework for Teaching* and its associated pedagogy was the failure to build appropriately on the evidence available at the time, and subsequently the questionable selective use of evidence (see Wyse, 2001, 2003). Instead it was developed primarily on the basis of the personal visions of Michael Barber, John Stannard and Laura Huxford (Barber had unprecedented personal influence on education policy as a reading of his book *The Learning Game* reminds us). This is not to say that research findings did not play any part in the thinking; the retrospective accounts of Beard/DfEE (1999) and much later of Stannard and Huxford (2007) argue that research did play its part. However, this was more a case of seeking research to fit the emerging story rather than a carefully considered process of review of theory and research in order to build, a priori, principles for effective practice.

The deficiencies resulting from the poor use of research evidence and appropriate theory were most evident in relation to the teaching of reading. When the NLS was implemented from 1998 onwards the approach to reading was described as a *searchlights* model that consisted of four strategies: 'phonic (sounds and spelling); knowledge of context; grammatical knowledge; word recognition and graphic knowledge' (DfEE, 1998, p. 3). The guidance said that, 'The range of strategies can be depicted as a series of searchlights, each of which sheds light on the text. Successful readers use as many of these strategies as possible' (op. cit.). This model did not appropriately reflect the evidence base of the time and was bedevilled from the outset by inconsistencies, for example how graphic *knowledge* could be defined as a strategy, and how this might differ from the spelling aspect of phonic knowledge. Also 'phonic' or 'phonics' normally refers to a teaching approach rather than to a strategy or to a facet of knowledge. Although the rationale for the model of reading was only superficially explained in the documentation for the NLS it appears to have been a combination of Stannard's personal vision, revealed in the searchlight metaphor and the intensification of the phonological and grammatical elements, but also with some recognition that a model based on semantic/syntactic/graphophonic *cueing* was popular at the time. It also looked remarkably similar to a diagram presented in Clay's (1979) influential book.

The NLS pedagogy also suffered from over-complexity and a rather eclectic combination of ideas. The structure of the daily literacy hour was one part of this complexity. The timed segments of the hour originally required the following: (1) approximately 15 minutes shared reading and writing – whole class; (2) approximately 15 minutes word-level work – whole class; (3) approximately 20 minutes guided group and independent work; (4) final 10 minutes – plenary session with the whole class. This structure was applied to reading *or* writing but the balance between the time for, and the timing of, the teaching of reading and writing was not made clear. A further layer of complexity was added by the decision to categorise all teaching objectives as word level, sentence level or text level (organised by primary school year group term by term from age 5 to age 11) with no convincing theoretical rationale for doing this offered.

Evidence of success?

The answer to the question of whether the NLS pedagogy was effective is made difficult to answer because it was not subject to rigorous large-scale experimental trial. However there is now a significant amount of evidence in general about the effectiveness of the NLS: Wyse *et al.* (2010b; Wyse and Torrance, 2009) summarised this by reviewing studies of primary classrooms and analysing trends in national test outcomes. Although reading showed slightly better gains than writing according to some sources, the overall trend in national test scores can be explained as modest gains from a low base as teachers learned to prepare pupils for statutory tests, then a plateau in scores as no further gains could be achieved by test coaching. Overall, the intense focus on testing and test results in the period of the NLS resulted in a narrowing of the curriculum driving teaching in the opposite direction to that which research indicates will improve learning and attainment.

One of the first attempts to evaluate the strategies was commissioned by the New Labour government. Earl *et al.*'s (2003) evaluation of the NLS and NNS included collection of data from schools as follows: (a) two postal surveys (in 2000 and 2002), each to two samples of 500 schools, one for literacy and the other for numeracy. Parallel questionnaires went to head teachers and teachers; (b) a postal survey to all literacy and numeracy consultants in LEAs across England in 2002; (c) repeated visits to ten selected schools (with various sizes, locations, pupil populations, levels of attainment) and their LEAs, with four to six days in each school. The research team interviewed head teachers and teachers, observed literacy and mathematics lessons, and analysed documents; (d) interviews with literacy and numeracy managers and consultants from LEAs of the ten selected schools. The researchers also attended training sessions and staff meetings in some of those LEAs; and (e) observations and interviews in 17 other schools (including special schools) and LEAs. Three of these were one-day visits to schools early in 2000, while the others were single visits as part of shadowing regional directors or HMI, or attending meetings locally.

Earl *et al.* (2003) found that the strategies had altered classroom practice, in particular greater use of whole-class teaching, more structured lessons and more use of objectives to plan and guide teaching. Teachers' views about the strategies were more variable than head teachers who were more likely to be in favour. Head teachers and teachers were more supportive of the NNS than they were of the NLS. For the most part, both teachers and head teachers believed that NNS has been easier to implement and had had greater effects on pupil learning than the NLS. Overall Earl *et al.* report a wide range of variation in teachers' opinions of the NLS ranging from positive to negative.

Non-government-commissioned research explored a range of issues in relation to the strategies. For example, a series of research studies all reported that the recommended pedagogy of the NLS literacy hour was resulting in rather limited teacher–pupil interaction which was tending towards short initiation–response sequences and a consequent lack of extended discussion. Observation schedules were used in studies such as those by Hardman *et al.* (2003), English *et al.* (2002) and Mroz *et al.* (2000). Mroz *et al.* (2000) noted the limited opportunities for pupils to question or explore ideas. English *et al.* (2002) found that there was a reduction in extended teacher–pupil interactions. Hardman *et al.* (2003) found that the NLS was encouraging teachers to use more directive forms of teaching with little opportunities for pupils to explore and elaborate on their ideas. Skidmore *et al.* (2003) used audio recordings of teacher–pupil dialogue combined with video of non-verbal communication to support their finding that teachers were dominating interaction during the guided reading segment of the literacy hour. Parker and Hurry (2007) interviewed 51 Key Stage 2 teachers in 2001 and videotaped observations of the same teachers in class literacy sessions focusing on teacher and pupil questions and answers. They found that direct teacher questioning in the form of teacher-led recitation was the dominant strategy used for reading comprehension teaching and that children were not encouraged to generate their own questions about texts. Lefstein's (2008, p. 731) extended case study of one primary school found that open questions were suppressed as a result of 'teacher knowledge and policy support, conditions of teacher engagement with the curricular materials, and the durability of interactional genres'.

The reading debates continued

In 2006, concerns expressed by many in education that the NLS approach to reading teaching had not worked led to a government-commissioned review into the teaching of early reading in England. It was hoped that this might result in a more rigorous analysis of research evidence as the basis for a carefully considered approach to how to improve reading teaching. This unfortunately was not the case. The outcome of the review was the decision to prescribe synthetic phonics as the sole method for teaching reading, something that caused controversy (Ellis, 2007; Goouch and Lambirth, 2008; Kershner and Howard, 2006; Lewis and Ellis, 2006; Wyse and Styles, 2007). As Wyse and Goswami (2008) point out the report did not sufficiently draw upon the large amount of high quality research evidence that was available.

The tension at policy level between narrow forms of reading instruction versus other forms such as *balanced teaching* (Pressley, 2006) can also be seen in other countries. In the United States the National Reading Panel (NRP) (National Institute of Child Health and Human Development (NICHD), 2000) concluded that reading teaching should not focus too much on the teaching of letter-sound relations at the expense of the application of this knowledge in the context of reading texts. Also phonics should not become the dominant component in a reading programme, so educators 'must keep the end in mind and insure that children understand the purpose of learning letter-sounds' (2–96). The importance of the cautions about phonics becoming a dominant component are given added weight if we consider the findings of Camilli *et al.* (2003). Camilli *et al.* replicated the meta-analysis from the NRP phonics instruction report and found a much smaller effect for systematic phonics instruction versus less systematic phonics instruction. They found that the effect for individual tutoring was larger than the effect for systematic phonics and that the effect for systematic language activities was slightly larger but comparable with that for systematic phonics. These findings resulted in their conclusion that 'systematic phonics instruction when combined with language activities and individual tutoring may *triple* the effect of phonics alone' (Camilli *et al.*, 2003).

Unfortunately the measured and generally appropriate conclusions of the NRP and Camilli *et al.* may not have been sufficiently reflected in policy on reading pedagogy in the USA. Policy on the teaching of reading became strongly influenced by federal government through the legislation of *No Child Left Behind*. Phonics instruction frequently received more attention than other important aspects of reading pedagogy sometimes *in extremis* (Cummins, 2007). Allington (2010) argues that federal education policy adopted a narrow, ideologically defined notion of 'scientifically-based reliable, replicable' reading research (SBRR). This determined the kind of reading pedagogy that states had to implement in order to receive federal funding. However, to date there is no compelling evidence that reading standards have improved as a result of the *No Child Left Behind* legislation which includes the requirement for SBRR, in fact there is some evidence of more limited reading curricula and decreased curricular and instructional coherence (op. cit.).

The difficulties of maintaining research-informed reading pedagogy in the context of policy formation and implementation are also revealed in Australia. The Commonwealth government in Australia carried out a review of research on literacy, influenced by the work of the NRP, but effectively restricted its focus to the teaching of reading. Although the report recommended that 'teachers [should] provide an integrated approach to reading that supports the development of oral language, vocabulary, grammar, reading fluency, comprehension and the literacies of new technologies' (Australian Government. Department of Education Science and Training, 2005, p. 14) and 'no one approach of itself can address the complex nature of reading difficulties. An integrated approach requires that teachers have a thorough understanding of a range of effective strategies, as well as knowing when and why to apply them' (op. cit.). Sawyer (2010) argues that the synthetic phonics approach was foregrounded and particularly favoured by the report. Of particular concern to Sawyer was the use of the study by Johnston and Watson (2005) as the basis for the suggestion in the report that the case for synthetic phonics was clearly proven whereas the research showing the significance of balanced reading instruction was 'assertion'.

Contrasts between the personal and the public are revealed in the limited number of topics that have been part of the debates about the teaching of English, language and literacy. Personal political agendas frame debates in limited ways and are fuelled by the media. For the teaching of reading this has revolved around the subject of phonics. For the teaching of writing in the NLS the debate was about the teaching of grammar then the achievement of boys. As a consequence of media and public interest politicians often focus on these topics, because they become high profile issues, in favour of arguably more deserving aspects that might be addressed.

Developing English, language and literacy teaching in future

The failure of the NLS to substantially improve English, language and literacy teaching, the removal of funding for the strategies, and the start of a Conservative–Liberal Democrat coalition government in 2010 resulted in another important moment in the modern history of education in England, but it was a moment characterised by considerable uncertainty about future curriculum development. Much more freedom over the curriculum was once again to be offered by government through a process of removing local education authority control and devolving power to schools themselves, for example through the idea of *free schools*. But one potential risk of this approach is the lack of opportunity to develop shared understanding of effective teaching based on rigorous consideration of evidence from research and practice. Although the networks of consultants that were part of the professional development model of the NLS were marred by an inappropriate drive to impose a particular pedagogy, the networks themselves could have been a powerful vehicle for supporting professional development if ownership of pedagogy was invested more in the participants. If this ownership is established there is more opportunity for democratic development where cases for changing practice on the basis of developments in research and scholarship can be introduced to further stimulate thinking.

The review of the NLS in this chapter, and the context of the political uncertainty at the time of writing, leads me to propose some suggestions for the future. The need to improve policy and practice in the short term needs to be balanced against the need to take sufficient time to develop policy that is appropriately informed by research, theory and professional practice. The negative aspects of policy overload are now better understood (Moss and Huxford, 2007). But there is also a need for greater recognition of the longer timescales that are characteristic of the way that new knowledge and understanding, particularly in a discipline like education, are acquired. The negative pressures of short-term policy cycles and truncated evaluation periods need to be avoided.

New policy needs to be explicitly built on sound interdisciplinary knowledge both theoretical and empirical. Appropriate theory for the development of policy and practice should account for the role of teachers in relation to English, language *and* literacy, not just reading, writing *or* literacy. There is also the need for coherent understandings of teaching as a part of the whole curriculum. One way to theorise this is *contextualised teaching*. Although I have previously articulated this in relation to reading (Wyse, 2010) contextualised teaching is applicable to the teaching of English, language and literacy more generally. Contextualised teaching privileges the holistic over the partial, the theorised vs. instrumental, the complex vs. the simple, the nuanced vs. the crudely straightforward. It recognises the socio-cultural context in which teaching is located but emphasises the pedagogical aspects of the socio-cultural context. Contextualised teaching is an approach to teaching of English, language and literacy that is driven by the use of and creation of whole texts (in the broadest sense to include electronic media and spoken texts) to locate teaching about the smaller units of language. The use of whole texts is situated in contexts that are meaningful to children. This context enables them to better understand reading and writing processes and to learn, apply and develop skills and understanding. The teacher or other adult as expert language user facilitates children's learning by responding to their interests and building on these in ways that are informed by careful assessment of children's development informed by knowledge of typical patterns evident from research and professional experience.

Contextualised teaching requires connection with explicit linguistic principles as an appropriate backdrop for effective practice (Wyse, in press):

- Communication of understandable meaning is the driving force of language
- The classroom context established for English/language teaching influences the quality of teaching and learning
- Analysis of language in use is the basis for appropriate knowledge for pupils and teachers
- As a consequence of the natural processes of language change descriptive accounts of language are more appropriate than prescriptive accounts
- Experiencing and reflecting on the processes of reading and writing are an important resource to enhance teaching and learning
- Language and social status (or power) are inextricably linked.

If we accept that these principles are appropriate to guide effective teaching then there are a series of implications. I conclude the chapter with some illustrative examples.

Since communication of understandable meaning is a driving force of language the aims and objectives of teaching will ensure that meaning is a constant point of reference and a purpose for language activities and interaction. Too many exercises that narrowly focus on small components of language and literacy, at the expense of whole texts and at the expense of understanding of meaning, are inappropriate. This principle is related to the second principle about context. For example the teaching of writing is most effective when the emphasis is on the process of writing coupled with structured teaching such as strategy instruction (Graham, 2010). This contrasts with more decontextualised teaching such as formal grammar teaching which has not been shown to have a positive impact on children's writing (Andrews *et al.*, 2004; Wyse, 2001, 2006).

The importance of the analysis of language in use, the third principle, can be seen in relation to grammar. Understanding of language which explicitly recognises the historical changes to English including the influences of English as a world language and influences from new technology (Crystal, 2004) is more appropriate than prescriptive conceptions of language. A knowledge of language in use is also built on recognition of the importance of grammars created on the basis of corpus data (Carter and McCarthy, 2006) as opposed to those based on Latinate rule-based assumptions. Although some conventions of language are relatively stable (spelling for example) others are subject to much more change. Vocabulary is a particularly noticeable example of language change but new ways of combining words and phrases are also part of the changing linguistic landscape. Perhaps one of the most dramatic features of this language change is the way that English progresses as a world language, and what the linguistic consequences of this are for teachers around the world (Wyse *et al.*, 2010a).

Teachers are experienced readers and writers relative to their pupils and have a personal linguistic expertise and resource to draw upon. Their experience needs to be enhanced by the opportunity to reflect upon their own processes of reading and writing, as a means to better understand the processes that their pupils might experience. Greater knowledge of the processes of writing can come, for example, from psychological accounts (Hayes, 2006), but knowledge of the craft of writing acquired by professional writers, which is increasingly accessible in published forms (Gourevitch, 2007), is also relevant, notwithstanding the differences between expert and novice writers that teachers also need to understand.

The final principle reflects the idea that linguistic knowledge needs to include understandings about the language backgrounds of people in school communities that teachers are likely to encounter. The central concern here is not only the way in which Standard English(es) is(are) established but also the implications that conceptions of Standard English, and its deployment, have on citizens. A particularly unfortunate example of (mis-)conception of Standard English is the way in which trainee teachers who use non-standard oral varieties of English are sometimes criticised on the basis that their language does not represent a good model of English – in spite of the fact that their meaning is entirely clear to their pupils. This brings us back to the first principle: if communication of under-standable meaning is the driving force of language, then the question is not whether a teacher uses Standard English or not, but rather whether they can be understood, and whether their communication helps their pupils learn. Empirical evidence on this specific point is scarce.

The move in England from a period pre-1988 when local control of the curriculum was dominant to post-1988 when state control of the curriculum, and increasingly pedagogy, was dominant, needs to be superseded by a much more rigorous and subtle balancing of personal and public ownership of the curriculum. Wyse (2008) argued for a 50–50 ratio of power as a guiding principle. Subsequently the House of Commons committee (House of Commons Children Schools and Families Committee, 2009) and Alexander and Flutter (2009) suggested greater local control with slightly different ratios. While the idea of a balance between personal and public is conceptually straightforward there is insufficient understanding of how this could work. State obligations can too easily negatively impinge on local decision-making. This can happen directly through curriculum requirements and guidance, and indirectly through the inspection system and statutory assessment systems. A substantial pilot project that engages educationists, policy makers and teachers, and that runs long enough for a full evaluation to be completed, could be a very important way to develop better understanding, including of the necessary checks and balances. Any subsequent national approach to new policy and practice should be facilitative, evidence-focused, democratic and inspiring to those who might benefit from it.

References

Alexander, R.J. and Flutter, J. (2009). *Towards a new primary curriculum: A report from the Cambridge Primary Review. Part 1: Past and present.* Cambridge: University of Cambridge Faculty of Education.

Allington, R. (2010). Recent federal education policy in the United States. In D. Wyse, R. Andrews and J. Hoffman (eds), *The international handbook of English, language and literacy teaching.* London: Routledge.

Andrews, R., Torgerson, C., Beverton, S., Locke, T., Low, G., Robinson, A., *et al.* (2004). The effect of grammar teaching (syntax) in English on 5 to 16 year olds' accuracy and quality in written composition. *Research Evidence in Education Library.* Retrieved 5 February 2007, from http://eppi.ioe.ac.uk/cms/.

Australian Government. Department of Education Science and Training. (2005). *Teaching reading. Report and recommendations. National enquiry into the teaching of literacy.* Barton, Australia: Department of Education, Science and Training.

Ball, S. (1997). Policy sociology and critical social research: A personal review of recent education policy and policy research. *British Educational Research Journal, 23*(3), 257–74.

Ball, S. (2008). *The education debate.* London: Policy Press.

Barber, M. (1997). *The learning game: Arguments for an education revolution.* London: Phoenix.

Beard, R. and Department for Education and Employment (DfEE). (1999). *National Literacy Strategy: Review of research and other related evidence.* London: DfEE.

Brooks, G., Nastat, P. and Schagen, I. (1996). *Trends in reading at eight.* Slough: National Foundation for Educational Research (NFER).

Camilli, G., Vargas, S. and Yurecko, M. (2003). Teaching children to read: The fragile link between science and federal education policy. *Education Policy Analysis Archives, 11*(15). Retrieved 1 March 2006, from http://epaa.asu.edu/epaa/v11n15/.

Carter, R. and McCarthy, M. (2006). *Cambridge grammar of English.* Cambridge: Cambridge University Press.

Clay, M. (1979). *The early detection of reading difficulties* (3rd edn). Auckland: Heinemann Education.

Coffield, F., Steer, R., Allen, R., Vignoles, A., Moss, G. and Vincent, C. (2007). *Public sector reform: Principles for improving the education system.* London: Institute of Education.

Crystal, D. (2004). *The stories of English.* London: Penguin/Allen Lane.

Cummins, J. (2007). Pedagogies for the poor? Realigning reading instruction for low-income students with scientifically based reading instruction. *Educational Researcher, 36*(9), 564–72.

Department for Children Schools and Families. (2009). *Your child, your schools, our future: Building a 21st century schools system.* Norwich: The Stationary Office.

Department for Education and Employment (DfEE). (1997). *The implementation of the National Literacy Strategy.* London: DfEE.

Department for Education and Employment (DfEE). (1998). *The National Literacy Strategy Framework for Teaching.* Sudbury: DfEE Publications.

Earl, L., Watson, N., Levin, B., Leithwood, K., Fullan, M., Torrance, N., *et al.* (2003). *Watching and learning: OISE/UT evaluation of the implementation of the National Literacy and Numeracy Strategies.* Nottingham: DfES Publications.

Elley, W.B. (1992). *How in the world do students read?* Hamburg: International Association for the Evaluation of Educational Achievement.

Ellis, S. (2007). Policy and research: Lessons from the Clackmannanshire synthetic phonics initiative. *Journal of Early Childhood Literacy, 7*(3), 281–97.

English, E., Hargreaves, L. and Hislam, J. (2002). Pedagogical dilemmas in the National Literacy Strategy: Primary teachers' perceptions, reflections and classroom behaviour. *Cambridge Journal of Education, 32*(1), 9–26.

Goouch, K. and Lambirth, A. (2008). *Understanding phonics and the teaching of reading: Critical perspectives.* Maidenhead: McGraw-Hill/Open University Press.

Gourevitch, P. (ed.). (2007). *The Paris review interviews* (Vol. 2). Edinburgh: Canongate.

Graham, S. (2010). Facilitating writing development. In D. Wyse, R. Andrews and J. Hoffman (eds), *The Routledge international handbook of English, language and literacy teaching.* London: Routledge.

Hardman, F., Smith, F. and Wall, K. (2003). 'Interactive whole class teaching' in the National Literacy Strategy. *Cambridge Journal of Education, 33*(2), 197–215.

Hayes, J.R. (2006). New directions in writing theory. In C. MacArthur, S. Graham and J. Fitzgerald (eds), *Handbook of writing research.* New York: Guilford.

House of Commons Children Schools and Families Committee. (2009). *National Curriculum. Fourth report of session 2008–09. Volume 1.* London: House of Commons.

Johnston, R. and Watson, J. (2005). The effects of synthetic phonics teaching of reading and spelling attainment: A seven-year longitudinal study. Retrieved 10 December 2006, from http://www.scotland.gov.uk/Resource/Doc/36496/0023582.pdf.

Kershner, R. and Howard, J. (2006). *Psychology of Education Review, 30*(2), 1–60.

Lefstein, A. (2008). Changing classroom practice through the English national literacy strategy: A micro-interactional perspective. *American Educational Research Journal, 45*(3), 701–37.

Lewis, M. and Ellis, S. (eds). (2006). *Phonics: Practice research and policy.* London: Paul Chapman.

Literacy Task Force. (1997). *A reading revolution: How we can teach every child to read well. The preliminary report of the Literacy Task Force.* London: Department for Education and Employment.

Moss, G. and Huxford, L. (2007). Exploring literacy policy making from the inside out. In L. Saunders (ed.), *Educational research and policy-making: Exploring the border country between research and policy.* London: Routledge.

Mroz, M., Smith, F. and Hardman, F. (2000). The discourse of the literacy hour. *Cambridge Journal of Education, 30*(3), 380–90.

National Institute of Child Health and Human Development (NICHD). (2000). *Report of the National Reading Panel. Teaching children to read: An evidence-based assessment of the scientific research literature on reading and its implications for reading instruction:*

Reports of the subgroups (NIH publication no. 00–4754). Washington, DC: US Government Printing Office.

Parker, M. and Hurry, J. (2007). Teachers' use of questioning and modelling comprehension skills in primary classrooms. *Educational Review, 59*(3), 299–314.

Pressley, M. (2006). *Reading instruction that works: The case for balanced teaching* (3rd edn). New York: Guilford.

Sainsbury, M., Schagen, I., Whetton, C., Hagues, N. and Minnis, M. (1998). *Evaluation of the national literacy project cohort 1, 1996–1998*. Slough: NFER.

Sawyer, W. (2010). English teaching in Australia and New Zealand. In D. Wyse, R. Andrews and J. Hoffman (eds), *The international handbook of English, language and literacy teaching*. London: Routledge.

Skidmore, D., Perez-Parent, M. and Arnfield, D. (2003). Teacher–pupil dialogue in the guided reading session. *Reading Literacy and Language, 37*(2), 47–53.

Stannard, J. and Huxford, L. (2007). *The literacy game: The story of the National Literacy Strategy*. London: Routledge.

Tatto, M.T. (2007). *Reforming teaching globally*. Oxford: Symposium Books.

Tikly, L. (2004). Education and the new imperialism. *Comparative Education, 40*(2), 173–98.

Wyse, D. (2001). Grammar. For writing? A critical review of empirical evidence. *British Journal of Educational Studies, 49*(4), 411–27.

Wyse, D. (2003). The national literacy strategy: A critical review of empirical evidence. *British Educational Research Journal, 29*(6), 903–16.

Wyse, D. (2006). Pupils' word choices and the teaching of grammar. *Cambridge Journal of Education, 36*(1), 31–47.

Wyse, D. (2008). Primary education: Who's in control? *Education Review, 21*(1), 76–82.

Wyse, D. (2010). Contextualised phonics teaching. In K. Hall, U. Goswami, C. Harrison, S. Ellis and J. Soler (eds), *Interdisciplinary perspectives on learning to read: Culture, cognition and pedagogy*. London: Routledge.

Wyse, D. (in press). Control of language or the language of control. In S. Ellis and E. McCartney (eds), *Applied linguistics and primary school teaching*. Cambridge: Cambridge University Press.

Wyse, D. and Styles, M. (2007). Synthetic phonics and the teaching of reading: The debate surrounding England's 'Rose Report'. *Literacy, 41*(1), 35–42.

Wyse, D. and Goswami, U. (2008). Synthetic phonics and the teaching of reading. *British Educational Research Journal, 34*(6), 691–710.

Wyse, D. and Torrance, H. (2009). The development and consequences of national curriculum assessment for primary education in England. *Educational Research, 51*(2), 213–28.

Wyse, D. and Opfer, D. (2010). Globalisation and the international context for literacy policy reform in England. In D. Wyse, R. Andrews and J. Hoffman (eds), *The Routledge international handbook of English, language and literacy teaching*. London: Routledge.

Wyse, D., Andrews, R. and Hoffman, J. (2010a). Introduction. In D. Wyse, R. Andrews and J. Hoffman (eds), *The Routledge international handbook of English, language and literacy teaching*. London: Routledge.

Wyse, D., McCreery, E. and Torrance, H. (2010b). The trajectory and impact of national reform: Curriculum and assessment in English primary schools. In R. Alexander, C. Doddington, J. Gray, L. Hargreaves and R. Kershner (eds), *The Cambridge Primary Review research surveys*. London: Routledge.

Index

A levels 14, 53, 126, 129
Achievement Initiative 89, 99
achievement monitoring 98–100
action plans 70
action research 28
activity theory 39–40
Adobe premiere 17
advertising 9, 137, 148–9
Afghanistan 152
aisthesis 17
Alexander, R. 53, 167
Alexander Review 5, 32
Allington, R. 164
alphabet 139
American Educational Research
    Association (AERA) 115
Americans 27
Andrews, R. 59
Anglo-Saxon 46
anthropology 38–9
Aristotle 13, 16–17
Armitage, S. 16
art-house cinema 12
Asian children 88
Asimov, I. 12
assessment literacy 77
Assessment Resource Banks (ARBs) 99
Assessment Tools for Teaching and
    Learning (aTTle) 90, 99–101
Atkins, R. 151
attainment 67–8, 70, 73, 78, 81, 107, 162
Attainment Targets 139
attendance 35, 123, 142, 145
audience 11–14, 16, 22–3, 50, 72, 152
audits 31
Austen, J. 13
Australia 1, 5, 45, 92, 100, 117, 119, 164
Australian Genre School 92

autonomous literacy model 109, 111
autonomy 29, 118, 130, 138

Babbage, C. 9
Baker, K. 48–9
Bakhtin, M.M. 22, 113
balanced teaching 163
Ball, S. 158
Barber, M. 1, 3, 29, 52, 67, 70, 122, 161
bardolatry 12
Barnes, D. 79
Barthes, R. 16
basics 3, 49
BBC 138, 141
Beard, R. 2, 63–86, 161
bias 8
bidialectalism 59
big bang theory 29, 31, 33
Bingham, L.-M. 143, 145–6
Black Papers 48
Blair, T. 3, 27–9, 31, 52, 157
blockbusters 12
Bomer, R. 45
books 19, 31, 35, 38, 60, 139, 161
boredom 31, 146–7
bottom sets 34, 36
Bourdieu, P. 17
Bourne, J. 49
boys 31, 67, 69, 71, 87–8, 90, 98, 101
British Educational Communications and
    Technology Agency (BECTA) 118
Britton, J. 50
Brontë, E. 12
Brooks, G. 159
Buckingham, D. 8
Bullock, A. 2, 137
Bullock Report 2, 47–50, 52, 119, 122,
    137–48

bullying 29
bureaucracy 32, 42, 114
Burn, A. 8–26

Cajkler, W. 54, 58
Cambridge Primary Review (CPR) 31–2, 81, 108, 111–12, 114
camera obscura 12
Cameron, D. 49, 53, 58
Camilli, G. 163–4
Canada 45
canonicity 12, 24, 47
Carter, R. 50, 53, 120
Cartesian dualism 30
case studies 53, 163
Cawkwell, G. 87–105
Caxton, W. 15
CD-ROMs 15, 98
centralisation 64–6
Changing Rooms 149
Chapman, J. 102
Chatterton, T. 16
Chaucer, G. 13
China 27
Choices 98
cinema 9, 12, 18, 23
Classics 46, 119
Clay, M. 97, 161
Coalition government 113–14, 165
coercion 28, 33
Coffield, F. 158–9
cognitive psychology 20
Coles, M. 80
collaboration 60
colonialism 46
comics 9–12, 19–20, 22, 24
commodification 149
Commonwealth 164
community capability 96
computers 9
Conservative governments 1–3, 47, 52, 113, 120–1, 141, 165
construction 102, 109
consultants 4–5, 27, 34–5, 67; criticisms 81; evidence 162; implications 70; informed prescription 121; knowledge 40; large-scale reform 75; New Zealand 97
contextualised teaching 165–6
control groups 160
Cookson, C. 12
core skills/subjects 46, 113

course work 118, 131
Cox, B. 48
Cox Report 11, 47–50, 52, 120
creativity 11, 20–2, 42, 75; evaluation 77; implications 113; informed prescription 124, 128; professional 33; public sphere 140
Creemers, B.P.M. 70
Crevola, C.A. 70
crime 143, 146
critical literacy 5, 11, 13–20
crusade discourse 121–2, 124, 160
3-Cs model 11, 22
Cultural Studies 11, 13
cultural-history activity theory (CHAT) 39–41
culture 8–9, 11–13, 19, 22–5, 46, 136
current affairs 148, 152
The Curriculum in Successful Primary Schools 79

Daguerrotye 9
dance 18
Dancing with the Pen 94
databases 66
DC Comics 20
de-professionalisation 29
deficit view 107
deformed restriction 1–7
delivery systems 134
democracy 136, 165, 168
demography 88
Denmark 46
Department for Children, Families and Schools (DCSF) 126
Department for Education and Employment (DfEE) 161
Department for Education and Skills (DES) 50, 159
dialect 35, 49, 59
dialectic 46
dialogism 22
Dick, P.K. 12
Dickens, C. 13, 16, 130
differentiation 90
digital cameras 13
distortion 66, 74, 76, 111, 129
divisions of labour 39
Dix, S. 87–105
Dixon, J. 47
documentary tradition 11–12
Dolby Sound 15

drama 9, 16, 18–19, 24, 38, 125, 129
Durran, J. 11, 15, 23
DVDs 98, 123–4, 132

Eagleton, T. 46
Earl, L. 162
Early Childhood Primary Links via
    Literacy (ECPL) Project 96
Early Years Foundation Stage (EYFS) 114
earnings 74
Economic and Social Research Council
    (ESRC) 111
economics 136, 143, 157–8
Education Department of Western
    Australia 92
Educational Reform Act 139
Effective Literacy Practice 96, 98, 102
Ekstrom, M. 136
Electronic Arts (EA) 15
Elley, W. 93
Ellis, V. 27–44
employment 74
Engeström, Y. 39
England 1–4, 10–12, 19; criticisms 78–9;
    curriculum development 30; evidence
    163; future trends 165, 167; grammar
    46–7, 50; implications 63–5, 69–70,
    111, 114–15; informed prescription
    117, 120; large-scale reform 76; NLS
    implications 63–86; NZ comparison 87,
    90–5, 97; personal issues 157, 159;
    professionalism 33; public sphere 142;
    standards 27
English as an additional language 69–70
English at the Crossroads 31
English, E. 163
English in the National Curriculum 47
English in the New Zealand Curriculum
    (ENZC) 90, 92–3
English for Speakers of Other Languages
    (ESOL) 97
English-teaching history 119–24, 137–48,
    157–70
Entertainments Leisure Software
    Publishers Association 15
entextualisation process 151
environmental pedagogy 38
epistemology 41, 64, 109
ethics 32
ethnicity 70, 88–9, 102
ethnography 39, 108–10, 141
ethos 13

Europe 1, 8–9, 12, 15, 45–6, 88–9
evangelism 121, 124–5, 133
Evetts, J. 32–3
evidence 165, 167–8
examinations 14, 78, 130–1
expansive learning 39, 41
expert practitioners 33–4, 37, 39, 149–50

fact/fiction divide 9
fairy tales 37
Feed Me Better Campaign 150
Feed the Mind 96
field force 67
film 9–12, 15–16, 18–20, 22, 24, 37
Final Report 69, 81
financial crisis 152
Finland 4, 39
First Steps Writing 92
Fisher, R. 71
Flanders, N.A. 79
Flutter, J. 167
Ford, H. 12
formalism 48–9, 52, 108, 113
formative assessment 98
Forum Comment 93
A Framework for Teaching English 5,
    27–8, 31, 33–5; grammar 52, 54;
    impact 117–35; implications 67, 69–70,
    73, 80, 111; NZ comparison 95;
    problems 160–1; professionalism 42;
    public sphere 140; teachers 38, 40
franchises 20
free school meals 31, 69
free schools 165
Fries, C. 46
From Good to Outstanding 151
Functional English 133
fundamentalism 8
Funke, O. 46
Further Literacy Support (FLS) 72–3, 78
future trends 165–8

game-box covers 14–15
games industry 14
gaming 9, 12, 14–15, 19, 22–4
GCSEs 14, 53, 118, 129
gender gap 20, 88, 94, 100–1
genre 37–8, 40, 92, 100; evidence 163;
    fiction 12; news reports 148–52; policy
    108; proliferation 136–56; public
    sphere 150–2; television 137; theory 28
Genre School 100

Germany 46
Gibb, N. 114
Gilbert High School 33–4, 38–40
girls 31, 67, 69, 88, 101
Glasswell, K. 100
globalisation 112, 158–9
Golding, W. 12
Goodwyn, A. 1–7, 114, 117–35
Goswami, U. 112, 163
grammar 19–20, 23–5, 28, 72; concerns
    164; future trends 166–7; informed
    prescription 119–20, 131; New Zealand
    92; policing 45–62; problems 161;
    public sphere 139–40
The Grammar Papers 52–3
Grammar for Writing 54, 56–7
graphic novels 19
group work 68–9
Gunter, H. 152
Gurrey, P. 45
Gutiérrez, K. 115

hagiography 12
Hall, C. 80
Halliday, M. 50
Hammersley, M. 114
Hardman, F. 163
Harris, G. 146, 150–1
Harris, J. 146
Harry Potter and the Chamber of Secrets 15
head teachers 4, 71, 73, 75; evidence 162;
    informed prescription 120, 123–4;
    public sphere 142–3, 145–6
Helmand Province 152
Her Majesty's Inspectorate (HMI) 66, 69,
    71, 73, 160, 162
heuristic of suspicion 8–26
Hill, P.W. 70
Hillocks, G. 38
Hislam, J. 58
history 8–11, 118–24, 137–48, 157–70
home language gap 88
Hong Kong 64
House of Commons 140, 167
Hudson, R. 46, 50, 54–5
Hurry, J. 71, 163
Huxford, L. 1, 27–9, 31, 41, 67, 90–1,
    94–5, 97, 117, 161

identity 22–3, 46, 118, 128, 133, 137
illiteracy 110, 121
imagery 54

imagination 20–2, 33, 124
imperialism 125, 158
income gap 89, 102
information and communication
    technology (ICT) 9, 113
information technology (IT) 118
informed prescription 1–7, 95, 117–35
Inner London Educational Authority
    (ILEA) 139
International Association for the
    Evaluation of Educational Achievement
    (IEA) 88, 93, 159
International Association for the
    Improvement of Mother Tongue
    Education 119
Internet 9, 12
interrogation strategies 8
investment 31, 81

Jackson-Cash, G. 143, 146, 151
Jespersen, O. 46
Johnston, R. 164
Jones, S. 45–62
journalism 14–15, 136, 148, 150
Junior Journals 97

Keith, G. 53
Kelly, R. 141
Key Stage 1 4, 114
Key Stage 2 4, 27, 30, 34, 106, 111, 122,
    160, 163
Key Stage 3 4–5, 27, 34, 47, 52, 54, 56,
    122–3, 127, 129–31
Key Stage 4 56, 106, 127–31
Key Stages 120
King, B. 136
Kingman Report 47–9, 52, 54, 120
Knight, R. 48
Knorr-Cetina, K. 41
Knott, R. 48
knowledge economy 158
Kress, G. 23
Kulick, D. 110

Labour government (NZ) 87
Labour government (UK) *see* New Labour
    government
laissez-faire 27
'Language Across the Curriculum' 2
A Language for Life 2
Language in the National Curriculum
    (LINC) 50, 53, 120

Language in Use 120
Latin 47–8, 167
Lave, J. 38
leadership 71, 73, 91, 96–7, 152
league tables 4, 65–6, 102; distortion 76; informed prescription 122–3; personal issues 158–9; public sphere 142
The Learning Game 161
Learning Media 97
Learning through Talk: Oral Language 98
learning-progression statements 90
Leavis, F.R. 8–10, 125
Lefstein, A. 136–56, 163
Letters and Sounds 142
lexis 20
LibDems 113, 165
libraries 80
Limbrick, L. 89
linguistics 46–7, 49–50, 52–3; future trends 166–7; grammar 54–6, 58–60; implications 108, 112; New Zealand 92; public sphere 148
literacy definitions 1, 121
Literacy Experts Group 88
The Literacy Game 1–2, 27–44, 106–17, 120–1
Literacy Hour 3–5, 67, 69–70; criticisms 79–80; evidence 162–3; implications 111; informed prescription 121–2; internal evaluation 71; longitudinal evaluation 74; New Zealand 95; problems 161; public sphere 140; status 76
Literacy Impact tests 73
Literacy Initiative for Teachers (LIFT) 68–71, 79
The Literacy Learning Progressions: Meeting the Reading and Writing Demands of the Curriculum 98
Literacy Professional Development Project (LPDP) 97, 100
Literacy Progress Unit: Sentences 58
Literacy Task Force 1–2, 67–8, 70, 159–60
Literacy Task Group 110
Literacy Taskforce (NZ) 88, 90–4, 97
Literacy Training Pack 67, 111
literature 124–33
lived culture 11
local education authorities 2, 4, 29, 35; evidence 162; future trends 165; implications 69; professionalism 33–4, 40; public sphere 143

Locke, T. 87–105
logos 13, 16
London School of Economics 74
Long, J. 142–3, 145–7, 150–1
Luhrmann, B. 17, 19

Machin, S. 74
McNally, S. 74
magazines 14
Mair, E. 145
makeover television 136–56
managerialism 32
manifesto texts 118, 126
Manovich, L. 9
Maori children 87–91, 96, 98, 101–2
market forces 30
Martin, J. 100
Marvel Comics 20
Marxism 8
MAs 118
Maths Champions 3
media 8–26, 124, 136, 139, 141, 164–5
media arts model 18
Mercer, N. 53
metalanguage 50, 54, 93
metaphor 16, 54, 96
mind 29–30
Miskin, R. 141–51
misrepresentation 8
missionaries 110
mixed ability policy 34
monitoring of achievement 98–100
montage 18
moral protectionism 8
Moss, G. 77–8, 111
mother tongue educators 119
Mroz, M. 163
multiculturalism 11, 33, 112
multimodal texts 19
multinational companies 15
multiple literacies perspective 107
music 9
music video 17, 137, 148
Myhill, D. 45–62

name-calling 22
narratology 16
National Association for the Teaching of English (NATE) 50, 119
National Council of Teachers of English (NCTE) 45

National Curriculum 2–4, 10, 16, 45–6;
critical literacy 19; evaluation 64–5, 73;
grammar 47–52, 54–6; implications 69,
114; informed prescription 119–20,
122, 124–5, 133; personal issues 158,
160; professionalism 33; public sphere
139, 142
National Curriculum Council 50, 65
National Education Monitoring Project
(NEMP) 88, 93–4, 99, 101
National Exemplars 99
National Foundation for Educational
Research (NFER) 69, 73
National Literacy Project (NLP) 68–71,
110, 160
National Literacy Strategy (NLS) 1–6, 45,
52–9; centralisation 66–7; concerns
164; criticisms 78–80; evidence 162–3;
experience 124–7; external evaluation
73–4; future trends 165–8; generic
lessons 77–8; implications 63–86,
106–16; informed prescription 117–23,
127–33; internal evaluation 71, 73;
large-scale reform 75–7; longitudinal
evaluation 74–5; New Zealand 87–105;
NZ comparison 90; origins 63–86;
personal issues 157–60; problems
160–1; professionalism 34, 41–2; public
sphere 140–2, 150; standards 27–8,
30–1; versions 106–16
National Numeracy Strategy (NNS) 3–4,
63, 73–4; criticisms 79, 81; evidence
162; informed prescription 120; large-
scale reform 77; longitudinal evaluation
75; personal issues 157
National Oracy Project 30, 33
National Party 89
National Primary Strategy (NPS) 63, 75,
77–8
National Reading Panel (NRP) 163–4
National Standards 92, 99
National Theatre 12
National Writing Project 30
neoliberalism 30
New Guinea 110
New Labour government 1–3, 10, 52, 78;
evidence 162; implications 110, 113;
informed prescription 120–1; personal
issues 157, 159; public sphere 139;
standards 27–8, 30
New Literacy Studies (NLS1) 106–16
new moral order 27

New Opportunities Fund 118
New Perspectives on Spoken English 53
New Public Management 30–2
New Zealand 1, 5, 45, 87–105, 119
New Zealand Curriculum Writing
Exemplars 99
Newbolt Report 46, 119
news reports 136–52
Newsnight 137–8, 141–5, 147–8, 150–2
newspapers 8, 138
No Child Left Behind 164
Northern Rock 152
Norwegians 27
Not Whether But How 53
novels 12, 80, 125
nutrition 150

Observation Survey 101
occupational professionalism 32
OFCOM 9
OFSTED 4, 31–2, 34, 66, 76, 79–80,
118, 122, 139, 151
Oliver, J. 150
Ontario Institute for Studies in Education
(OISE) 4, 30, 74–8, 80
Opfer, D. 158
oracy 12, 38, 64, 79–80, 98, 113, 164,
167
organisational professionalism 32, 40
orthography 144
Orwell, G. 12
outsourcing 31

Pacific children 88
Pakeha children 101
parents 15, 23, 77, 91–2, 96, 150–1
Parker, M. 163
parsing 47, 49, 52
parts of speech 45, 52
Pasifika children 87, 89, 96–8, 101–2
pathos 13
pedagogy 4–5, 15, 32, 38; attainment
67–8; concerns 164; criticisms 81;
evidence 162; future trends 165–7;
grammar 50, 59–60; implications 108,
110, 113; informed prescription 123,
126; longitudinal evaluation 74; New
Zealand 90, 92–7; personal issues 158;
problems 160–1; professionalism 42
Perera, K. 48, 53
performance 4–5, 31–2, 35; implications
64–5, 70; large-scale reform 77;

longitudinal evaluation 74–5; New
Zealand 94, 97, 99–100; personal issues
159–60
Performance in International Reading
Literacy (PIRLS) 64
personalized learning 132
PGCEs 118, 127
philosophy 20, 38, 137
phonemes 65, 77, 138, 142, 144–5, 151
phonics 65, 69, 71–3, 76–7; implications
107; New Zealand 88, 102; problems
161; synthetic 28, 40, 112–13, 137,
149–52, 163–4; systematic 164
photography 9
pilot research 34–5
plays 125
Plowden Inquiry 112
Poetics 16
poetry 9, 12–13, 16, 18, 22, 50, 80, 125,
128–9
polemics 19
policy 59–60, 74, 77, 81; concerns 163–4;
future trends 168; implications 106–16;
personal issues 157–8, 160; problems
161; television 137–48
political economy 15
politics 29–30, 41–2, 49, 78; concerns
164–5; definitions 31; grammar 45,
52–3, 59; implications 108, 111, 115;
informed prescription 117, 121–2, 124;
personal issues 158–9; television 137
popular culture 10, 12, 22, 24–5
Postman, N. 136, 147
power relations 110
PowerPoint presentations 27, 31
precipitating factors 68–71
predisposing factors 67–8
prescription 3–5, 32, 114; future trends
166; grammar 48, 52–3, 55; informed
95, 117–35; longitudinal evaluation 75;
public sphere 146–8
presentational pedagogy 38
The Press 89
primary curriculum 3–4, 28, 31, 54–5, 58,
120–2, 161
*Primary Framework for Literacy and
Mathematics* 77, 79
prime time 136–7
principals 91, 97
prior knowledge 108
privatisation 30
product placement 149

professional development 60, 63, 67,
75–6; capability 96–8; creativity 33, 42;
future trends 165; implications 111;
New Zealand 90–2, 95; public sphere
140
professionalism 3, 32–3, 41, 60, 75
Programme for International Student
Assessment (PISA) 4
programmes of study 51–2
Progress in International Reading Literacy
Study (PIRLS) 101
progress monitoring 98–100
Progression in Phonics 140
Progressive Achievement Tests (PATs) 99
progressive model 119, 126
propaganda 112
prosody 16
protectionism 8
public sphere 136–7
publishers 15
Pullman, P. 12
punctuation 36, 56
puppet shows 37–8

Qualifications and Curriculum Authority
(QCA) 10, 52–3, 118, 124

racism 27
rational thought 20–2
Read Write Inc. 141, 143–7
reader response view 133
reading 2, 4, 9–10, 28; achievement 87;
attainment 73; concerns 163–5;
criticisms 78–80; evidence 162; future
trends 165–7; guided 4, 68–9, 71, 73,
95, 98, 161, 163; implications 64–5,
70, 72, 106–9; independent 64, 67;
informed prescription 120–1, 124–7,
130–1, 133; New Zealand 87–8, 91,
93–4; personal issues 160; problems
161; public sphere 137–8, 140, 142–6,
151; teacher knowledge 31, 35, 37
Reading Literacy Study 93
Reading for Pleasure and Profit 80
Reading Recovery 91, 95, 97, 102
A Reading Revolution 159
Reading Wars 137
*Reading, Writing and Mathematics
Proposals (RWMP) pool* 97
Ready to Read 97–8
reality television 137, 148–52
regulation 15, 28, 32, 158–60

reification 4, 99
Renewed Framework for English 55–6, 67
Report of the Literacy Task Force 87, 93
research 1–2, 12, 19, 28; attainment 67; concerns 164; criticisms 79–81; evidence 162–3; future trends 165–6; generic lessons 77; grammar 45, 47, 53, 58, 60; implications 63, 65, 68–9, 71–2, 107–9, 111–15; informed prescription 117–23, 126–7, 129, 133; internal evaluation 71; linguistics 46; New Zealand 93–5, 97, 100; personal issues 159; problems 161; professionalism 34–5, 40; public sphere 138–41, 148; standards 27, 30
resource allocation 30–1
Resource Teachers of Reading 91
retail 14
Review of Research and Other Related Evidence 80
Reynolds, D. 73
rhetoric 13–20, 23–4, 27, 30; experience 124; grammar 46, 54; informed prescription 121, 126, 133; New Zealand 90
Richards, T. 136
Riley, J. 110–11
role-play 14, 19
Romanticism 22, 27
Romeo and Juliet 17, 19
Rose, J. 137, 141
Rose Report 108, 111–14, 137–48
Rosenblatt, L. 133
rote learning 48
Rousseau, J.-J. 48
Rowling, J.K. 12, 16
Rubra, C. 147–8
Rumbold, A. 48
Russian Federation 64

SATs 120, 122, 124, 129–30
Sawyer, W. 164
scaffolding 92
Scheerens, J. 70
schemes of work (SOW) 70, 128
Scheuer, J. 136–7
School Dinners 150
School Entry Assessment (SEA) 99
School Evaluation and Assessment Council 50
School Improvement Partners (SIPs) 157

School Journal Story Library 98
School Journals 98
school meals 31, 69, 150
School Support 97
Schools' Council 30
Schwarzenegger, A. 12
scientifically-based reliable replicable (SBRR) research 164
Scotland 140
Scribner, S. 30, 38–9
searchlights model 140–1, 161
seating arrangements 74
Second World War 113
secondary curriculum 4–5, 28, 54–6, 58, 120–2, 133
Select Committee on Education and Skills 140
selective tradition 11
semiotics 10, 16, 19–20, 22–4
Shakespeare, W. 12, 16–17, 129, 131
simple model 141, 159
Singapore 64
situated cognition 38–9
Skidmore, D. 163
Slavin, R.E. 70
Slovenia 64
social networking 15–16
social practice approach 106
social sciences 28, 30, 38
socio-economic status (SES) 89, 102
sociology 20, 32, 41
Socrates 76
software 14, 17, 22
Sound-bite Society 141
Special Needs 33, 69, 72
speech 37, 45, 52–5, 139
spelling 35, 54, 69, 93, 138, 144, 161
Sponsored Reading Failure: An Object Lesson 139
Standard English 45, 47, 49; future trends 167; grammar 52–3, 56, 59
standards 1–3, 27, 29, 31; criticisms 79–81; evaluation 70; generic lessons 78; grammar 45, 49–50; implications 63, 69, 111, 113–14; informed prescription 120, 126, 134; large-scale reform 76; New Zealand 92–3, 99–100; personal issues 160; public sphere 139, 141
Standards and Effectiveness Unit 52, 70
Stannard, J. 1, 27–9, 31, 41, 67, 69, 90–1, 94–5, 97, 117, 160–1

storytelling 37–8, 136
Street, B. 106–16
Stroud, C. 110
structuralism 16
struggle 117–35
Stubbs, M. 48–9
student teachers 5, 34, 37–8, 127–8, 130, 167
Study of Written Composition 93
superheroes 20
supplemental programmes 73
Supplementary Tests of Achievement in Reading (STAR) 99
suspicion 8–26
sustainable development 27
Swift, J. 13
syntax 23, 36, 40, 45, 54, 161
synthetic phonics 28, 40, 77, 112; concerns 163–4; personal issues 161; public sphere 151–2; television 137, 149–50

Talk for Learning 113
target setting 4, 30–2, 66–7, 71, 107, 126
Task Force on Literacy 2
taste regimes 16–17
Tatto, M.T. 158
teacher training 3, 28–30, 47, 60; experience 124; future trends 167; informed prescription 118, 120, 123, 127, 132, 134; personal issues 158; public sphere 144
teachers 1, 3–6, 8, 22; assessment 73; common cause 24; concerns 164; creativity 20; critical literacy 14, 16–17, 19; criticisms 78–9, 81; culture 12; evidence 162–3; future trends 166–8; grammar 47–50, 52–4, 57–60; implications 63, 65, 69, 106–7, 109, 111–14; informed prescription 117–35; internal evaluation 71; knowledge 27–44; longitudinal evaluation 74–5; New Zealand 87–93, 95–100, 102; personal issues 158; prescription 32, 117–35; professionalism 33–6, 39–40, 42; public sphere 139–40, 142, 144–8, 150–1; standards 28, 31; understanding 75–6
Teacher's TV 151–2
teaching assistants 73, 144, 146
teaching to test 4, 63, 78, 124

The Teaching of Writing in Primary Schools: Could do better 71
Technical Accuracy Project 53
technology 136, 164, 167
television 8, 10, 19–20, 24, 136–56
tendering 31
test scores 4–5, 32, 34, 63; criticisms 78–9; evaluation 65–6, 70–1, 73; evidence 162; implications 69, 107; large-scale reform 76–7; longitudinal evaluation 74; New Zealand 101; personal issues 160; problems 160; public sphere 140
textuality 10, 16, 20–2
Thatcher, M. 2–3, 48–9
thingification 38
Thomas, S. 146–8
Thomson, P. 152
The Times Education Supplement 15
Training and Development Agency (TDA) 118
trials 162
Tunmer, W. 101–2
Turner, J. 145
Turner, M. 139
Twain, M. 115
tweenhood 22
Tymms, P. 32

underachievement 71, 143, 159
uninformed prescription 3
unions 5, 124, 146–8
United Kingdom (UK) 8–9, 14–15, 24; criticisms 79–81; implications 63–4, 66, 106, 108, 110, 112; standards 30; television 149
United States (US) 1, 5, 8; concerns 163–4; Congress 137; criticisms 79; grammar 45–6; implications 65, 114; informed prescription 117, 119; television 149
universities 46, 127
University of Auckland 97, 99
University of London Institute of Education 67–8

value for money 74
Van Leeuwen, T. 23
video editing 17
violence 8, 146
Vulliamy, G. 74–5
Vygotsky, L. 20, 30, 33, 39

Waiting for a Jamie Oliver 150
Wales 47, 50, 124, 142, 159
Walmsley, J. 46, 54–5
War Poets 13
Wark, K. 142, 150
Warner Bros 12, 15
Wasik, B.A. 70
Watson, J. 164
Wave 2 children 97
Webb, R. 74–5
websites 124, 126, 151
Welsh Office 11
West 109, 136
whole-class teaching 5, 37, 68–9, 74, 95, 161
whole-language teaching 137, 144
whole-school literacy 133
Wilkinson, I. 88, 90
Williams, R. 11–13, 22–3
Williams Review 3

withdrawal groups 73
word processors 38
working class 31
Wray, D. 58
writing 10, 19, 28; attainment 73; criticisms 78, 80; evidence 162; frames 40; future trends 165–7; grammar 49, 52–3, 57–8; guided 4; implications 64–5, 69–70, 106–9; informed prescription 121, 124–5; issues 71–2; large-scale reform 76–7; New Zealand 87–8, 91–4; problems 161; programmes of study 51–2; public sphere 140; standards 30–1, 35–8
Writing Assessment Results 93, 101
Writing Developmental Continuum 92
Writing Resource Book 92
Wyse, D. 112, 157–70

youth culture 11